D1295814

MANAGING COMPETITION

MANAGING COMPETITION
A Blueprint for Economic Policy

By Douglas N. Thompson

/ '/

Crossroads Research Institute
50 South Main Street, Suite 1090
Salt Lake City, Utah 84144

Crossroads Research Institute is a nonprofit
organization engaged in economic research.

Crossroads Research Institute
50 South Main Street, Suite 1090
Salt Lake City, Utah 84144

Library of Congress catalog card number: 89-062668
Library of Congress classification: HB238

ISBN 0-9624038-0-6

To My Family

ACKNOWLEDGEMENTS

The support of Joseph S. Peery, Professor Emeritus, University of Utah, has been of extraordinary importance in this project. He has always been ready with suggestions and encouragement, and has served as a friendly adversary in the testing of ideas. Professor Peery also supervised the University of Utah Inflation Project which cooperated in this research venture. Special thanks must go to Dr. Peery.

Garry K. Ottosen, Senior Research Analyst, has been a major contributor to this book. He has reviewed hundreds of professional books and articles, has done nearly all of the statistical work, and has written most of the analyses in appendix B.

The financial support of Douglas A. Elkins has been important, and is deeply appreciated.

Peter A. Lawson brought us into the computer age and prepared some of the analyses in appendix B. Lorraine Anderson, writer and editor of Palo Alto, California, helped so much to make the manuscript more coherent and readable. Katie Clayton provided a helping hand to speed the final proof reading.

Douglas N. Thompson
Salt Lake City, Utah, 1989

MANAGING COMPETITION
A Blueprint for Economic Policy

CONTENTS

Chapter 1

Basic Considerations in the Management of Competition

Poverty and homelessness have become highly visible in the United States. In large part these problems are due to government errors of the past.

These errors, in turn, often have been the result of sincere but misguided compassion. An outstanding example is the grievous error made by the Federal Reserve in the late 1960s. It let inflation get out of hand, ending a long period of price stability. It accepted an accelerating rate of inflation because its "compassion" kept it from risking even a small recession with the accompanying hardships. This unfortunate decision ushered in a decade and a half of serious recessions alternating with periods of accelerating inflation. As we shall see, this Federal Reserve mistake was far more important than the Vietnam War or the oil shocks in creating the many dislocations and hardships of the 1970s and early 1980s. Marginal workers suffered the most, and are, in fact, still suffering. Misguided compassion is one of the greatest enemies of responsible government behavior.

Poverty and homelessness are getting so much attention that grave danger exists of another outburst of misguided compassion. The solution to the poverty problem does not depend on transferring large additional funds from those living above the poverty line to those living below the poverty line. On the contrary, it requires improving the basic factors that allow a market–managed economy to function effectively, thereby increasing job opportunities and the relative incomes of the poor.

But how do we improve the market–managed economy? Much of the solution to poverty, homelessness, and other economic problems lies in enhancing the effectiveness of competition, especially in markets where it is now weak. And whether we like it or not, that task rests ultimately in the hands of government. Better management of competition by government can avoid many of the errors induced by a misguided compassion.

1

By management of competition we do *not* mean just the traditional restraint on monopoly by antitrust legislation. Rather, we include—surprisingly—management of competition by Federal Reserve policy, government fiscal policy, labor law, and policies dealing with international trade. These policies affect the intensity of competition in extremely important ways. But their impact on competition is often neglected in policy decisions, and the adverse effects are not widely understood.

Effective competition is essential to the proper operation of a free enterprise system. It is Adam Smith's "invisible hand" that turns the self–interest of the individual into actions that benefit others. It is both motivator and disciplinarian. Self–interest is a powerful force. But as we have seen in thousands of instances all over the world, the self–interest of those who run our economic systems often leads to grotesque behavior when that self–interest is not properly directed by effective competition.

Monopoly is the opposite of competition. Entrenched monopolies—whether they are in corporations, labor unions, governments, universities, professions, or perhaps even churches—usually end up having an adverse impact on human society. Arrogance, insolence, inefficiency, and complacency are too often the hallmarks of monopoly.

Effective competition does not happen automatically. It must be carefully protected and nurtured. It must be managed. And that is what this book is about.

THREE POLICIES NECESSARY FOR THE PROPER MANAGEMENT OF COMPETITION

Just three policies, properly implemented, would go a long way toward improving the management of competition to, in turn, alleviate the problems of poverty, homelessness, inflation and slow productivity growth. These policies are as follows:

Policy #1: The Federal Reserve should drive the inflation rate back down to a low level, say 2 or 3 percent, and then maintain as top priority the prevention of the acceleration of inflation. The second priority should be to keep demand, production and employment growing as rapidly as possible without the acceleration of inflation. These priorities appear to be nearly in place.

Although it is not often recognized, the Federal Reserve is directly and substantially involved in the management of competition. As we shall see, the Federal Reserve restrains inflation by manipulating the intensity of a special kind of competition. Federal Reserve policy is, indeed, an important part of the management of competition.

Policy #2: The Federal Government should speed the movement toward balancing its fiscal budget and complete that balance within 4 to 5 years—not with gimmicks but with real spending cuts and tax increases. Then it should hold the deficit near zero except in times of recession.

One of the most important reasons for eliminating the deficit is to improve the intensity of competition. For example, the fiscal deficit is a major cause of our large trade deficit, and the very large trade deficit is making people believe that the United States cannot compete in the world economy. Consequently, we are drifting toward protectionism. If that trend lasts, we will lose much of the international competition that is such a vital element of our domestic competition.

For over half a century this country has been moving toward free international trade with a gradual reduction of tariffs. Since World War II, both exports and imports have become a much greater part of total merchandise produced and consumed in this country, rising much faster than industrial production. Now, all of a sudden, we are worried about our ability to compete in international markets, and many groups are fighting for protectionist legislation. Surely, this shift in attitude is largely a product of our very large trade deficit in recent years, which has made many believe we can't compete in open international markets.

A loss of a significant part of our precious international competition would be a tragic result of imprudent management of fiscal policy. And that is just one of the ways in which poor management of the budget adversely impacts competition.

Policy #3: Governments should take steps to improve the intensity of "structural competition" (reduce monopoly power) in both product and labor markets.

Improved structural competition is necessary so that when the Federal Reserve stimulates demand, production and employment will rise—not wages and prices. And when the Federal Reserve restrains demand, employment will be restricted less and wages and prices will be restricted more. Improved structural competition will also alleviate the poverty problem and increase productivity. This third policy is of vital importance. It is the catalyst that makes the other two policies really work. Unfortunately, it is the most neglected of the three policies. (Structural competition is defined more precisely later in this chapter.)

As will become evident throughout this book, these three policies are all interrelated, but we should point out a special relationship between policy #1

3

and policy #3. Policy #1 directs the Federal Reserve to prevent inflation from accelerating *even if such action increases unemployment*. This policy has been recommended in different forms at times in the past, but has always seemed harsh and unyielding. It has seemed to say that unemployment is not important, or that we are helpless to do anything about it. Consequently, anti–inflation policy has often been abandoned when inflation control has threatened greater joblessness.

But policy #3 comes to the rescue. It points the way for us to do something about unemployment even while maintaining a rigorous anti–inflationary monetary policy. We are not helpless in facing the problem of unemployment. If it is too high under restrictive monetary policy, it can be brought down by paying rigorous attention to improving structural competition. In providing a more compassionate outlook, policy #3 is an essential adjunct to restrictive monetary policy. It may be the only way we can strengthen Federal Reserve resolve when rising unemployment brings forth demands for more expansive monetary policy even in the face of threatening inflation.

Benefits from the Three Policies

A number of benefits can reasonably be expected from the implementation of the three policies. Some of them are products of improved management of competition. Some of them, in turn, improve the effectiveness of competition. Others are simply pleasant side effects that should encourage the prompt implementation of the prescribed policies. These benefits are as follows:

- "Full employment" without inflation. With the three policies in place, there would be no serious recessions or double–digit inflations. Unemployment would probably be held around 4 to 4.5 percent, except in an occasional mild recession, when it would rise to no more than 6%.

- Improvement of the lot of marginal workers. Marginal workers are insecure, low–paid workers. Since 1969 they have suffered most from unemployment and have seen their relative wages continually decline. They are a major part of the poverty problem in America today. Indeed, we will argue that the implementation of the three policies is the only way we can solve the poverty problem in America.

- Decline in interest rates. This benefit would in turn have a number of positive effects. For instance, there is no reason why mortgage rates could not drop to 6 percent. At 6 percent, the monthly payment on a $100,000, 30–year mortgage is $600; on a $70,000, 20–year mortgage the monthly payment is $502. The American dream would become a reality for many more families. Another positive effect of a decline in interest rates would accrue to the less–developed countries (LDCs). A problem constantly in the news is the high debt owed to banks by the

LDCs. About 70 percent of these loans have floating interest rates. A sharp decline in interest rates would help significantly to reduce the financial pressure on the LDCs. In addition, as we shall see, low interest rates would have a dramatic effect in speeding the modernization of third world countries and thus would help to alleviate the poverty problem around the world. In the United States lower interest rates would make possible increased spending on the country's infrastructure by state and local governments and more spending by corporations on highly efficient equipment. Both would improve the productivity of the American economy.

• Rapid progress toward closing the trade gap.

• Improvement in the quality of government. This benefit would result because the three policies would require a better balancing of benefits and costs in governmental programs, as will be demonstrated later in this book.

• Improvement in our standard of living. This benefit would result because the increase in the intensity of competition would stimulate productivity.

Can This Program Really Be Achieved?

On the surface it is not readily apparent why all these benefits should accrue from the implementation of the three prescribed policies. The relationships will become clear in succeeding chapters.

The scenario of this book may seem naively optimistic and hopelessly impractical to many. But these goals can be achieved. *We're already halfway there!* The proper Federal Reserve policy is apparently nearly in place. Small steps have been taken to reduce the federal budget deficit, and almost everyone recognizes that much more should be done. Even the strengthening of structural competition is well under way. In spite of all the alarmist literature of recent years, we are tantalizingly close to achieving these objectives. It would be tragic if we were to fritter away the wonderful opportunities that are so near to being realized. Of course, serious short–term problems exist. We *may* accidentally stumble into a small recession as we adjust to a lower trade deficit and budget deficit. And domestic consumption must *certainly* slow its rate of growth until these two deficits are reduced. But the long–term prognosis is very good.

CONTRAST WITH OTHER IDEOLOGIES

This book stakes out a kind of ideological middle ground. We argue that the details of the production process (such as wages and prices) can best be managed by a competitive market (Adam Smith's "invisible hand") rather than by government. But we also argue that competition, itself, must be managed by government. Effective competition does not automatically happen. If left alone, competition often destroys itself.

Even more important, most government programs impact the intensity of competition one way or another. Unless government responsibility for the management of competition is explicitly recognized, competition often becomes an unintended victim of these government programs. This has been demonstrated by past Federal Reserve policies, and by government policies dealing with the budget deficit, labor law, international trade, and a host of regulatory activities. Programs are constantly being adopted without adequate recognition of their impact on competition.

Government management of competition—as an ideology—is bounded on the left by traditional socialism and much liberalism, which seek direct government management of the details of the production process. On the right it is bounded by the conservative claim that competition needs no management. Some conservatives, in their effort to minimize government activity, argue that if monopolies are left alone, new competitors will find a way to destroy them. Therefore, competition needs little or no government protection; effective competition is expected to survive on its own.

We shall throughout this book try to defend the middle ground, that it is the responsibility of government to protect and promote competition and then allow competition to regulate the details of the productive process. This approach allows a very important but very limited role for government in the management of the economy. It is much closer to the right than to the left.

THE PLAN OF THE BOOK

A glance at the table of contents will indicate that most of the chapters discuss the problem of managing competition. Chapters 2 and 3 examine the management of basic *structural* competition built into the corporate and labor markets. Chapter 4 looks at the management of another kind of competition: below–capacity competition. Then chapters 5 and 6 change the focus a little and evaluate the management of competition for two specific purposes: to reduce poverty and to improve productivity. Chapter 7 looks at a special kind of competition among countries, and chapter 8 ties it all together.

But before we can begin these detailed analyses of the management of competition, we must examine, in this chapter, five important topics that must be mastered in order to understand this book. These five topics are:

- The trade–off between using two different types of competition to control inflation.

- The role of the Federal Reserve in controlling prices and wage–gain norms.

- The relationship between the federal budget deficits and interest rates.

- A general theory of inflation.

- A record of the changing intensity of competition over the past thirty years.

THE TRADE–OFF BETWEEN TWO TYPES OF COMPETITION

How can improved management of competition by the implementation of the three prescribed policies reduce the magnitude of both inflation and recession? The answer lies mainly in the trade–off between using two different kinds of competition to curb inflation. It is one of the most important—and most neglected—trade–offs in all of economics.

The Role of Competition

To understand this critical trade–off, we must examine two simple propositions.

First, in a free enterprise economy, competition among sellers, in both product and labor markets, is the force that limits gains in wages and prices. In fact, it is the *only* significant force that restrains inflation. As we will argue throughout this book, *the intensity of competition is the primary determinant of the rate of inflation.*

Everywhere in the marketplace sellers must constantly decide whether to increase prices or to increase the quantity of goods or services sold. The decision for increased quantity leads to greater production and employment plus a higher standard of living. The decision for increased prices leads to inflation. It is competition—and only competition—that tilts those decisions toward increased quantity. That statement should be self–evident to anyone familiar with the day–to–day operations of business.

Second, due to various factors described throughout this book, *the intensity of competition among sellers is constantly and rapidly changing.* As the intensity of competition decreases, inflation accelerates. Conversely, as competition increases, inflation slows.

To curb inflation, then, it is necessary to increase the intensity of competition. But there are two basic kinds of competition: *structural* competition and *below–capacity* competition.

Structural Competition

Structural competition is the total competitive restraint resulting from all the market factors that limit the power of sellers to increase wages and prices. These factors are built into the structure of markets, but they are not unchanging. Some of them change rapidly.

Put another way, *weak* structural competition means sellers have considerable monopoly power over the markets in which they sell their goods and services. *Strong* structural competition indicates the absence of monopoly control of markets.

A few examples of the factors that limit the market power of sellers should help clarify this important definition.

Increased international trade limits the market power of domestic producers to raise wages and prices. That is, it tilts that ubiquitous price–quantity decision away from increased inflation toward increased production. The degree of freedom in international trade, then, is one important determinant of the intensity of structural competition. Also, on a day–to–day basis fluctuating international exchange rates affect the intensity of competition as they change relative costs and prices among countries.

A large number of firms in an industry (resulting in a low concentration rate) limits the ability of sellers to raise prices through informal collusion or any other means. Hence, a large number of firms usually adds to the intensity of structural competition in a industry, while a smaller number of firms tends to diminish that competition.

When labor unions "take wages out of competition" by organizing most of an industry and establishing relatively uniform wage rates, it becomes easier for workers to demand and get higher wage rates, and easier for the firms to pass those higher wages on to the consumer in higher prices. Thus, the price–quantity decision is tilted toward increased inflation. The intensity of structural competition is diminished by high unionization rates.

Government regulations that limit the number of sellers in a market give existing sellers some degree of control over prices in their markets, and thereby limit the restraining force of structural competition.

To repeat, all of the many factors built into the structure of both labor and product markets that restrain or fail to restrain the ability of sellers to raise wages and prices, are counted as determinants of the intensity of structural competition.

Below–Capacity Competition

Below–capacity competition is the increased intensity of competition that prevails when the economy is operating below full capacity. What does that mean? At full capacity operation, markets are generally referred to as sellers' markets. Business firms have nearly all the orders they can handle. Raising prices is easy because customers have no other suppliers to whom they can easily turn. Resisting union demands for large wage increases is difficult because strikes are disastrous when customers are in urgent need of supplies. Replacement of striking workers is difficult. At full capacity operation, then, competition is weak. Both unions and corporations have considerable market power enabling them to increase wages and prices.

On the other hand, when the economy is operating well below full capacity as in recession, markets are generally described as buyers' markets. Firms are vigorously competing with one another for new orders so they can put to work their idle facilities or operate more efficiently. Wage demands are easier to resist. Market power of both unions and corporations is limited by competition.

The intensity of below–capacity competition is determined by the size of the gap between full–capacity operation and the actual prevailing level of output. Important *changes* in the intensity of below–capacity competition are determined largely by *changes* in the level of output since capacity to produce changes but slowly.

Below–capacity competition becomes stronger the further we fall below full–capacity operation. In deep, prolonged recessions, the increased intensity of competition induced by operating below capacity becomes very powerful as an inflation–limiting force.

Putting it another way, below–capacity competition amplifies the effectiveness of the economy's basic structural competition. *That is, it reduces monopoly power.*

Total Competition

The intensity of competition resulting from all the factors that make up structural competition, plus the amplifying force of below–capacity competition, make up the total competitive discipline that limits the power of sellers to raise wages and prices in their markets.

The difference between below–capacity competition and structural competition is real and important. A clear understanding of these two types of competition is absolutely essential to grasping the analysis of this book.

The Trade–off

The critical trade–off lies in the decision as to which of these forms of competition is used to control inflation. In general, increasing the use of one reduces the need to increase the other. The problem in the United States has often been that structural competition in product and labor markets is so weak the Federal Reserve has to supplement it by increasing below–capacity competition to restrain inflation.

The Side Effects

There is a world of difference in the performance of the economy depending on whether governments and the Federal Reserve increase below–capacity competition or structural competition to curb inflation.

When most of the elements of structural competition are strong, the economy can operate very close to full capacity (and full employment) without causing inflation to accelerate. When structural competition is weak (monopoly is widespread), the economy must operate well below full employment in order for below–capacity competition to amplify the effectiveness of the weak structural competition. Weak structural competition (monopoly) is a major cause of high unemployment.

Put in different terms, to increase below–capacity competition means, of course, that economic growth must be slowed so that the economy is operating at less than full capacity. Increasing below–capacity competition *substantially* to curb strong inflationary forces produces a recession with high unemployment and, as documented in chapter 5, sharply increases the burden of the marginal worker.

If, however, governments take the necessary steps to improve all those factors that intensify structural competition in both product and labor markets, less below–capacity competition will be needed. Therefore, the economy can operate closer to full capacity with faster growth and lower unemployment. The marginal worker who makes up such a large part of the poverty problem in America will be the greatest beneficiary.

The choice seems clear. Anyone interested in reducing unemployment and improving the lot of the marginal worker must work toward improving all of those elements that make structural competition effective in both product and labor markets. Proper government policies are not likely to be formulated without a clear understanding of the trade–off between structural competition and below–capacity competition.

THE ROLE OF THE FEDERAL RESERVE SYSTEM

Most democratic countries have the luxury of using both government fiscal policy and central bank monetary policy to control the level of business activity, and, of course, thereby determine the intensity of below–capacity competition. But the United States cannot rely on fiscal policy because the fragmentation of political power makes fiscal action too slow and cumbersome. Hopes must remain modest as to our ability to improve the fiscal policy mechanism.

Our central bank, the Federal Reserve System, was set up in 1914 to be the *lender* of last resort. It has become the *stabilizer* of last resort. No matter what errors are made in fiscal policy, international trade, antitrust decisions, labor negotiations, and so on, the Federal Reserve must stand ready with a policy to prevent both inflation and deep depression. It is not an easy task. But the Federal Reserve is the only existing body with power and the ability to act quickly.

The Federal Reserve has not always accepted the role of stabilizer of last resort. Nevertheless, in this book we shall lay upon it the final blame for stabilization failures, and give it final credit for stabilization successes. Sometimes good fiscal policy makes monetary policy decisions easy. Sometimes bad fiscal policy makes monetary decisions difficult. Nevertheless, the final responsibility for stabilization must reside with the Federal Reserve.

How Does the Federal Reserve Influence the Inflation Rate?

As indicated earlier, the Federal Reserve influences the inflation rate by changing the intensity of competition. Many economists seem surprised to read that statement, but it is true. The mechanism is simple.

By well–established techniques, the Federal Reserve eases or tightens money, changing the availability of loanable funds, the rate of interest borrowers must pay, and the supply of money available for spending. This monetary manipulation encourages or discourages spending for goods and services by consumers, businesses and sometimes even governments. In turn, the change in *spending* (demand) for goods and services calls forth additional or lesser *production* of goods and services.

In periods of monetary restraint, declining spending for goods and services causes the level of production to drop further below full capacity, increasing the intensity of below–capacity competition. Increased below–capacity competition, of course, tends to restrain inflation.

The file steps by which Federal Reserve policy restrains inflation are as follows:

- The Federal Reserve tightens money.

- Tight money reduces spending for goods and services.

- Lower spending slows the production of goods and services, dropping output further below full capacity.

- A wider gap between the level of production and capacity increases below–capacity competition.

- Increased competition reduces the inflation rate.

Put still another way, when the Federal Reserve wants to slow the inflation rate, it administers a dose of monetary restraint, which in turn increases below–capacity competition to amplify the effectiveness of inadequate structural competition. There is no other significant way by which the Federal Reserve can curb inflation.

Surely every economist alive is aware of the very substantial change in the intensity of competition as we move closer to or farther away from full–capacity operation. But somehow this simple, straightforward explanation gets lost in the convoluted, almost mystical, explanations by which some economists have tried to explain the route by which monetary policy affects prices.

How Does the Federal Reserve Influence Wage–Gain Norms?

Wages and salaries represent about two–thirds of the cost of doing business in the American economy. Since prices must cover costs, the determination of wage and salary rates is of paramount importance in the control of inflation. And wage–gain norms are extremely important in the wage–setting process.

A *wage–gain norm* is a customary rate of wage increase. It is set by a particular competitive environment that lasts long enough for the wage gain to become traditional. For example, if a highly restrictive monetary policy maintains strong below–capacity competition for several years, low wage gains become customary or traditional or normal. This norm, then, has a powerful influence on wage setting policies in succeeding years for both union and nonunion workers.

Just as a wage–gain norm is established by a particular competitive environment, it is also changed by a changing competitive environment.

The Federal Reserve influences wage–gain norms because it influences, substantially, the intensity of below–capacity competition. A long period of restrictive monetary policy creates a competitive environment that establishes a norm of low wage gains–perhaps the single most important factor for a noninflationary, high–production economy. A long period of stimulative monetary policy can create a weak competitive environment and, therefore, a norm of accelerating wage rates that is highly inflationary and extremely difficult to break. Examples of each are included in the record of the changing intensity of competition described later in this chapter.

THE FEDERAL BUDGET DEFICIT AND INTEREST RATES

The important relationship between the federal budget deficit and interest rates keeps popping up throughout this book. We should, therefore, introduce it at the beginning. The relationship is simple and quite generally accepted.

In general, interest rates are higher with a large budget deficit than they would be with a small deficit or a balanced budget under the same circumstances. A large deficit increases total spending because the government is pouring more money into the economy via the spending route than it is taking out by taxation. This stimulative government action requires greater Federal Reserve monetary restraint—with higher interest rates—than would be necessary without the stimulating federal deficit.

In times of recession, when the stimulation of greater aggregate demand is needed, the Federal Reserve does not move to offset the impact of government deficits. There interest rates remain low. But in periods of business expansion, when danger of inflation is always present, federal deficits necessitate tighter money.

The relationship between the federal budget deficit and interest rates can be viewed in another way. The government finances its deficits by borrowing on the open market for loanable funds. In that market it is competing with private borrowers. When government borrowing is large, it absorbs a major part of the supply of loanable funds, driving interest rates up.

In summary, we can choose between a policy of large budget deficits with high interest rates or a policy of low budget deficits with low interest rates. We will argue throughout this book that low interest rates are better.

A GENERAL THEORY OF INFLATION

Much of the analysis of this book deals with the relationship between competition and inflation. It emphasizes the choice between using greater below–capacity competition or improving structural competition to curb inflation. How does competition figure into conventional theories of inflation?

The changing intensity of competition is the primary determinant of the changing rate of inflation. That statement could be described as a general

13

theory of inflation because it unifies most popular theories by pulling out the single strand—changing competition—that is the operative force in each of them.

Excessive demand is the most common explanation of the cause of inflation. Excessive demand gives rise to inflation when it pushes output close to capacity ceilings, permitting wages and prices to rise as the restraining force of below–capacity competition is reduced.

Excessive growth of the money supply has also been a recent popular explanation of inflation. It creates inflation *if* it induces excessive demand, which in turn reduces below–capacity competition. However, the economy at some times needs more money for normal growth than it needs at other times. Consequently, faster growth of the money supply does not automatically accelerate inflation. Growth in the stock of money, but without excessive demand, is not the cause of inflation.

The theory of cost–push inflation (which had considerable credibility many years ago) is simply a recognition of the weakness of some aspects of structural competition due to labor unions, oligopolies, and other factors.

The oil shocks of the 1970s are often blamed for being the main cause of the inflation of the same decade. They were simply a manifestation of the breakdown of structural competition in the oil industry as the OPEC cartel took control of prices. The oil shocks intensified inflation for a time, but did not by any means initiate it.

The worldwide speculation in commodities from 1972 through early 1974 is generally listed as an important aspect of the inflation of that period. It was merely a product of the strong demand that seriously reduced below–capacity competition on a worldwide basis. It was, of course, exacerbated by crop failures, a true "exogenous" shock unrelated to competition.

Government deficits are usually conceded to be a major cause of inflation. They do, indeed, cause inflation *if* they are large enough to create excessive demand, which in turn reduces below–capacity competition. However, if excessive government deficits are offset by restrictive monetary policy, as they likely will be in the future, then the government deficits bring about higher interest rates rather than accelerating inflation. Excessive government deficits, then, produce either inflation or high interest rates, each of which has serious adverse consequences.

Changing wage–gain norms have an important influence on the inflation rate, but they are merely a product of a previous competitive environment.

In summary, each of these "causes" of inflation works mainly by changing some aspect of competition or is a manifestation of some aspect of competition.

The general theory we have advanced cannot be tested empirically in total because so many factors affect the intensity of competition, some of which, like the impact of wage–gain norms, are impossible to quantify. But to anyone familiar with the day–to–day workings of the marketplace, the importance of competition should be self–evident. Competition is the force that tilts the ubiquitous price–quantity decision in the market away from increased wages and prices and toward increased quantity. In a free market, effective competition is the only disciplinarian of wages and prices.

For decades we have been looking at the "simple" solution to macroeconomic problems–turning on and off the spigot of dollar flows by fiscal and monetary policies. *This is important in the necessary control of aggregate demand, which is really the necessary control of below–capacity competition.* But it is not enough. We must now face up to the more difficult problem lying at the heart of our economic system: preserving and improving the effectiveness of the disciplinarian and motivator, competition. Then, when the Federal Reserve stimulates demand, production and employment will rise more; wages and prices will rise less.

A RECORD OF THE CHANGING INTENSITY OF COMPETITION

An economic history of the period since 1955 in the United States raises fascinating questions. What conditions made possible the economic golden age of the early 1960s with low inflation, low unemployment and rapid economic growth? Can these conditions be duplicated? Also of great interest is the record of adverse side effects during the two periods when below–capacity competition was used to shore up faltering structural competition. These two periods were the late 1950s and the 1970s.

Chart 1.1 should be used to help follow this historical analysis.

Period I, 1955 to 1960: Incipient but Controlled Inflation

As chart 1.1 shows, a sharp acceleration of inflation occurred in 1955–56. It followed a four–year period of price stability during the wage and price controls of the Korean War and the small postwar recession of 1953–54.

The cause of the price acceleration was a combination of weak below–capacity competition and weak structural competition. The economy in 1955 was operating near full capacity. Unemployment was only about 4 percent, so below–capacity competition was relatively weak.

But more important, structural competition was also weak. At the corporate level, a few large American corporations dominated each of the most important industries. The world was still recovering from the destruction and shortages of World War II. International competition was weak and just beginning to build. Many industries had substantial control over their markets.

15

UNEMPLOYMENT AND INFLATION

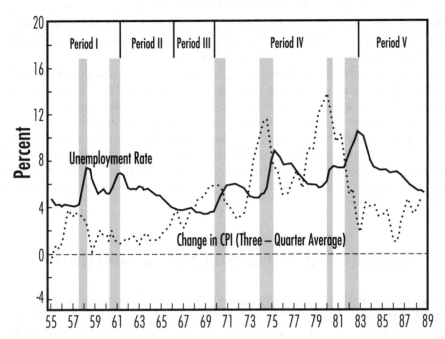

Chart 1.1 *Quarterly unemployment rate and quarterly (three-quarter average) changes in the Consumer Price Index (CPI). The shaded areas indicate periods of business contraction.[1]*

At the union level, the wages of members of powerful unions such as construction, autos and oil refining clearly led the acceleration of wages, substantially outdistancing wage gains in the nonunion and weak union industries throughout the period. This period was near the apex of the labor union movement as measured by the percent of workers unionized, and perhaps also the existence, interpretation, and enforcement of protective labor legislation. In this case unions were implicated in the onset of inflation, not just the perpetuation of inflation.

Restrictive monetary policy was used to restrain inflation. The side effects were those that are always present when below–capacity competition is increased to supplement inadequate structural competition. As Chart 1.1 shows, two recessions occurred, and, of course, unemployment rose, with an adverse impact on the marginal worker.

It is often argued that the Federal Reserve was overly restrictive in 1959 and 1960, unnecessarily creating the 1960 recession. Perhaps this is true. As chart 1.1 shows, it must have been acting as much out of a *fear* of serious inflation as it was responding to the small acceleration of inflation that occurred in 1959.

In summary, then, both corporations and unions were responsible during Period I for the weak structural competition, the acceleration of inflation, and the necessity for Federal Reserve restraint to intensify below–capacity competition with its adverse side effects. If greater below–capacity competition had not been forthcoming at that time, we would have witnessed in Period I the inflation that began in 1966 when such supplementary competition was *not* forthcoming. (It should be noted that in Period I restrictive monetary policy was supported by restrictive fiscal policy, making inflation easier to contain.)

Period II, 1961 to 1965: The Economic Golden Age

What was different in the markets of Period II to produce an economic golden age of steady growth, low inflation and a decline in unemployment to near 4 percent of the labor force?

Market power of corporations was still high as evidenced by, among other things, corporate profits rising strongly as a percent of corporate–generated income. The concentration of many industries had not changed much. International competition was still meager. Unionization, as a percent of the labor force, had not changed significantly.

But one important factor was different. A new norm of small wage gains had been established by the restrictive monetary policy and the consequent strong below–capacity competition of the previous period. It was this disciplining tradition or norm that kept wage gains at a very low level throughout the period. Such a norm of low wage gains is an absolute prerequisite to a low–inflation, high–production economy. The reestablishment of such a norm is one of several requirements for creating another economic golden age such as that of the early 1960s.

An unusually strong growth in productivity prevailed throughout much of Period II and undoubtedly had something to do with the favorable economic performance. A repetition of this rapid growth of productivity in the future is unlikely but not impossible. (See chapter 6 for a discussion of the determinants of the growth of productivity.)

Period III, 1966 to 1969: The Breakdown of Competition

Period III was a transition period, a tragic period, ending the economic golden age and ushering in the long period of inflation of the 1970s. As chart 1.1 shows, prices accelerated sharply from the inflation rate of the previous period. Unemployment declined slightly, dropping to just below 4 percent, as industrial production grew substantially.

17

What caused the sudden acceleration of inflation? It began with a break-down of below–capacity competition. Total spending in the economy rose, partly due to the delay in raising taxes to finance the Vietnam War, pushing total output up against the physical limits of capacity in a number of industries. In sellers' markets such as these, competition virtually disappears in many industries. Without competitive restraints, prices accelerate.

But the most important question is, Why didn't the Federal Reserve authorities tighten money to restrain demand, thereby slowing the economy and increasing below–capacity competition? They failed to do so because of a shift in priorities. Whereas earlier they had firmly accepted their responsibility for preventing inflation, they now felt more strongly the need for preventing recession. The gradual shift in priorities is clear from a reading of the Federal Reserve Open Market Committee minutes. This priority shift was probably the greatest mistake in the management of competition in the postwar era!

The change in Federal Reserve priorities was far more important than the Vietnam War in allowing excessive demand, production and inflation to develop. The Federal Reserve could have easily absorbed the excessive demand by a restrictive monetary policy. The federal budget deficit was only one–fourth as large (as a percentage of the gross national product) in the years 1965 to 1969 as it was in the years 1981 to 1984 when the Federal Reserve *did* break the inflationary spiral.

Another important factor that added to inflationary pressures was the collapse of the norm of low wage gains and its replacement by a norm of accelerating wage gains. A norm of accelerating wage gains is present when workers are accustomed to getting a better raise or contract settlement each time wages are negotiated, a condition that certainly prevailed throughout much of the 1970s.

Wage–gain norms are usually changed by major changes in the competitive environment, and this was no exception. The new wage–gain norm was a result of the collapse in below–capacity competition, due to the changed Federal Reserve policy.

The only aspect of *structural* competition to deteriorate during this period was the norm of low wage gains in both nonunion and union industries. Except for in the construction industry, strong unions did *not* lead wage acceleration as they had done in Period I. In fact, they lost ground very slightly to the nonunion and weak union industries. Corporate profit margins, though generally more than adequate to attract capital, were lower than in either Period I or Period II. Declining profit margins indicate a strengthening, not a weakening, of competition at the corporate level.

In summary, then, the collapse in below–capacity competition and the consequent replacement of the norm of low wage gains were the two major factors causing inflation to accelerate. Both were products of a change in Federal

Reserve priorities, placing the prevention of recession above the control of inflation.

Period IV, 1970 to 1982: The Inflation Era

As chart 1.1 indicates, Period IV was highly inflationary. Four recessions occurred, marking periods when the Federal Reserve felt compelled to apply strong doses of monetary restraint to increase below–capacity competition to prevent runaway inflation. At these times, rising wages and prices had become so serious that the Federal Reserve had no choice.

Side effects were as expected when strong below–capacity competition supplements weak structural competition. Economic growth was slow. Unemployment rose to a postwar high, topping 10 percent in 1982. Burdens increased for the marginal worker.

Where were the weaknesses in structural competition during this period?

Perhaps the weakest element of structural competition was the norm of accelerating wage gains inherited from the previous period. This norm was not a disciplining force holding down wage gains. Rather, it was a powerful stimulative force requiring ever larger gains. A norm of accelerating wage gains is extremely difficult to break. It survived through 1979.

A second weak element in structural competition was that in the labor markets, unions used their market power to *lead* the acceleration of wages. Unions expanded their wage premiums over nonunion industries until 1983. They did not do so because employment in union firms and industries was rising, thereby increasing demand for workers. On the contrary, the demand for workers in highly unionized industries was declining relative to the rest of the economy. Relative union wages did *not* rise because of difficulty in attracting workers. A queue of applicants was almost always waiting to get those good union jobs. Furthermore, relative quit rates in most highly unionized industries declined, a real indicator of how union workers appraised the attractiveness of their jobs. Also, relative union wages did not rise steadily throughout the 1970s to regain the relative position lost in the late 1960s; rather the catch–up was accomplished in a single year.

Some argue that the union wage gains of the 1970s were merely a union response to previous price hikes. Perhaps, in part, they were. But the critical point is that the strong unions had the market power to respond more vigorously to price increases than weak unions or nonunion industries. The strong unions expanded their *relative* wages (including fringes) throughout most of the period. Furthermore, their *real* total compensation expanded throughout most of the period. So we are right back at the same point. Union wage gains were primarily a product of market power—available and used.

As documented in chapter 2 and in the industry studies in appendix A, several important industries were losing market power during this period and consequently were having a lesser inflationary impact. However, significant areas of monopolistic power that still existed kept structural competition weak at the corporate level in a number of industries.

Furthermore, structural competition in a major industry—oil—collapsed in 1973 as OPEC took control of the industry. This event followed serious crop failures and roughly coincided with the end of a wage– and price–control program. Worldwide speculation in most commodities drove prices sharply higher. Together, these factors produced a substantial upsurge in inflation. The OPEC oil price increase was *not* the major cause of our inflationary problems of the 1970s, as has been so frequently argued. It was just one element of the weak structural competition of the period, certainly not the beginning of the inflationary era.

But finally, toward the end of the period a massive surge of international competition sharply increased structural competition in many manufacturing industries. The increased competition was effective at both the corporate and the union levels. This increased structural competition, combined with the below–capacity competition of the 1980 and 1982 recessions due to changed Federal Reserve policy, managed to break the norm of accelerating wage gains that had prevailed for so long. Inflation was brought under at least temporary control.

Period V, 1983 to 1988: Disinflation

As chart 1.1 indicates, inflation remained relatively low throughout Period V. Another recession–producing dose of monetary restraint was not needed. As for structural competition, three factors have so far dominated this period.

First, a sharp rise in the value of the dollar on the foreign exchange markets made American goods much more expensive than foreign–produced goods, and hence increased competition to American producers. This increased competition restrained both wage and price increases. Although the dollar valuation was reversed, the increased foreign competition still had some restraining effect.

Second, OPEC lost much of its control over oil prices, sharply increasing structural competition in this important industry. Oil prices declined.

Third and perhaps most important, a new low wage–gain norm seemed to be building due to the sharply increased competition of the early 1980s. As indicated earlier, if effective competition is allowed to prevail for a few years, this low wage–gain norm may solidify and lead to another economic golden age such as prevailed in the early 1960s.

20

THE NEXT STEP

The main thrust of this first chapter has been that improved management of competition will result in a far better performance of the American economy; and the management of competition should be directed mainly toward increasing the intensity of structural competition in order to reduce the need for below–capacity competition.

Once we have established the necessity for vigorous structural competition, the next step is to identify those areas in our economy where basic competition is weak. In chapter 2 we begin by looking at competition in corporate markets. In chapter 3 we look at competition in labor markets.

CHAPTER 2

MANAGING COMPETITION IN CORPORATE MARKETS

For nearly a century the United States has recognized a need for managing competition in corporate markets. Antitrust laws represent the government's effort to preserve competition in this important sector. Implementation of these laws, however, has often been halfhearted—sometimes almost nonexistent. Nevertheless, over the years an extensive literature and a large body of complex law have been built around this effort to limit monopoly power.

Antitrust laws now are under attack from both the left and the right. The attack from the left is rather feeble, although a couple of well-known names are associated with the effort. These economists generally prefer more direct government involvement in managing the details of economic processes via some kind of a "partnership" arrangement among government, business, and labor. They reject the notion that government should concentrate on preserving an effective competition and then let competitive markets manage the details of the economic system.

From the right a powerful attack is aimed at sharply reducing or eliminating antitrust restraints. This group of economists, spearheaded by the Chicago school, argues that antitrust laws are unnecessary and may actually have undesirable effects by preventing improvements in productive efficiency. They claim that little need exists for managing competition. Effective competition will automatically happen. In recent years these arguments have prevailed, at least to some extent. A significant weakening of antitrust enforcement has occurred.

Most mainstream economists probably support the middle ground when dealing with corporate markets. They feel that government should, by antitrust laws, maintain effective competition and let competitive markets manage details of the economic processes. Arguments about managing competition in the corporate sector are summarized briefly in appendix B and even more briefly toward the end of this chapter. But before we appraise those arguments we must look at the state of competition in corporate markets and see how and why it has been changing. To do so we must start with the problem of identifying monopolistic industries.

IDENTIFYING MONOPOLISTIC INDUSTRIES

The identification of monopoly power in individual industries is necessary for several reasons. First, we must know if and where structural competition can be improved by better antitrust activity. Second, we need to know the impact that changing monopoly power has on productivity. Third, we must judge whether union wage premiums come at the expense of monopoly profits or are passed on to consumers. And finally, government officials, workers, and the public in general should be aware that many industries are *not* monopolistic. The latter purpose is important for the following reasons.

- When corporate profits are perceived to be excessive (even when untrue), workers demand larger wage increases and are more militant in their demands. Furthermore, public sympathy tends toward support of those wage demands, even when the wage demands are excessive–and inflationary.

- The perception that profits are excessive encourages increased taxes of various kinds on corporations. Most of these taxes are eventually passed on to the public in higher prices, aggravating inflation, and triggering subsequent Federal Reserve restraint.

- A sense of economic fairness is important for the proper functioning of an economic system. A perception that most corporations are exploiting workers and customers by reaping monopolistic profits is more conducive to friction than to a smooth–running economy.

An example of misleading impressions can be found in the 1987 book *Secrets of the Temple* by William Greider.[1] The central theme of this book is that the Federal Reserve runs the country for the benefit of the banks and the rich at the expense of the poor. If this is true, why doesn't the favoritism of this powerful Federal Reserve show up as excessive bank profits? As appendix A shows, bank profit margins in the United States for nearly thirty years averaged less than the all–industry average. In only seven of those years have bank profit margins been above the all–industry average, and then only slightly. This is also true for the large money center banks.

Inaccurate perceptions such as those encouraged by Greider's book make for poor functioning of the economic system, and, if taken seriously, can result in unwise legislation.

In brief, an *antimonopoly* attitude is useful. An *antibusiness* attitude can be destructive. One of the purposes of this chapter is to provide a measure of monopoly power that will help distinguish between the two attitudes.

Monopoly as Viewed by the Economics Profession

Considerable controversy has raged in the economics profession over the extent of monopoly power exercised by American industries and the proper methods for measuring that power. At the present time, however, at least a majority of economists would agree on three points:

- American industry is generally very competitive, but it still has a sizable monopolistic fringe. (Argument persists about the size of the monopolistic fringe.)

- Competition has increased substantially in the past thirty years.

- Monopoly power cannot be identified by a single indicator. A number of indicators are required describing the structure, behavior and performance of each industry.

Only a few economists, however, have attempted to quantify monopoly power and estimate how much it has changed. One of these is William G. Shepherd. His excellent study uses the following factors to identify monopoly power:[2]

> The concentration of market share in one or a few firms.
> The existence of barriers to entry of additional firms.
> Price rigidity.
> Ability to set discriminatory prices.
> Ability to report above–average profit margins.
> Stability of market shares of individual firms.

Using these factors, Shepherd classified industries for each of the three years, 1939, 1958, and 1980 as follows:

TABLE 2.1   PERCENTAGE SHARE OF
NATIONAL INCOME IN EACH OF THE FOUR CATEGORIES

	1939	1958	1980
Pure Monopoly	6.2	3.1	2.5
Dominant Firm	5.0	5.0	2.8
Tight Oligopoly	36.4	35.6	18.0
Other (Competitive)	52.4	56.3	76.7

Industries in the first three categories have some degree of monopoly power. The rest are largely competitive. Shepherd's estimates indicate that American industry is largely competitive and that competition increased sharply between 1958 and 1980. His study ended before the massive increase in import competition of the 1980s that further increased competition.

But we cannot just accept these estimates and let the matter drop. A great deal of subjective judgment is involved in Shepherd's selection, analysis, and weighting of the factors that determine monopoly power. If a reader is to be convinced of the validity of the estimates, he should be able to examine the important industries that fall in each category. A reasonably informed person could then make a judgment about the credibility of the classifications and the extent of monopoly power.

To facilitate this kind of examination, we have included in this book an analysis of 42 industries. The analysis emphasizes (but is not restricted to) a single indicator—relative profit margins. Results for each of the industries are shown in appendix A where they are related to important aspects of the labor market and to changing productivity.

The Measurement Problem

No noncontroversial measure of monopoly power is available. We must, therefore, briefly explain and justify the methodology we have used.

At the core of our analysis is a fundamental principle of economics that we call the convergence principle: *In a competitive economy, the profit margins of industries tend to converge toward the all–industry average.* If transient economic forces such as an increase in demand cause profit margins in an industry to rise well above average, those high profits attract new investment from firms both within the industry and outside the industry. Competition increases, and profit margins are driven back down toward the all–industry average.

The convergence principle does not mean that profit margins of all industries are ever equal. While competition is driving profit margins of some industries down toward the average, transient economic forces are usually pushing profit margins in other industries above the all–industry average. Consequently, in a dynamic but competitive economy, each industry's profit margin fluctuates around the all–industry average; but over a period of time, profit margins for each industry tend to average fairly close to the all–industry average.

There is nothing new about the convergence principle, except perhaps the name. George J. Stigler summarized the concept when he wrote, "There is no more important proposition in economics than that, under competition, the rate of return on investment tends toward equality in all industries." [3]

Just as competition tends to drive profit margins down toward the all–industry average, monopolistic power allows the firms in some industries to maintain profit margins above the all–industry average for long periods of time. Barriers to entry tend to keep new investment from entering these high–profit–margin industries, so profit margins remain high.

One way to estimate the intensity of competition at the industry level, then, is to measure its effectiveness in driving down those high profit margins. *Any industry that can maintain profit margins (on equity) substantially and persistently above average, possesses monopolistic power.* These industries are not subject to the convergence principle. Their market power is not effectively contested by new competitors.

Some argue that high profit margins in an industry may be due to higher risk in that industry rather than to monopoly power. But it is difficult to believe that an industry that persistently generates above–average profit margins does have above–average risk. As we examine the industries that fall into this category, the high risk argument will quickly fade away. (There is, of course, high risk to new companies trying to break down barriers to entry, but not to those already entrenched.)

The profit margin test of monopoly power applies to entire industries, not to individual companies within an industry. In any industry, there are well managed firms and poorly managed firms. The well managed firms have profit margins above average for that industry, while the poorly managed firms have below–average profit margins. The above–average margins for an individual company are a reward for superior management and hence are economically justified if they exist within a competitive industry.

In our analysis we have generally used the profit figures as reported by corporations. In doing so we have been fully aware of the problems of diverse accounting practices and changes in the tax laws. We have also had serious problems with industry classifications, since the activities of many companies extend across several industries. Because of these and other complications, we have not attempted great precision in identifying monopolies. We have looked only for gross examples of above–average profit margins where accounting and other problems could not reasonably account for monopoly–identifying performance. *We must emphasize as strongly as possible this limited nature of our goals.* It is the primary justification for this methodology.

The profit margin test of monopoly power is a measure of the *performance* of an industry. It must be supplemented by an analysis of those elements of an industry that determine that performance. Changing international competition, barriers to entry, industry concentration, market shares, and changing government regulations are factors that determine the monopolistic or competitive performance of an industry. In short, a detailed study of each industry would be required to estimate its monopoly power.

Another question relating to monopolies and the convergence principle must be addressed. Could industries earning just average profit margins be monopolists that have their excessive profits taken away by labor unions in excessive wages? That question is explored in general terms in chapter 3 and on an industry–by–industry basis in appendix A.

The convergence principle has another side. When an industry's earnings fall below average, new investment in that industry is curtailed (at least for expansion purposes), cost–cutting efforts are initiated, product is improved, some firms drop out of the industry, and consequently after a period of time, profit margins in these industries usually rise to the all–industry average. Ordinarily, below–average profit margins set in motion these forces that bring recovery. This is the convergence principle in action.

Depressed industries that recover in just a few years can be referred to as short–term endangered. But a few industries go on for many years persistently earning below–average profit margins and these are classed as long–term endangered industries. For them the convergence principle doesn't work, or, at least, it takes a very long time to work. In this chapter and in appendix A we give examples of some long–term endangered industries.

In summary, an industry should be able to earn a profit margin high enough to attract capital to the industry. When it does not, it faces decline and eventual bankruptcy. There are many indicators of financial endangerment. In this book we will examine just three of them for each of our industries:

- Profit margins much below average for an extended period of time. This situation makes it difficult to obtain funds from retained earnings.

- High and rising long–term debt as a percent of total capitalization. This indicator means that this source of funds has been or is being exhausted. (At present, many American corporations are undergoing a "restructuring" fad, a by–product of which is often very high debt. Consequently, at the moment, rising debt may be due simply to fear of a hostile takeover rather than evidence of difficulty in raising capital.)

28

- Common stock prices below book value for a long period of time. This situation makes it extremely difficult for a corporation to raise funds by selling new stock. (Stocks usually sell at or above *replacement* value, which currently averages more than 50 percent above book value.)

No precise point exists at which a firm or an industry becomes financially endangered, but certainly the three indicators just named can point out industries that are in serious trouble.

Advantages of the Profit Margin Test of Monopoly Power

Economists have often been reluctant to use reported accounting profit margins to identify monopolies. Their reasons for preferring other approaches are surveyed briefly in "Measures of Monopoly Power" in appendix B. Most of the criticisms of the profit margin test of monopoly power can be met by using data covering long periods, by attempting to identify only gross examples of monopolistic performance, and by using the test in conjunction with an analysis of the structural factors that determine profit margins.

The profit margin test of monopoly power using reported accounting profits has the following advantages:

- Data are more readily available than they are for some other tests of monopoly power. Studies can be quickly brought up to date to detect changes in market performance, and they can be checked easily. Only the necessity for weighting makes the arithmetic at all cumbersome.

- The competitive profit margin pattern is sufficiently reliable to be used as a rough forecasting device for investment and other purposes. Whenever average profit margins for a competitive industry rise much above the all–industry average, we can be confident that competition will drive them back down again. Examples of industries for which this has been true are grocery stores, general merchandise stores, banks, paper, and oil. There are many others. Paying high prices for stocks in competitive industries with temporary high relative profit margins can be a costly mistake.

Many analysts on Wall Street have failed to use the predictive power of this simple concept. Reports are often written extolling the high profit margins of an industry or a company but with hardly a hint of how long it might take competition to reduce those margins. As indicated in appendix A, the stock market has rarely predicted a decline in relative profit margins due to competition, and worse, has sometimes taken years to recognize the disciplining force of competition even after it has occurred. An economic pattern upon which even rough predictions can be based should not be overlooked. Analysts interested in estimating long–term earning power rather than one–year earnings must certainly look at relative profit margins and the competitive environment of the industry.

- The profit margin test of monopoly power can be easily understood. Most people relate monopolists to excessive profits, so industries that have profit margins substantially and persistently above the all–industry average are perceived as having some monopolistic control over markets. The profit margin idea is easier to understand than, say, marginal cost pricing as an indication of monopoly power.

CLASSIFYING INDUSTRIES BY DEGREE OF MARKET POWER

An industry is defined as a group of companies that compete with one another. Historically, companies have been classified into industries according to the products and services they produce. But the problem of grouping companies by industry is becoming more difficult every year as more and more companies expand their activities into several fields. While acknowledging this difficulty, we have analyzed most of the major industries for which data are readily available and that have several participants, plus a few industries that have but three or four important participants. We have then grouped these industries into five categories according to degree of market power:

Long–term competitive.
Increasingly competitive.
Long–term endangered.
Decreasingly competitive.
Long–term monopolistic.

Following are descriptions of each category. (Appendix A presents considerable information about each of the forty–two industries we have analyzed. In particular, it relates monopolistic power in product markets to monopolistic power in labor markets, and to the rate of growth of productivity for the industry. The number of industries we have analyzed has been limited mainly by the problem of classifying companies that operate in several industries. More time and resources can go a long way toward solving this problem.)

Long–Term Competitive Industries

The convergence principle indicates that in a competitive economy, profit margins for each industry fluctuate around the all–industry average. Over a long period of time, the average profit margins for a competitive industry are close to the average profit margins for all industries for the same period of time.

The fourteen industries we have classified as long–term competitive match this ideal type quite closely. (See Table 2.2) By itself this fact does not *prove* that these are competitive industries, but it provides a strong presumption that they are, indeed, competitive.

In addition to the fourteen industries classified as long–term competitive, we have included in this category three regulated utilities whose profit margins tend to match those of competitive industries. Their productivity, however, is not necessarily comparable to that of competitive industries.

As for the market structure of these industries, all but the copper industry have fairly low and steady four–firm concentration ratios. (The *four–firm concentration ratio* is the percentage of the sales of the entire industry accounted for by the four largest firms.) The price of copper is set on international markets, so the domestic industry has no control over market prices. Most of these industries have witnessed significant new entrants, demonstrating that barriers to entry are not insurmountable. Small firms have often grown to substantial size, signifying changing market share, an important indicator of aggressive competition.

But we cannot be positive that these industries will remain competitive. If the present merger trend continues for many years, the effectiveness of competition may decline even in these industries. The airline industry is an especially good example of this dangerous trend. From 1968 to 1986 the airline industry had but one really good year. Some of the other years were very, very bad. But many of the industry's problems are now behind it. With numerous mergers already complete and with a growing shortage of landing slots and loading gates hampering new entries, the industry may gradually gain considerable monopolistic control over prices and profits.

TABLE 2.2 LONG–TERM COMPETITIVE INDUSTRIES, BY MAJOR TYPE

Major Type	Industry
Retail	Grocery stores
	General merchandise stores
Financial	Banks
	Savings & loans
Service	Hotels, motels
Transportation	Airlines
Manufacturing	Apparel
	Paper
	Oil (international integrated)
	Oil (domestic integrated)
	Furniture
	Copper
	Steel
	Tires
Regulated utilities whose profit margins are similar to those of competitive industries	Electric service
	Telephone communications
	Natural gas distributors

Increasingly Competitive Industries

This category includes seven of the forty–two industries we have analyzed. (See table 2.3) All of these industries have lost some market power over time. Six of the seven industries are manufacturing industries that have faced sharply increased foreign competition. The seventh industry–trucking–has faced increased competition partly due to deregulation of the industry.

Several of these industries were involved as active participants in pushing up prices to generate high profit margins in the incipient inflation of the 1950s, but not so much in the inflation of the 1970s. These industries had considerable monopolistic power in the early period but have since become more subject to the convergence principle.

The increased competition in these industries has not been due to a lower concentration ratio. Only aluminum and, to a lesser extent, chemicals have had significantly declining concentration ratios. But all the manufacturing industries have been subject to stronger foreign competition, as evidenced by rising import rates. Undoubtedly, increased foreign competition has been responsible for much of their loss of control of prices.

We must be careful in predicting the future of profit margins in these manufacturing industries, since their products are now becoming much more competitive with foreign goods due to the decline of the dollar on foreign exchange markets. Consequently, they are now experiencing sharp increases in profit margins. It is likely, however, that most, if not all of these industries, will remain competitive in the coming years, with profit margins fluctuating around the all–industry average, unless protectionism sharply reduces foreign competition.

TABLE 2.3 INCREASINGLY COMPETITIVE INDUSTRIES, BY MAJOR TYPE

Major Type	Industry
Transportation	Trucking
Manufacturing	Aluminum
	Cement
	Chemicals
	Lumber
	Motor vehicles
	Semiconductors

Long–Term Endangered Industries

These industries are identified, first, by profit margins well below average for long periods of time, and second, by a long–term difficulty in attracting capital as evidenced by stocks selling below book value and by rising debt as a percent of total capital. The convergence principle fails to return profit margins to the all–industry average in the few industries that fit the long–term endangered category.

Endangered industries do not all meet the same fate. Some go on year after year making valiant but unsuccessful efforts to improve margins. The textile industry has been an example to the present. The meat packing industry, on the other hand, went through a series of bankruptcies, forced reorganizations, restructurings, and sales of important divisions. (See appendix A.) The shoe manufacturing industry succeeded in restructuring itself. Large companies became shoe retailers, importing much of their product from abroad. Many small companies simply went out of business.

Many industries become *short–term* endangered, but are able to recover as the economy grows. Some firms go into bankruptcy. Survivors stop expanding, modify their products, and cut costs. This is the normal working of a competitive market. It is the convergence principle in action.

Only five of the forty–two industries, we have analyzed fall into the long–term endangered category. (See Table 2.4)

TABLE 2.4 LONG–TERM ENDANGERED INDUSTRIES, BY MAJOR TYPE

Major Type	Industry
Manufacturing	Farm Machinery
	Footwear
	Machine Tools
	Meat packing
	Textiles

Decreasingly Competitive Industries

Decreasingly competitive industries are those where vigorous competition destroys itself, leaving a few survivors able to exercise increasing control over outcomes of their markets. Two of the forty–two industries fall into this category: malt beverages and newspapers. (See Table 2.5)

The malt beverages industry is the only one we have analyzed that has shown a sharply rising concentration ratio. The concentration of most American industries has remained quite constant since the mid–1950s. Has this been due to fairly vigorous antitrust restraint on mergers between firms in the same industry? And if antitrust enforcement is further relaxed, might concentration increase substantially, bringing with it considerable monopolistic control over prices and the many adverse consequences of monopoly?

TABLE 2.5 DECREASINGLY COMPETITIVE INDUSTRIES, BY MAJOR TYPE

Major Type	Industry
Manufacturing	Malt beverages
	Newspapers

Long–Term Monopolistic Industries

Long–term monopolistic industries have profit margins that are substantially and persistently above average. It is precisely the pattern that would be expected when barriers to entry discourage other firms from entering the industry to take advantage of the high profit margins. This long–term, above–average profit margin pattern is evidence of monopolistic market power, but it does not guarantee that the high profits will continue. An analysis of each industry's market structure must be made to estimate how long the high profit margins might survive. Attracting capital has rarely been a problem for companies in these industries, as their stocks usually sell far above book value, and borrowing is made easy by low debt ratios and rising earnings.

Eleven of the forty–two industries we have analyzed fall in this category. (See Table 2.6) Surprisingly, eating places (major chains) and drugstores (major chains) are included because their profit margins have followed the monopolistic pattern. Appendix A explores the reasons why, and indicates that these two industries, together with security and commodity brokers and computer manufacturers, are losing their monopolistic position.

By far the largest industry in this category is one we call marketing conglomerates. This industry includes manufacturers of packaged foods, perfumes, cosmetics, personal care items, soaps, cigarettes, soft drinks, confectionery, proprietary drugs, and a number of miscellaneous industries such as household paper products. Marketing conglomerates sell small consumer products distributed principally through grocery stores and drugstores. Firms in this industry are *conglomerates* because they are active in several subindustries. The word marketing emphasizes that competition among them is generally more in selling rather than in design or production.

TABLE 2.6 LONG–TERM MONOPOLISTIC INDUSTRIES BY MAJOR TYPE

Major Type	Industry
Packaged goods manufacturing	Marketing conglomerates *Examples of subcategories* Cigarettes Perfumes and cosmetics Soaps and detergents
Service	Radio and TV broadcasting Advertising agencies
Retail	Eating places (major chains) Drugstores (major chains)
Financial	Security and commodity brokers
Manufacturing	Computers Drugs

How can we consider this large group of industries as a single industry? An industry is defined as a group of companies competing with one another. Companies included in the marketing conglomerates industry compete with each other in a number of ways. First, they are rapidly getting into each other's businesses. Second, they compete with each other for precious shelf space at the retail level. And finally, they compete for the customers' attention in all the advertising media.

Even though competition has spread across product lines in the marketing conglomerates industry, its intensity and nature have not yet been able to drive down the above–average profit margins. Indeed, the huge industry has shown a remarkable persistence in maintaining above–average profit margins. This fact comes as no surprise to economists who have long been aware of the market power of "product differentiation," whether real or created by superior merchandising. Product differentiation is really just brand name loyalty, and presents a serious barrier to entry to potential new competitors attracted by the high profit margins.

Although marketing conglomerates have market power sufficient to maintain profit margins significantly and persistently above the all–industry average, they do not have complete control over prices and profits. As indicated earlier, great rivalry exists among these many firms, and barriers to entry are not completely effective as they get into each other's businesses.

Profit margins for the marketing conglomerate industry have fluctuated around a level about 50 percent above the all–industry average. In trying to forecast future margins for this industry, one might anticipate that profit margins much more than 50 percent above the all–industry average would be so attractive that competition would be able to drive them down. The years 1986–1988 have witnessed extraordinary profit margins–double the all–industry average. Much of this gain in *relative* profit margins was due to the fact that poor performance (including large write–offs) in some manufacturing industries brought down the all–industry average. Undoubtedly, the extremely high relative profit margins will soon disappear. But profit margins for this industry will likely remain about 50 percent above the all–industry average as they have in the past.

Monopolistic firms, and divisions of monopolistic firms, producing items with brand name loyalty are being bought and sold regularly in the financial markets today. They are called consumer franchises. Considering the premium prices being paid for these monopolistic positions, Wall Street no doubt believes the monopolistic profits will continue.

What happens to monopolistic profits in the marketing conglomerate industry? The average firm in this industry faces a relatively slow rate of growth in demand for its products and yet experiences a significantly above–average–profit margin. *The combination of these two factors leads to an accumulation of cash*, over and above the amount required for internal investment. What happens to that cash? A very large part of it goes to the acquisition of other major firms within the marketing conglomerates industry.

Examples abound. Philip Morris acquires General Foods and Kraft; RJR Industries acquires Nabisco. These acquisitions have been going on for a long time, but have speeded up in recent years.

Although the antitrust authorities have recently seen fit not to oppose these mergers, such mergers may increase market power among the marketing conglomerates in at least two ways, even when the acquired company produces a substantially different product line.

First, the merger increases the total amount of money spent on advertising by a single company. There is an advantage in large–scale advertising. Large amounts of media exposure can be acquired at a lower price per unit than small amounts.[4] The cost of producing effective advertising is also less per unit of exposure for the large advertiser than for the small.

Second, in the competition for precious shelf space and for special attention by wholesalers and retailers, the large firm has a distinct advantage. Mr. Wilson, chairman of the newly formed RJR Nabisco, spoke of this power in a Wall Street Journal interview. He predicted that "the company will use its massive presence to pursue unique new relationships with the wholesale and retail trades."[5] That massive presence is largely a product of mergers, and adds to monopolistic power in the marketplace.

More aggressive antitrust restraint would prevent further buildup of market power among the marketing conglomerates through mergers and acquisitions, and it would probably divert some of that excess cash into other ventures, thereby increasing the number of participants and the intensity of competition in these new areas.

We should emphasize that the large cash accumulations of these monopolistic, slow–growing industries is the best source of funds for the development of new competitive products in other industries. Those funds are in the hands of capable managers possessing marketing skills, marketing organizations, and a strong desire to see their companies grow. But when funds are used for acquiring other large firms, the result is a decrease rather than an increase in competition.

What is the outlook for other industries we have identified as long–term monopolistic? As we noted earlier in this chapter, the function of high profit margins in a free enterprise economy is to attract new capital and additional participants to an industry. For those industries where profit margins are still high, one test of how well the market is working lies in whether or not additional participants and new capital are being attracted to the industry. If not, barriers to entry may exist that require antitrust or other direct action to remove.

Five of the eleven long–term monopolistic industries we have identified are attracting additional capital in a dramatic fashion. These industries are drugs, computers, security and commodity brokers, drugstores and eating places. In industries that make up the marketing conglomerates industry, the issue is not as clear–cut.

The drug industry, for example, has attracted new participants—in the form of start–ups—such as Genentech, Cetus, and Biogen to exploit one of the most promising areas presently on the drug horizon: genetic engineering. These companies are well capitalized. At the same time, nondrug companies–mainly chemical firms–have entered the drug market directly. Companies specializing in generic drugs have entered the market and dramatically expanded to take advantage of the relaxation of regulatory rules protecting the existing position of companies whose drugs have gone off patent. And foreign companies in Europe and now Japan have entered the United States market in significant numbers.

The net result is a wide array of effective new drugs coming to market, a huge amount of new funds being devoted to research, and reduced prices for some drugs coming off patent. Competition has not yet fulfilled its function of driving profit margins down to the all–industry average, but at least the high profit margins have attracted new capital and new participants. In any practical sense, this seems like a market that is, in general, working fairly well. High profit margins are performing their legitimate function, at least in part.

The same kind of new competition is setting in on the computer industry. The days of its above–average profit margins are probably limited.

Appendix A points out the growing competition and almost inevitable decline in profit margins of three other high–profit–margin industries–eating places (major chains), drugstores (major chains), and security and commodity brokers.

Conclusions from Industry Analyses

The evidence seems to indicate that the management of structural competition in the corporate sector since World War II has been reasonably effective. The intensity of the basic competition built into the structure of corporate markets has shown considerable improvement. Also, a very large percentage of the corporate sector is now evidently very competitive.

Whatever can be said about the power of corporate America, one fact is clear. Most industries have not, in recent years, had sufficient monopolistic power to keep their profit margins much above the all–industry average for any appreciable period of time. That is, most industries are subject to the convergence principle. There are, of course, still industries with monopolistic power, undoubtedly more than we have identified in our analysis.

But basic structural competition must be strong enough to perform two other functions besides preventing individual industry profit margins from straying too far above the all–industry average. It must be strong enough to force aggressive cost cutting—that is, increasing productivity. And competition must also be strong enough to restrain *average* corporate profit margins.

The effectiveness of competition in improving productivity will be appraised in chapter 6. We must now look at the impact of competition on *average* profit margins.

COMPETITION AND AVERAGE PROFIT MARGINS

The convergence principle is sufficiently effective to keep profit margins in most industries from straying too far or too long from the all–industry average. But what about *average* profit margins? How effective has competition been in restraining *average* profit margins? And how high will average corporate profit margins be in the coming years? This question is of vital importance to those worried that corporations are siphoning off too large a share of corporate revenues at the expense of workers and consumers. The question is also of great importance to investors and business executives.

Has Competition Reduced Average Profit Margins?

For a considerable time after World War II, U.S. corporations were dominant in the world. But finally the destruction and scarcities created by the war were overcome, and competition began to build. Two sources of data indicate that average corporate profit margins in the United States have come under greater competitive pressures since the mid–1960s.

Chart 2.1 shows corporate profits, after tax, as a percent of total income generated in the corporate sector. That share of corporate income fluctuated around 10 to 12 percent from 1953 to the mid–1960s. It dropped sharply in the late 1960s, and since then has moved irregularly sideways. Apparently the competitive environment has prevented corporations since the mid–1960s from raising prices sufficiently to maintain profits at the earlier share of income.

From a second point of view, common sense suggests that in a highly competitive economy some relationship should exist between profits from the use of capital (corporate profit margins) and the cost of capital. When profit margins are substantially above the cost of capital, corporations will obtain new funds to add to capacity, output will be expanded, and the increased supply will force profit margins downward toward the cost of capital. The

CORPORATE PROFITS AFTER TAX AS A
PERCENTAGE OF CORPORATE DOMESTIC INCOME

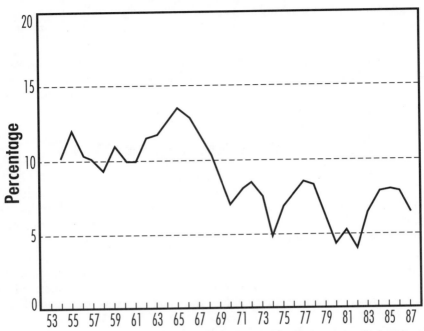

Chart 2.1 Corporate domestic profits after tax, with inventory valuation and capital consumption adjustments, as a percentage of corporate domestic income.[6]

speed of such a process will, of course, depend upon many factors including executive views of the outlook for the continuation of those high profit margins, and the rate at which demand increases to absorb the additional output.

The most important single *external* source of capital is borrowing, and for large corporations this usually means issuing bonds. Chart 2.2 shows the relationship between corporate profit margins as represented by the average return on equity of the Standard & Poor's index of 400 industrial companies, and the interest yields on an index of newly issued corporate bonds, a measure of the cost of borrowed capital.

(The relationship between the cost of *borrowed* capital and the return on *equity* capital is rather complex. But the theoretical and empirical relationships are so loose that elaboration is probably not warranted at this time.)

During the period of weak competition up to the mid–1960s, profit margins were 2.5 to 4 times the cost of borrowed capital. But in the more competitive environment after the mid–1960s, corporations were unable to maintain the previous large profit–margin premium over the cost of borrowed funds.

Profit margins surely must command a premium over bond yields, but the size of that necessary premium is very difficult to estimate. We can, however, make some conjectures as to the probable size of the premium and its implication for corporate profits in the coming years.

The Outlook for Average Corporate Profit Margins

The question of how high average corporate profit margins will be in the coming years is an important one for investors, corporations, and governments. As chart 2.2 shows, in 1988 corporate profit margins on equity rose above 17 percent, the highest return of the previous thirty–five years. A good possibility exists that by 1995 margins will drop below the lowest point we have seen since World War II. Why?

Extreme pressure is building in this country and among our creditors around the world for the United States to reduce the federal budget deficit. Also, the Federal Reserve appears committed to maintaining a low rate of inflation. These two programs, if realized, will bring interest rates on corporate bonds down again, probably to around 6 to 7 percent, but still half again above the level that prevailed in the early 1960s. The question then arises, Will profits on equity remain high as they were in the early 1960s or will they decline along with interest rates? They probably will decline. *At no time in the period between 1953 and 1988 did low interest rates and strong structural competition in the corporate sector occur simultaneously.*

Until the mid–1960s, when interest rates were low, structural competition in the corporate sector was weak, allowing high profit–margin premiums to prevail. Later, as structural competition in the corporate sector strengthened, interest rates were high. But now a distinct possibility exists that low interest rates and strong structural competition at the corporate level will co–exist. If this happens, the profit–margin premium over the cost of borrowed capital should narrow to, say, the roughly 50 percent premium that has prevailed since the late 1960s except for the extraordinary period of recession and high interest rates of early 1970s. That will put profit margins at about 9 to 10 percent. Such a decline in profit margins will just about offset the normal rise in corporate revenues over a five–year period, leaving corporate earnings flat for that period. Cries of profitless prosperity will certainly be heard on Wall Street. That leveling–off of corporate profits may be just one or two years away.

41

RETURN ON COMMON STOCK EQUITY
AND CORPORATE BOND YIELDS

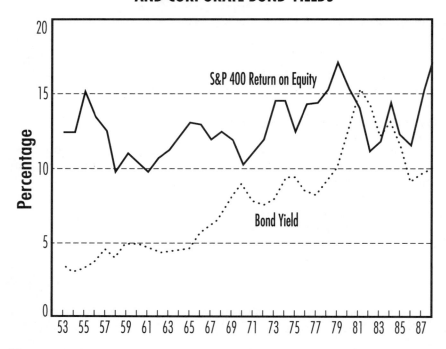

Chart 2.2 Average return on equity (after tax) of Standard & Poor's 400 industrial companies and yields of newly issued high-grade corporate bonds.[7]

Of course, putting even approximate numbers on a forecast of this sort is hazardous, but the trend is very likely to occur. Our growing foreign debt will give rise to increasing pressure to reduce the budget deficit. If the Federal Reserve tries to back away from the policy of attacking inflation early, the financial markets (stock, bond and foreign exchange) will likely force it to reverse its policy. The inflation rate, then, is likely to remain low, interest rates are likely to decline, and the spread between corporate profit margins and interest rates is likely to narrow, reducing profit margins to the lowest level that has prevailed since World War II.

BELOW–CAPACITY COMPETITION AND CORPORATE PROFITS

So far we have discussed the effect on corporate profit margins of *structural* competition built into markets. We also need to look briefly at how corporate profits respond to changes in *below–capacity* competition.

Corporate profit margins are very sensitive to changes in below–capacity competition. Chart 2.3 shows the relationship in the manufacturing sector of the economy.

Capacity utilization nearly always begins to decline *before* the actual downturn in business activity at the beginning of recessions. This is true because output begins to slow while capacity continues to expand. As capacity utilization declines, competition becomes more vigorous, and corporate profit margins immediately come under pressure.

MANUFACTURING RETURN ON EQUITY
AND CAPACITY UTILIZATION

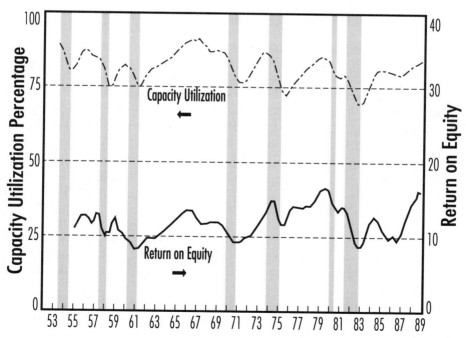

Chart 2.3 Manufacturing return on equity and capacity utilization, four–quarter average. The shaded areas indicate periods of business contraction.[8]

Putting it another way, corporate profit margins are the first casualty of Federal Reserve efforts to slow the economy to curb inflation. (Chapter 3 will show the far different response of wages to such Federal Reserve restrictive action.) At the trough of business activity, profit margins also respond immediately to increases in capacity utilization. They are the first beneficiaries of expanding business activity.

In summary, it is easier for the Federal Reserve, by managing below–capacity competition, to affect corporate profits than it is to influence any other income sector in the economy.

THE OUTLOOK FOR COMPETITION IN CORPORATE MARKETS

Evidence from analyses of both industry and aggregate profit margins indicates that structural competition in corporate markets in the United States has improved somewhat since the mid–1950s. What have been the causes of this increased competitiveness, and will it continue to improve?

The Causes of Increased Competitiveness

The natural working of the market over a long period of time has been an important factor in improving competition in the corporate sector. In some industries, such as the huge chemical industry, it took considerable time for high profit margins to attract sufficient new competition to drive those margins down to the all–industry average. The convergence principle often acts slowly. Also, the recovery of the world economy after World War II took many years to produce a rigorous international competition in many industries.

But in addition to these general causes of increased competitiveness, three government policies have been critical in the improvement of competition in corporate markets:

- A positive commitment to greater international trade. The result has been a growth rate for both exports and imports that has been much faster than the rate of growth in industrial production in the United States.

- A fairly aggressive enforcement of antitrust legislation. Both antitrust restraint and the *threat* of antitrust restraint have been important in preserving and improving competition.

- Deregulation of some industries where competition was limited by government regulation–particularly trucking and air transportation.

The worrisome prospect is that all three of these policies *may* be reversed. Some reversal has already begun. Almost everyone agrees that at least some relaxation of antitrust enforcement has occurred. Also, a growing protectionist movement has appeared in this country. The sharp decline of the dollar is already reducing the extreme foreign competition of the past few years. There is even a little talk of reregulating some of the industries that have been deregulated.

Competition in the corporate markets at the moment is in reasonably good shape. But to achieve our goal of reducing the need for below–capacity competition we must preserve the past improvements in structural competition and find ways to achieve an even better performance. The problem of preserving and enhancing international competition is considered in the final chapter. But we now need to review briefly the arguments over antitrust enforcement.

The Battle over Antitrust Enforcement

The main battle over the management of competition at the corporate level, as indicated at the beginning of this chapter, is being waged between the conservative Chicago school, which argues for substantial relaxation of antitrust restraints, and mainstreamers who argue for the maintenance of stringent antitrust enforcement. The Chicago school has been winning the battle. Lawyers friendly to that view have lately dominated the enforcement policies of the Justice Department and the Federal Trade Commission, and have been supported by a batch of new federal judges friendly to the conservative position.

The central *issue* of the debate is the amount of freedom business executives should have in merging their firms with others. The Chicago school argues that many mergers are necessary to take advantage of efficiencies that come with large–scale operations. And they argue that business executives, not government officials, are best able to estimate those efficiencies. Furthermore, they argue, if businesses should merge just to reduce competition and to reap monopoly profits, new competitors would quickly arise, increasing competition and destroying those high profit margins.

Mainstream economists disagree on every count. They argue that bigness is often not necessary for efficiency, that claims of economies of scale are frequently illusory. They point out that business executives are too often motivated by the quest for monopoly profits rather than just striving for efficiency; therefore, they should not be allowed complete freedom to merge as they wish. And mainstreamers attest that, most important of all, once monopolies become entrenched, it is often very difficult and very time consuming for new competitors to enter the business; in the meantime, great damage is done by the monopolies.

The central *fact* of the debate is lack of knowledge. It is difficult to estimate in advance the effects a merger will have on productive efficiencies or on monopoly pricing. It is even difficult to measure these effects after the fact of a merger. Statistical techniques are not adequate to determine precisely the point at which industry concentration will begin to create monopoly profits or to affect productive efficiency. (Indeed, we will argue in chapter 6 that monopoly is more likely to *reduce* productive efficiency than to increase it.) Given these judgmental difficulties, we must ask how the greatest damage might occur: with a too–lax or a too–tight restraint on business combinations.

If antitrust enforcement were too tight, damages would not be great. Too–tight enforcement would simply mean that some firms would not be allowed to merge even though such mergers would truly create productive efficiencies due to economies of scale and even though monopoly pricing would not result. But if economies of scale really were possible, then the firms denied the right to merge but convinced of those economies, would certainly expand internally, becoming more efficient. The error of too–tight enforcement would be corrected. Not much would be lost by erring somewhat on the side of too–tight enforcement.

If, on the other hand, antitrust enforcement were too lax, serious losses might prevail. Too–lax enforcement would mean that firms would be allowed to merge when the result would be a significant boost in monopoly prices rather than in production efficiency. The Chicago school, of course, argues that in this event new competitors, attracted by the high profits, would quickly arise, increasing competition and driving down the high profit margins. But what if barriers to entry were sufficiently strong to discourage most new competition? Certainly there are important industries in the United States–particularly in the marketing conglomerate area—where barriers to entry are significant. In such cases monopoly profits would remain high, and all the other adverse consequences of monopoly would be aggravated.

The Chicago school's analysis is a bit inconsistent. It argues that economies of scale are important, frequently requiring large operations. At the same time it argues that barriers to entry are low. Actually, when economies of scale are important, existing large producers have a substantial advantage over new competitors, and, therefore, barriers to entry are substantial.

In a 1986 paper, Judge Frank H. Easterbrook of the Seventh Circuit Court of Appeals, a proponent of the Chicago school's skepticism of antitrust enforcement, emphasized our lack of understanding of the effects of mergers and other business practices. He concluded that since we are not sure of the results, government should back away and not interfere with market processes except in very clear–cut cases of cartels and monopolies. Government interference might do more damage than good.[9] But contrary conclusions can be drawn from an awareness of our lack of knowledge.

If we relax antitrust restraints substantially, and the policy turns out to be wrong, creating many entrenched monopoly situations, it will be extremely difficult to reverse policy and break up those monopolies. There is grave danger in a precipitous relaxation of antitrust enforcement, if that policy turns out to be in error.

The relaxation (not abandonment) of antitrust enforcement for just a short period of time has been partly responsible for the wave of mergers and acquisitions. But, business executives are carefully testing antitrust authorities to see how far they can go. We do not know what would happen if a full implementation of the doctrine that "business knows best" were allowed over a long period. It could be disastrous.

In the best of times, the effects of mergers on competition are not known for some time after the merger becomes effective. At present the problem is especially acute. A merger might not reduce competition now, but may do so as foreign competition declines as we close the trade gap. Also, mergers that now seem harmless may become virulent as we attempt to operate close to full employment for extended periods with minimum below–capacity competition.

And, finally, in view of our lack of knowledge, too much of the debate has been expressed in strong ideological terminology. It would be more reassuring if the proposals were more flexible, such as a proposal to relax antitrust restraint where international competition is intense and to tighten restraint in other areas such as the marketing conglomerates industry where for decades the convergence principle simply hasn't been effective. To repeat, competition built into the structure of markets is a precious thing. It must be carefully protected and nurtured. The burden of monopoly is very heavy.

Chapter 3

Managing Competition in Labor Markets

After examining the problem of managing competition in corporate markets, we can now shift to an analysis of the management of competition in labor markets. Two extremely important aspects of *structural* competition in the labor markets must be considered in this chapter—labor unions and wage—gain norms. We will also consider the effect of *below-capacity* competition in labor markets.

THE IMPACT OF UNIONS ON LABOR MARKET COMPETITION

The management of competition in labor markets—as related to labor unions—has taken a much different path from the management of competition in corporate markets.

Until the 1930s, government influence on union activity was largely expressed through court decisions, and most of it was adverse to the unionization of workers. But in the 1930s, landmark legislation, especially the National Labor Relations Act, followed by very supportive executive and court decisions sharply increased the power of unions in the labor market. By these actions, competition among workers in the wage setting process was deliberately reduced. Although executive and court decisions have in recent years diminished the monopolistic power of unions, government support of workers' right to organize and bargain collectively remains formidable. What has been the economic impact of unions on structural competition and thereby on the inflation process, unemployment, and on the spread between high-wage and low-wage industries?

The Union Wage Premium

Union workers receive substantially higher wages than similarly qualified nonunion workers doing similar work. This differential is called the union wage effect or the union wage premium. When fringe benefits are included, it becomes the union compensation premium. Put another way, the union wage premium is the amount over and above the wage that would be necessary to attract and retain qualified workers if the union were not present.

Unions are able to achieve this wage premium for their members because they have considerable control over their markets. Control over markets is the definition of monopoly power. Hence, this wage premium is often called a monopolistic wage premium. It is a measure of monopolistic power, or conversely, a measure of the weakness of competition.

The union wage premium results in an excessive wage. Wages in an industry or occupation should be just high enough to attract workers to that industry or occupation—that is, to induce workers to get the proper training, to put up with the dangers, monotonies, insecurities, and other negative aspects of the job, and to put forth a proper effort to perform in that job. Any wage above that level is an excessive wage. It performs no economic function. The union wage is clearly above the wage necessary to attract workers to the job.

How large is this union wage premium? Many efforts to measure the union wage premium have been made. Gregg Lewis of Duke University has done the seminal work in this field. He estimates that the *average* union wage premium in the late 1970s for the United States was between 15 and 20 percent.[1]

The union wage premium is countercyclical. Unions have a higher wage premium in periods of recession and slow growth than in periods of strong economic growth and prosperity. As we shall show in chapter 5, low–paid, marginal workers have in the past narrowed the gap between their wages and the high wages of workers in the strong unions only in times of high employment such as the latter part of the 1960s. (An extreme case was World War II, when the gap apparently nearly closed.)

But using wage data alone is misleading because the greatest advances in compensation, particularly by the strong unions, have been in fringe benefits. Richard Freeman and James Medoff estimate that the average union total compensation effect is about one–quarter higher than the union wage effect.[2]

Also, *average* union wage premium figures for the United States have limited usefulness. There are strong unions and there are weak unions. What we really need to know is the effect unions have on wages and fringe benefits for each individual industry. The statistical problems involved are horrendous, primarily because of the inadequacy of the data.

50

Freeman and Medoff have attempted a study of union wage effects for individual industries but apparently have not, as of the publication date of this book, published it. They do, however, report some findings: the union wage effect is 0 to 4.9 percent for thirteen industries, 5 to 14.9 percent for seventeen industries, 15 to 35 percent for twenty–four industries, and over 35 percent or more for eight industries.[3]

To roughly estimate the union effect on *total compensation* we could increase these figures by one–quarter, the approximate average for all industries. (Actually, our studies indicate that higher–wage industries have fringe benefits that are greater proportionately than the fringe benefits of low–wage industries.) The resulting estimates are as follows: the union total compensation effect is 0 to 5.9 percent for thirteen industries, 6 to 18.9 percent for seventeen industries, 19 to 44 percent for twenty–four industries, and 44 percent or more for eight industries.

A. Gary Shilling, of an economic consulting firm by that name, has completed a study in which he estimates union total compensation effects for some thirty–two industries. (These were three–digit industries under the Standard Industrial Classification Code.) One–third of those industries showed a union effect on total compensation in excess of 30 percent—ranging from 34 percent to 83 percent.[4]

Peter Linneman and Michael Wachter, using very broad industry classifications, report union wage premiums up to 62 percent with premiums for over half of the industries they analyzed over 30 percent. They do not include fringe benefits in their analysis.[5]

Considering the enormous statistical problems involved, one should treat all the figures on union wage premiums and union total compensation premiums for individual industries with a fair amount of skepticism. However, the evidence does suggest that several industries with strong unions have achieved total compensation premiums in the 30 to 60 percent range. Anecdotal information indicates some may go considerably higher.

Another Way of Looking at Union Wage Premiums

Union wage premiums are generally estimated by elaborate statistical procedures that attempt to measure the wage differentials for comparable workers in union and nonunion industries. Following is another useful approach for estimating the adequacy of wage rates and the size of union wage premiums.

We have argued that in a highly competitive economy, wage rates for an occupation or an industry will be just high enough to attract the necessary workers to that occupation or industry in the face of available alternative employment. Any wage above that amount includes a wage premium that serves no economic function.

But how can we estimate the wage rate necessary to attract workers? The only people qualified to judge the adequacy of wage rates in an industry or occupation are those working in that industry and those deciding whether or not to enter that industry in the face of alternate employment opportunities. Bureaucrats are not qualified to make the judgment for other people.

The judgment of those working in an industry is estimated by their quit rates. Rising quit rates indicate growing dissatisfaction with the job package; declining quit rates the opposite. For example, *relative* quit rates in industries with strong unions and high wages during the inflationary 1970s generally were declining, indicating growing worker satisfaction with relative wages and working conditions. (See appendix A.) Wages were not driven up out of a need to attract or retain workers. (It should be noted that the judgment of workers as to job satisfaction must be measured by what workers do rather than what they say. In polls, union workers generally are more critical of their jobs than nonunion workers. But their relative quit rates indicate greater satisfaction with their jobs.)

Unfortunately, the government has stopped gathering quit rate data, thus eliminating one valuable source of information about the adequacy of wages in individual industries.

The judgment of workers outside an industry as to wage sufficiency is determined by looking at the numbers of those applying for jobs. Hiring new workers has rarely been a problem for high-wage industries, and often an announcement of a small hiring program will bring tens of thousands of applicants to stand in line for hours or even days just for a small chance at a high-paying job. The behavior of these job applicants tells us that these high-paying jobs carry substantial wage premiums.

This approach to estimating the wage rates necessary to attract workers does not allow us to put precise dollar amounts upon the necessary wage rates or upon the existing union wage premiums for a given industry. However, it can be very useful in many cases for making judgments as to whether wage increases are necessary to attract workers or whether they simply add to the union wage premiums.

Who Pays the Union Wage Premium?

The evidence cited suggests that *a large part of the union wage premium is shifted on to the consumer through higher prices*. Like a regressive consumption tax, that part of the union wage premium that is shifted is paid disproportionately by low income consumers. Many of those paying the union wage premium are earning less than half the amount earned by members of the strong unions receiving those wage premiums.

The evidence also suggests that of the union wage premiums absorbed by corporations through lower profit margins, a large part has been absorbed by companies in competitive industries, hurting their competitive positions and reducing their growth and their employment. Only a small part of the union wage premium effectively reduces monopolistic profits.

These statements are in sharp contrast to much of economic literature. A recurring theme in the literature has been to the effect that monopolistic unions are merely capturing part of the excessive profits of monopolistic corporations, and hence no serious damage is being done.[6]

Indeed, the very justification of the National Labor Relations Act in 1935 was the perceived need to equalize bargaining power between the worker and the corporation. What did that phrase mean? As applied to wages, it implied that corporations were getting too large a share of corporate revenue and the worker too little. It was a clear expression of the notion that higher wages would come at the expense of excessive corporate profits. The lawmakers apparently did not consider the possibility that higher union wages would be paid disproportionately by low income consumers.

(For those who wish to pursue the professional literature as to who pays the union wage premium, a brief survey is presented in appendix B under the title "How Do Unions Affect Corporate Profits?")

To determine who pays the union wage premium we must examine six different market situations:

- Federal, state and local governments employ over five million union members–over one–fourth of all union members in the United States. Since governments make no profit, the monopolistic union wage clearly must be paid by the taxpayer, or by higher user fees, such as for postal services. State and local governments and federal service organizations such as the post office hire most of the unionized government workers. State and local tax systems are often somewhat regressive. User fees to a large extent are business costs and are reflected in the prices of consumer goods. These too are regressive. Therefore, monopolistic wages of government union workers are clearly paid by state and local taxpayers and by the consumer. Low–income people pay a disproportionate share of such excessive wages.

- Public utilities employ another three–quarters of a million union workers. The profits of these firms are regulated in such a manner that all costs—including union wage premiums—are passed on to the consumer. Utility costs, along with the cost of other necessities such as food, rest heavily on low–income families. (See appendix A for an analysis of the behavior of utility profits.)

Governments and public utilities together hire nearly one–third of all the union workers in the United States. Certainly union wage premiums in these areas do not come out of profits.

- Monopolistic industries may or may not pass union wage premiums on to the consumer. Monopolistic industries are defined as those having control over outcomes of their markets. But control over markets is always a matter of degree. Within the limited control they have, how do they set prices?

    Monopolistic industries rarely try to maximize profits in the short run.[7] Rather, they set general goals such as growing at some rate faster than the general economy, or maintaining some designated profit margin, or just holding market share. Perhaps the most common goal among monopolistic firms is to earn above–average profit margins that will allow superior growth but that will not be so high as to induce *potential* competitors to break down industry barriers and become *real* competitors.

    It would seem, then, that monopolistic industries earning a profit margin that had achieved these goals, would maintain that satisfactory profit margin and pass increases in union wage premiums on to the consumer. It is difficult to find clear–cut cases where the union wage premium effectively reduces the profit of monopolistic industries. Undoubtedly, some such situations exist, but documentation is difficult.

- Companies in a *competitive industry that is almost entirely unionized* generally face similar labor costs as far as wage rates, fringe benefits, and many working conditions are concerned. Unions in these industries have achieved their goal of taking wages out of competition. Since all firms pay about the same wages, these wages can be passed on to the consumer without hurting any individual firm's competitive position. It is usually done even when the rising prices bring slower growth in product demand and reduce employment for the industry. Hotels and stores in a fully unionized city, the steel industry before foreign competition became so onerous, are examples of industries where wages have been taken out of competition.

- In *competitive industries that are substantially but not fully unionized*, nonunion companies often pay wages close to union scale to avoid being unionized. This is the union threat effect, and often serves to take wages out of competition. When this happens, wages become a uniform cost and must be passed on to the consumer just like material costs.

- In those competitive industries where *unionization is not nearly complete and wage rates do not become uniform*, the companies paying the union wage premium are at a disadvantage. They find it difficult to shift the wage premium on to the consumer because their competitors have lower wage costs and can cut prices. Absorbing the union wage premium is equally difficult in these industries since profits would be sharply reduced or even eliminated. In this third case, then, it is not clear how much of the union wage premium is passed on to the consumer in higher prices and how much is absorbed by reduced profits.

One fact is clear. In the aggregate, unionized companies and industries have been losing market share. In oversimplified terminology, unions, by forcing excessive wage premiums, have priced their workers out of the market.

In the May 1986 issue of the *American Economic Review*, two articles document the loss of market share by companies and industries paying the union wage premium. The first article, by Peter Linneman and Michael Wachter, concludes, based on a study of the period 1973–84, that "the so-called deindustrialization of America appears to be a union–specific phenomenon, at least at the one–digit level." [8] (One–digit level refers to the Standard Industrial Classification, a broad industry classification.) In the second article, Richard Edwards and Paul Swaim observe, "In effect, labor's changing circumstances seem to be reflected in a quantity rather than a price adjustment: the union wage differential has not changed, and instead there has been a rapid substitution of nonunion for union workers." [9] (Data were for the period 1979 to 1984, when the high wage premiums were leveling off but union employment was sharply declining.)

In summary, then, unionized companies in competitive industries either pass the union wage premium on to the consumer or lose market share. Which of these events occurs depends largely on whether or not the unions succeed in taking wages out of competition by nearly complete unionization of the industry.

In 1978, Charles Brown and James Medoff claimed that unions increased productivity enough to offset the wage premium so that neither of the adverse results just cited would have to occur.[10] Evidence provided by Linneman and Wachter seems to indicate otherwise. (A further analysis of union effects on productivity will be presented in chapter 6 and in appendix B, "Union Effects on Productivity and Union Work Rule Effects on Efficiency.")

The previous argument that much of the union wage premium is passed through to consumers does not imply that such action is *immediate*. In many cases it takes a good deal of time—sometimes several years—for the shifting to take place, and in the meantime, a rise in union wage premiums adversely impacts corporate profits.

Evidence from Industry Analyses

It is not an easy task to determine precisely on an industry–by–industry basis how much of the union wage premium is passed through to the consumer, how much is absorbed by lower profits in competitive industries, and how much is absorbed by lower profits in monopolistic industries. An examination of the forty–two industries in appendix A will help to give a feel for the possibilities. In our study of those industries we have used three main approaches to estimate who pays the union wage premium:

- An analysis of whether the union has been able to take wages out of competition by extensive organizing. Companies in industries that are fully unionized and that have relatively uniform wages, find it easier to pass union wage premiums on to the consumer. This is true whether they are in monopolistic or competitive industries.

- A comparison of the relative sizes of labor costs and pretax profits. The higher labor costs are in relation to pretax profits, the harder it is to absorb union wage premiums via lower profits. Most of the large corporations we have looked at have employee costs three to eight times pretax profits. Obviously, absorbing significant wage premiums through reduced profits would be extremely difficult for such corporations. In a few industries such as the oil industry, total employee costs are very close to pretax profits. In such cases the question of whether union wage premiums are absorbed by profit reduction must be answered by other evidence.

- A comparison of the *timing* of important changes in relative wage rates and relative profit margins. If monopolistic industries have lost market power as evidenced by declining relative profit margins at a time when relative wages have been rising, it might be argued that the loss in monopoly profits *could* have been caused by the rising relative wages. However, the loss of monopoly power has usually come at a time when relative wages have *not* been rising.

What has been the relationship between the timing of changes in relative wages and changes in relative profit margins in our forty–two industries? Eighteen industries showed sustained rising relative wages throughout the inflationary period of the 1970s and early 1980s. But of those eighteen industries with rising relative wages, only seven experienced concurrent declines in relative profit margins: steel, cement, chemicals, copper, tires, aluminum and drugs. Each of these industries, except the drug industry, experienced at the same time major increases in competition from rising

56

imports and other factors that could easily have caused the decline in profit margins.

In looking at details of the record, one would be inclined to judge that the declining relative profit margins in the seven industries (except for the drug industry) were due in large part to increased competition rather than to increased relative wages, although increased wages may have exacerbated the decline. In any event, if the decline in relative profit margins was caused by the rising relative wages, the profits were taken from competitive industries, not monopolistic industries. The six industries were already competitive before the relative profit margins declined. In appendix A we argue that we cannot determine for sure whether or not the rise in relative wages in the drug industry came at the expense of monopolistic profit margins.

We can look at the question of who pays the union wage premium in still another way. Any industry subject to the convergence principle will sooner or later shift wage increases on to the consumer through higher prices. If the total wage increase cannot immediately be passed on to the public, profit margins will be reduced. But then under the convergence principle, new investment in that industry will slow, other adjustments will be made, and finally the normal growth in demand will allow prices to rise. Some endangered industries, of course, may go for quite a period of time before prices can be raised to regain average profit margins.

In summary, then, firms will shift wage premiums on to the consumer by raising prices when it is relatively easy to do so, and when it is difficult to absorb them by reducing profits.

- It is easy to pass wage premiums on to the consumer when unions have taken wages out of competition and wages are reasonably uniform across an industry.

- It is easy to pass wage premiums on to the consumer when firms have considerable monopolistic control over their markets.

- It is difficult to pass wage premiums on to the consumer when demand for the industry's product is highly elastic—that is, when an increase in prices will result in a sharp decline in the quantity purchased, as in the case of an industry with substantial foreign competition.

- It is difficult to absorb wage premiums by reducing profits when the wage bill is very high in relation to pretax profits.

In summary, then, the evidence cited in this chapter and in appendix A suggests that *much*, but not all, of the rising relative wages–and wage premiums–has been successfully shifted on to the consumer in rising prices.

Conclusions from Industry Analyses

Two obvious conclusions can be drawn from our analyses. *First, labor negotiations, including strikes, are not just a system by which corporate revenues are divided between the corporation and its workers. Rather, they are more a process for determining the size of the union wage premium that consumers must pay.* If one accepts the earlier analysis that much of the union wage premium is shifted on to the consumer through higher prices, this conclusion is inescapable.

Second, if excessive union wage increases are passed on to consumers in higher prices rather than being absorbed by corporations in lower profits, then unions are engines of inflation whenever their monopolistic power over labor markets is exercised.

From a different point of view, if most industries do, indeed, pass union wage premiums on to the public in higher prices, then it is not likely that competitive industries with profit margins near the all–industry average are really monopolistic industries with excessive profits being captured by monopolistic unions.

Very little economic research has been done on an individual industry basis to deal with the question: Who pays the union wage premium? The question is of such vital importance that it should be the subject of intense economic research and debate. A great deal of information can be obtained to help answer the question for many individual industries. On the other hand, a few broad statistical studies have been made using data covering many industries in an effort to answer that difficult question. These studies are referenced and reviewed briefly in appendix B under the heading "How Do Unions Affect Corporate Profits?"

Some of these studies arrive at conclusions somewhat different from ours. They claim that a substantial part of the union wage premium reduces *monopolistic* profits but not so much the profits in competitive industries. They are saying, in effect, that industries that have considerable power over pricing in their markets choose to absorb the wage premium through lower profits rather than by raising prices; while industries that do not have power over their markets manage to pass the wage premium on to customers through higher prices. Such assertions as these are not quite credible.

When Has Union Monopolistic Power Been Used?

Unions have used their market power to increase their wage premiums mainly in the period of incipient inflation from 1955 to 1960 and then again in the inflationary era from 1970 to 1982. In both these periods wages (plus fringe benefits) of strong unions pulled way ahead of weak union and nonunion wages. (See chapter 5.) Therefore, unions bear part of the responsibility for the monetary restraint needed to curb inflation during those two periods.

Union power was not used to increase union wage premiums in the economic golden age of the early 1960s. Why not? Because they were under the disciplining force of a well–established low wage gain norm, a product of the restrictive monetary policy of the 1950s. Most unions acted responsibly under the informal discipline of the wage norm. In the late 1960s that norm was breaking down, but unions (except for construction and a few miscellaneous unions) still did not use their market power to increase their wage *premiums*. The reason may have been that unions underestimated the inflation rate when signing their typical three–year contracts. Not many of them had cost–of–living escalator contracts at that time.

How Extensive Is the Impact of Union Power?

Unions clearly weaken the intensity of structural competition. How important is that union effect on total competition? Evidence indicates that it is not trivial.

Employment costs make up nearly two–thirds of the entire cost of doing business in the United States. The Bureau of Labor Statistics gave a weight of 35 percent to the union workers' share of the entire employment cost index for 1977. This represented a 26 percent union share of the nonagricultural labor force plus the higher–than–average wage of union workers. Considering that this 35% of employment cost included an average wage premium, including fringes, of 20 to 25 percent due to market control, it is clear that at that time unions caused a substantial weakening of structural competition.

In addition, there is the "spillover effect." When strong unions demand and get large wage increases, efforts are made by other unions to match as closely as possible the strong union gains. So the initial wage settlements have a magnifying effect on inflation because of the effect on other wage settlements as well as on nonunion wages. This is called the spillover effect.

We have looked at some twenty professional articles attempting to measure the spillover effect. Although results are not completely conclusive, the weight of evidence indicates that large union wage settlements influence other wage settlements through several channels—from union firms to nonunion firms in the same industry, from union firms in one industry to both union and nonunion firms in other industries, and from union workers to white–collar workers in the same company. (See appendix B, "Union Wage Spillover.")

It seems unbelievable that wage increases in the union sector, which amounted to 35 percent of the country's total employment cost in 1977, would not have a substantial impact on lagging nonunion wages. The impact would result from (1) the simple imitation effect on nonunion firms, (2) the necessity for nonunion firms to follow union wage increases to keep from losing their best workers, and (3) the direct effect on the cost of living caused by the union wage increases.

At least some spillover, then, and probably a substantial amount must amplify the effect of union market power. This union market power can be a powerful impediment to the effective operation of structural competition in holding down wages and prices, as it was from 1955 to 1960 and again from 1970 to 1982. Equally, the below–capacity competition required to offset this impediment to effectively operating structural competition can be substantial and harmful.

(Since 1977, the Bureau of Labor Statistics' weighting of union workers' share of the employment cost index has declined from 35 percent to about 25 percent. Unions, therefore, now have a somewhat smaller effect in limiting the efficacy of structural competition than they did in the inflationary era of the 1970s.)

Summary

In summary, we believe that the following assertions can reasonably be made as to the union impact on labor market competition.

First, the existence of substantial union wage premiums demonstrates the market power that unions have to force wages above the level that would prevail in a competitive market—that is, above the level necessary to attract and retain qualified workers.

Second, increases in union wage premiums are largely passed forward to the consumer in higher prices, thus intensifying inflation and causing the Federal Reserve to tighten money, slowing the growth of the economy. The shifted wage premium is paid disproportionately by low–income workers.

Third, the magnitude of the union wage premium plus a spillover effect indicates that the union impact in exacerbating inflation has been substantial; therefore, unions must bear significant responsibility for forcing restrictive monetary policy with its adverse consequences.

Fourth, union power has also had an adverse impact on employment in unionized industries. By exercise of their market power, unions have priced themselves out of the market. Unionized industries have lost substantial market share.

And finally, union power over markets has not always been exercised. In the golden age of the 1960s, unions respected the informal discipline of the low wage–gain norm. It could happen again.

COMPETITION AND WAGE–GAIN NORMS

Probably the most important single factor in the determination of wage rates is the prevailing wage–gain norm.

What is a wage–gain norm? A wage–gain norm is a customary rate of wage increases. When a particular rate of wage gain prevails for a period of time, it gradually becomes a tradition, a custom, a norm that guides in the setting of future wage rates. Since it is a force that helps direct or control the size of wage settlements and is built into the structure of markets, it is considered to be part of the prevailing intensity of structural competition. In a formal sense it is a still active residual of a previous competitive environment.

A wage–gain norm is created by a specific degree of competition—structural competition plus below–capacity competition—that survives for a period of time. A wage–gain norm is changed by a substantial change in the degree of competition. The strength of a wage norm depends in part on its duration: it gains strength the longer it lasts.

Wage–gain norms have frequently been analyzed in economic literature–by George Perry, Arthur Okun, Michael Wachter, Daniel J. B. Mitchell, and Charles Schultze among others.[11] Other terms, such as wage traditions, wage–setting habits, and wage precedents have been used to describe much the same phenomenon.

A Review of Changing Wage–Gain Norms

Chart 3.1 shows changes in average hourly compensation since 1953, and helps us to review the changing wage–gain norms described in chapter 1. In the 1953–60 period a low wage–gain norm was established by rigorous monetary policy, creating considerable below–capacity competition to shore up weak structural competition and reverse the incipient inflation of 1955–56. This wage–gain norm was strong enough to be an important factor in establishing the noninflationary economic golden age of the early 1960s. But in the 1965–69 period, below–capacity competition virtually disappeared under stimulative monetary and fiscal policy. The sharp decrease in competition shattered the low wage–gain norm and created a norm of accelerating wage gains.

A norm of accelerating wage gains is one in which larger raises are expected at each contract negotiation for unions, and at each regular wage adjustment for nonunion workers. The many announcements made by unions during the 1970s that "this is the best settlement we have ever received" underscores the then–prevailing norm of accelerating wage gains.

CHANGES IN AVERAGE
HOURLY COMPENSATION

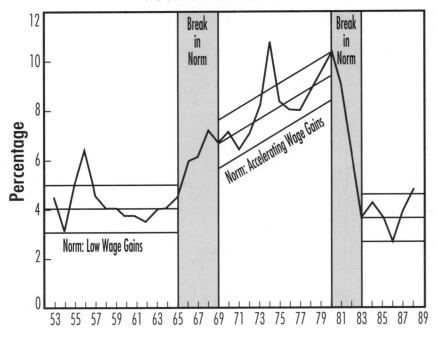

Chart 3.1 Annual percentage change in average hourly compensation.[12]

The norm of accelerating wage gains was temporarily put on hold by the two recessions of the 1970s, but these recessions were too short to break the prevailing wage–gain norm.

In economic literature, reference is often made to an upward shift in the wage norm in the 1970s. A norm of accelerating wage *gains* is far different from and much more dangerous than a single upward shift in the wage norm. This distinction must be emphasized. A norm of *accelerating* wage gains will, if allowed to continue, eventually get out of control, as it nearly did in 1978–79. Such a wage–gain norm is extremely hazardous. It has no natural limits.

The new norm lasted through the 1970s until a huge increase in below–capacity competition induced by restrictive Federal Reserve policy and a powerful surge in structural competition from burgeoning international trade broke the high wage–gain norm. We now seem to be in the process of rebuilding a new low wage–gain norm somewhere in the area of 3 to 5 percent. But it will take several years to become fully effective.

In summary, restrictive Federal Reserve monetary policy was largely responsible for the low wage gain norm of the late 1950s and early 1960s. Extremely permissive Federal Reserve policy in the late 1960s created the accelerating wage–gain norm of the 1970s. The break in the norm in 1980–82 was partly engineered by the Federal Reserve. It is apparent, then, that the Federal Reserve not only can substantially influence the degree of below–capacity competition, but it can also influence considerably the strength of structural competition by maintaining or changing the wage–gain norm.

It should be emphasized that wage–gain norms apply to both union and nonunion workers. Different wage–gain norms may, however, develop for different sectors of the economy. In the golden age of the early 1960s, union and nonunion wage–gain norms were the same. In the late 1950s and the 1970s, the union wage–gain norms were much stronger.

Why Do Wage–Gain Norms Persist?

What is the economic reason for the persistence of wage–gain norms? Probably two factors account for much of their strength:

- The need on the part of both worker and employer to have some notion of future wage gains for planning purposes.

- The influence of uncertainty. When severe uncertainty prevails, we tend to do what is customary.

For example, the calculation of an appropriate wage settlement in a typical three–year labor contract involves many difficult forecasts of an uncertain future. These forecasts encompass the possible response of customers to price changes, changes in material costs and technology, changes in interest rates and foreign exchange rates, costs of a possible strike, and reaction of competitors, to name just a few elements.

Though the future is uncertain, we must take action based on some kind of forecast. The most common method of forecasting is to extrapolate from the recent past into the future. And that is just about the same as saying that decision makers tend to do what is customary.

The Importance of Maintaining a Low Wage–Gain Norm

A low wage–gain norm is very important in the economic scheme of things. It is mandatory that we do not allow temporary disturbances such as, say, food price hikes due to crop failures, to have a permanent impact by changing the wage–gain norm.

For that reason, we prescribed as policy #1 at the beginning of this book the Federal Reserve's responsibility to keep inflation from accelerating, even if it involves accepting a small recession. After several years of such policy, wage and salary gains of, say, 3 to 4 percent will become the expected standard, and we will be able to move closer to full employment for extended periods without causing inflation to accelerate.

A brief note should be inserted here about the influence of the guideposts established in 1962 by the president's Council of Economic Advisors. These guideposts set limits that wage increases were not to exceed. They survived for about four years. Were these guideposts partly responsible for the low increases in wage rates of the golden age of the early 1960s?

A number of efforts have been made to measure the impact of the guideposts on wage increases. Not surprisingly, these studies have been unable to separate the influence of the guideposts from other factors that affected wage rates.[13] The studies are inconclusive.

It is instructive to note that the guideposts of the early 1960s *supported* the prevailing norm of low wage gains. The guideposts were not seriously violated until 1966. In the late 1970s, guideposts were used again, this time in an effort to *break* the prevailing norm of accelerating wage gains. These guideposts were totally ineffective.

The Impact of Below–Capacity Competition on Wage–Gain Norms

Wage gains are generally slowed when below–capacity competition increases, but the amount and timing of such deceleration are irregular from one cycle to another. In (and following) the relatively deep recessions of 1957–58, 1973–74, and 1980–82, response in the form of slower wage gains was substantial. In the smaller recessions of 1960–61 and 1970, response was mild. (See chart 3.1.) But in no case did wage *rates* actually decline because of recession. This is in contrast to corporate profits which are very vulnerable to increased below–capacity competition.

The question of how much wage–gains decelerate in response to recession does not seem so important now. But it was of burning importance in the 1970s when the general belief among economists was that it would take several years of recession—or depression—with unemployment over 10 percent to bring wage inflation down to the 3 or 4 percent level. And indeed it might have taken that long if the substantial increase in structural competition, mainly foreign competition, of recent years had not supplemented the increase in below–capacity competition. The important point is that the economy must suffer serious recession for below–capacity competition to reduce high or accelerating wage–gain norms significantly. Therefore, we must never again allow wage gains to accelerate. The correction is too painful.

(Since we have put so much emphasis on wage–gain norms in this book, we have included a section on related literature in appendix B entitled "Wage Norms.")

HOW THE CHANGING PRICE LEVEL RELATES TO WAGES

In economic literature, the changing price level is prominent among the factors listed as determinants of wage changes. We cannot review the extensive literature at this time, but a few observations should be made.

Price changes are not the *basic* causal force controlling wage changes. Rather, they are, like wages, a manifestation of the changing intensity of competition. The intensity of competition is the *fundamental* force controlling both prices and wages. Competition restricts wage increases directly, and it restricts wage increases indirectly by restraining prices and corporate profits.

There is a great deal of interaction between wages and prices, popularly referred to as the wage–price spiral. Prices affect wages, and wages affect prices. Much of the popular debate about this spiral is centered around the question of who started inflation–business or labor. It has not been a highly productive debate. Both wage and price changes are a product of the changing intensity of competition.

Wages and prices must move fairly closely together since prices must cover costs, and wages (in the broadest sense) represent about two–thirds of the cost of doing business for the nation as a whole. However, random factors from outside the economic system such as weather–induced crop failures also affect prices. Furthermore, wages and prices respond somewhat differently to the business cycle. Increases in productivity, of course, allow wages to grow faster than prices.

(For a detailed study of the relationship between prices and wages, see Daniel J. B. Mitchell's excellent book *Unions, Wages, and Inflation*, Chapter 4.[14])

THE OUTLOOK FOR COMPETITION IN LABOR MARKETS

Three important factors have sharply improved structural competition in labor markets: (1) the beginning of a new norm of low wage gains, (2) the improvement in global competition, and (3) the sharp decline in the percentage of the labor force that is unionized. If future management of competition preserves and enhances these gains, we can be optimistic about operating near full employment without inflation most of the time. Besides these three factors, changing interpretation of labor law and a trend toward profit sharing may also impact the future of competition in labor markets.

The New Norm of Low Wage Gains

Since 1983, the average annual increase in compensation has been in the range of 3 to 5 percent. (Different indexes show different rates of change. See chart 3.1) Workers generally have no thought of receiving, nor do employers have any thought of granting, the 9 to 10 percent annual increases common in the late 1970s. A new norm, or custom, or tradition now exists in the wage–setting process, and it has some disciplining power. If the Federal Reserve, by judicious management of below–capacity competition, should hold compensation gains at around the 3 to 4 percent level for another ten years, the norm would become a powerful influence in restraining inflation even when the economy is operating close to full capacity for an extended period.

A 3 percent annual compensation increase coupled with a possible 1.5 percent annual improvement in productivity (output–per–man–hour) would yield an inflation rate of 1.5 percent–but only after the dollar has found the level on international exchange markets necessary to close the trade gap and stabilize import prices, and only if the government does not add new hidden taxes or various requirements that increase business costs.

The new norm of low wage gains is a product of the courageous but painful Federal Reserve policy that broke the 1970s norm of accelerating wage gains by throwing us into the back–to–back recessions of 1980 and 1982. These recessions were the price we paid for earlier Federal Reserve errors, particularly the permissive monetary policy of the late 1960s. Since 1982, inflation has begun to accelerate twice, in 1983–84 and again 1987. In each case the Federal Reserve has tightened money and brought inflation under control *before wage rates began to accelerate, and without creating a recession.* As this is being written, inflation has begun to accelerate again, and this time it is being accompanied by a slight acceleration of wage rates, providing a sterner test of Federal Reserve resolve. But our successful experience of the past few years provides encouragement for the future.

Perhaps "gradualism" represents the greatest risk for future Federal Reserve management. A small increment to wage gains may be excused by a weak Federal Reserve Board on the ground that it is due to temporary factors or because it is not enough to warrant restraining action. And so wage gains will ratchet upward. As we become accustomed to that higher rate of wage gains, another small "temporary" upward move may be allowed. Soon we may find a norm of slight but still accelerating inflation. Even that would cause pain to correct.

This discussion must surely raise the question of whether the Federal Reserve can possibly manage below–capacity competition with such precision. In chapter 4 we argue that it can and most likely will. It will represent the implementation of our prescribed policy #1.

The Globalization of Competition

The globalization of competition has become apparent to almost everyone. It includes the general increase in international trade, the appearance on the economic scene of participants from many newly industrialized nations, and the setting up of manufacturing operations in the United States by a number of foreign corporations that had never been here before.

The globalization of competition is important in maintaining competition in the labor markets. It is virtually impossible for unions to take wages out of competition when an industry from one country is in competition with industries in other countries that have different cost structures. Many of the strong unions that led the acceleration of wages in the late 1950s and again in the 1970s such as the steel, auto, and oil refinery unions are in the manufacturing sector, which is especially subject to international competition.

All three of our prescribed policies are intimately involved in the management of international competition. The subject is so important that a special section in the final chapter of this book has been reserved to discuss the several ways by which the implementation of these policies can improve international competition.

The Decline of Unionization

As is well known, union membership as a percentage of total employment has declined sharply. The result, of course, has been a significant increase in competition in the wage setting process.

Two main reasons exist for the membership decline. First, unions have used their monopolistic power to drive up wages and price many of their workers out of the market. Second, several unions have lost part of their monopolistic power due to the increase in international competition and the reduction in regulation of the trucking and airline industries. Consequently, unionized firms have lost market share.

Will union membership continue to decline, or might union power experience a resurgence as international competition diminishes somewhat with the closing of the trade gap and as we attempt to operate more consistently near full employment? There is another important question. Will unions use their power to force their *relative* wages upward or will they act responsibly, accepting low–wage gain settlements as they did in the golden age of the early 1960s? We cannot answer these questions for sure, but if there is a major resurgence of labor power, and that power is used to drive wages upward, the proper management of competition will require a change in labor law to increase competition in labor markets.

Conflicts Over Interpretation of Labor Law

Just as a battle is being waged over implementation of the law governing the management of competition in corporate markets, so, also, is there conflict over implementation of the law concerning the management of competition in labor markets. In this case, the struggle is joined mainly in the National Labor Relations Board (NLRB) and the courts, but also in the political arena where elections determine who will appoint the board members and the judges who interpret the law. The issue involves a myriad of rulings that strengthen or weaken the power of unions to press their demands against employers.

Calls are occasionally heard for scrapping the entire National Labor Relations Act (NLRA), allowing labor–management relations to be determined under basic law governing contracts, torts, and property rights. Most argument, however, centers around interpretation of the NLRA rather than its elimination.

Labor leaders generally argue that recent interpretations of the NLRA have seriously curtailed the proper functioning of labor unions. Management, on the other hand, argues that recent decisions of the NLRB only serve to counterbalance the earlier decisions that were excessively in favor of labor. Perhaps most observers would argue that the effective impact of changing interpretation has been moderate.[15] The decline in unionization has more likely been due to the factors mentioned earlier—the increase in competition, and unions pricing their workers out of the market.

A major shift in labor legislation could, of course, have a substantial impact on competition in labor markets. If an important legislative shift toward strengthening labor's bargaining power were to occur simultaneously with a move to protectionism and a further relaxation of antitrust enforcement, there is little doubt but that greater Federal Reserve restraint would be required to curb inflation, and we would soon be operating much farther below full capacity and full employment.

No great movement is under way at present to make major changes in labor law. But two changes may become necessary, to allow increased union–management cooperation, and to bring competition to labor unions.

Union–Management Cooperation

In recent years the United States has seen a resurgence of interest in employer–employee cooperation. Evidence of this resurgence can be found in the academic literature and in the popular press. For instance, academic studies by Irving H. Siegel and Edgar Weinberg; Michael H. Schuster; Charlotte Gold; and Edward Cohen–Rosenthal and Cynthia E. Burton all show an increase in the incidence of and interest in such cooperative efforts as in–plant labor–management committees, quality of work–life programs, productivity sharing plans, and area labor–management committees.[16] In *Business Week* magazine, John Hoerr noted that by 1982 at least seven hundred plants of both union and nonunion firms had quality of work–life programs.[17] Such programs were rare in the mid–1970s. In 1984 a New York Stock Exchange survey indicated that 41 percent of the companies with more than five hundred employees had worker–management participation programs.[18] In addition, Cohen–Rosenthal and Burton have provided evidence of union–management cooperation in virtually every sector of the American economy.[19] Labor–management cooperation is not yet the norm, but without

doubt it is increasing. And the startling fact is that a great many of these cooperative arrangements may be illegal.

The NLRA, the basic labor law of the United States, set up a clear–cut adversarial relationship between unions and management. Cooperative plans between unions and management were prohibited. The purpose was to eliminate all the old "company unions" that were frequently subject to company domination. The Supreme Court in the 1938 Newport News Rule entrenched the adversarial relationship when it held that even a cooperative plan with which employees are satisfied and that involves no improper motives on the part of the employer is illegal.[20] Subsequent court decisions have made it clear that this rule applies very broadly to all aspects of union–management relations.

Recently, some circuit courts have seen fit to allow union–management cooperative organizations to remain intact based on employer and employee satisfaction with the plan. But the old Supreme Court decisions still stand. No significant case challenging recent cooperative plans has been pressed clear to the Supreme Court.

The adversarial relationship between unions and management set up by the NLRA certainly must have impeded union–management cooperation over the past half century. How important is union–management cooperation?

We took the time to read a hundred or so issues of periodicals published by various unions for their membership. In the area of worker–employer relations, a single theme was dominant. The corporation (or at least management) is the enemy. It is out to exploit the workers and will succeed in doing so unless the workers have union protection. This is the union side of the adversarial relationship. Undoubtedly, in most cases, the adversarial attitude is as strong on the management side.

How is it possible to have improving productivity, a feeling of teamwork, or a decent personal work environment when adversarial attitudes are dominant? They make for suspicion, inefficiency, inflexibility, and persistent squabbling.

In any event, union–management cooperative organizations are burgeoning. It may be that the movement will continue so that if the practice is challenged and gets to the Supreme Court, the practice will be so widespread that the Court will be reluctant to uphold the old adversarial decisions. Otherwise, a change in the NLRA will be required.

The movement toward cooperation might also result in a further decline in the union movement as the adversarial attitudes diminish. A number of labor leaders have expressed fears that this might happen.

The spread of union–management cooperation mainly in the areas of productivity improvement and quality of work life does not solve the problem of monopoly. If the company is in a monopolistic position, and can pass wage increases on to the consumer, unions and management may cooperate in granting inflationary wage increases as well as maintaining monopolistic profit margins. Also, if the industry is highly competitive, but the union has organized sufficiently to take wages out of competition, and if prices can be raised by the whole industry without too great a loss of sales volume, then union–management cooperation can still result in inflationary wage settlements.

In summary, union–management cooperation may have substantial benefits in improving productivity and making better the quality of work life, but it does not fully solve the problem of inflationary wage settlements.

Bringing Competition to Labor Unions

Over 80 percent of workers in the United States are without the protection of labor unions. They are not helpless. They are protected by law from various kinds of discrimination and against arbitrary discharge. Considerable protection is provided by law against unsafe working conditions. But more important they are protected by their abilities and willingness to perform productive work, and the fact that employers must provide sufficient compensation and satisfactory working conditions to attract workers to the job.

In offering their services to employers, workers are competing *individually* with other workers. They receive the compensation and enjoy the working conditions that the employer must provide to attract and retain workers. Union workers receive the same compensation plus an additional union wage premium which is the amount over and above the compensation necessary to attract and retain workers. As indicated earlier, this union wage premium does not perform any economic function.

When unions, by strike threat, force large wage gains on to corporations, the corporations can respond in several ways to avoid raising prices:

Reduce labor costs by automating.

Contract out part of the production process.

Hire temporary or part–time help.

Relocate plants.

Lease workers.

The use of these defenses to high wage costs has been growing, and, not surprisingly, is being resisted by unions. If excessive union wage gains prevail in the future, it may be desirable to change the labor laws to make it an unfair labor practice for unions to bargain to prevent the use of any of these defense mechanisms. Such a change in the law would put union workers closer to the competitive discipline faced by the over 80 percent of the rest of the labor force that is nonunion.

However, a major difference would exist between union and nonunion workers. Most nonunion workers compete with one another on an individual basis. Union workers would be competing *as a team*, trying to improve productivity (and holding down wage demands) to prevent contracting out, plant relocation, or any of the other defense mechanisms. Productivity in such an environment might improve in a spectacular manner. Cooperation would exist among workers within the union, but competition would prevail among groups of union and nonunion workers. Cooperation among individuals *within* groups where loyalty and teamwork are important plus competition *among* groups that do not have close personal ties may be the ideal form of economic organization.

Competition among corporations can be divided into many different functional categories; for example competition in design, research, production, advertising, selling, and in attracting and motivating workers. As we improve the basic structural competition of the American economy and operate closer to full employment for extended periods, competition in attracting and motivating employees will become more and more important in determining the success of a business. Business firms will have to continually improve their employee relations to become known as a good place to work. There will undoubtedly be many innovative forms of compensation and other rewards for superior performance. Profit sharing may be one of them.

The Trend toward Profit Sharing

As we noted earlier in this chapter, neither union nor nonunion wage rates are very responsive to restrictive monetary policy that slows the economy. Nonunion wages are somewhat more responsive than union wages, but all wage rates are resistant to the restraining force of increased below–capacity competition.

On the other hand, as we noted in chapter 2, corporate profits are very vulnerable to the restraining force of increased below–capacity competition. Corporate profits usually begin to decline at about the same time that the gap between output and capacity begins to rise, before the peak of the business cycle is reached. And they decline sharply as below–capacity competition increases in the contraction phase of a recession.

It follows, then, that if a significant part of wage rates (including salaries) were tied to corporate profits, wage rates like corporate profits would become more sensitive to Federal Reserve restraint. The result would be extraordinarily beneficial to the economy as a whole. When inflation threatened, a slight tightening of monetary policy would have as much impact in reducing wages, costs, and prices as it would have in reducing profits, output, and employment. Recessions would be much smaller, perhaps almost nonexistent, because the required Federal Reserve restraint would be so mild.

This policy is basically profit sharing. To be effective it would have to involve a substantial part of the wage rate. The trend seems to be in the direction of wage and salary bonuses based on profits, instead of outright wage increases. The trend should be encouraged. Besides helping to stabilize the economy, it should have a substantial impact on productivity. Profit sharing should also increase the savings rate, as workers face the uncertainty of not knowing what their total incomes will be until the end of the year, and, therefore, are inclined to postpone spending.

Profit sharing has been recommended in the United States for over one hundred years. It always sounds so good, but it has never really caught on. It has been used by a number of well–known companies in a minor way to determine the amount of contributions to pension funds. But true profit sharing of a substantial nature has been used successfully by only a few companies.

Recommendations have been made to encourage profit sharing by giving compensation from profit sharing some kind of tax break.[21] Such a program enters the dubious area of narrowing the tax base (probably substantially), thereby requiring higher rates on the remaining tax base.

Profit sharing would be a desirable addition to compensation techniques, but it should not be regarded as a panacea. Bringing greater competition to labor markets will probably require many innovative programs currently not even being considered.

COMPETITION IN OTHER SECTORS OF THE LABOR FORCE

Before we bring this chapter to a close, we should acknowledge other sectors of the labor force that have not been analyzed due to limitations of time and resources. The ones we regret most having passed over are the executive and professional sectors.

Top executive compensation may not amount to a large part of the total dollars paid as employment cost, but its visibility is so great that it often plays a large role in weakening structural competition.

Corporations must resist excessive union wage demands in order to reduce the need for monetary restraint to create greater below–capacity competition to restrain inflation. But how can corporations resist wage demands when top executives are granted large and highly visible salary increases?

Junior executives' salaries are generally restricted by rigorous competition in a market where such executives can and do move rather freely from industry to industry. But what discipline is there on top executive salaries?

If the evidence of extraordinary salaries paid to top executives were not enough to indicate the magnitude of top executive power to advance their personal fortunes, spectacular events of the last few years provide that evidence:

- The payment of blackmail (euphemistically called greenmail) to raiders by top corporate officers just to keep their jobs but against the interests of stockholders.

- The adoption of expensive "golden parachutes."

- Willingness to leverage up a corporate balance sheet to make the company less attractive to a raider. That is, top executives are willing to put their company in jeopardy to protect their jobs.

These are examples of the power of top executives. Evidence leads to the conclusion that the present structure of corporate management provides little competitive discipline to the salaries of top executives.

Professionals have occasionally had protected incomes due to the inability of new participants to enter the field. Prima facia evidence is the number of qualified people wanting to get into a profession but denied the ability to do so.

Within professions, little areas that have been immune to effective competition have often been staked out by specialists.

We do not yet have data to estimate the degree to which such barriers act as impediments to structural competition.

CHAPTER 4

MANAGING
BELOW–CAPACITY COMPETITION

In the previous two chapters we have focused mainly on the management of *structural* competition in corporate and labor markets. We now turn to the management of *below–capacity* competition. The main purpose of this chapter is to demonstrate that it is feasible for the Federal Reserve to manage demand–and therefore the intensity of below–capacity competition–sufficiently well to avoid both accelerating inflation and deep depression, and to keep recessions mild and infrequent. This represents the implementation of policy #1 prescribed in chapter 1.

THE BUSINESS CYCLE AS A MANAGED CYCLE

Since World War II, we have been living in a new and different kind of world as far as the business cycle is concerned. During this postwar period the business cycle has been a *managed* cycle. It will continue to be so.

Managed cycles have somewhat different magnitudes, frequencies and determinants from unmanaged cycles. Cycles since World War II are clearly of a different breed from the largely unmanaged cycles of the previous century. Periods of business contraction are less frequent, shorter, and of smaller magnitude. Even with some terrible management errors, the record of the managed cycles is far superior to that of the unmanaged cycles of the previous century. (See chart 4.1. A chart showing the *depth* of declines would be even more striking than this chart, which shows only the *length* of the periods of contraction.)

A COMPARISON OF MANAGED
AND UNMANAGED BUSINESS CYCLES

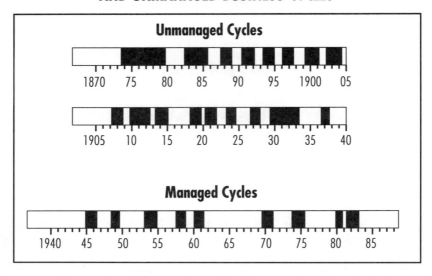

Chart 4.1 Managed versus unmanaged business cycles. The shaded segments indicate periods of contracting business activity.[1]

Business cycle management generally involves only the management of aggregate demand, within which the market mechanism performs the traditional functions of distribution of income, allocation of resources, and so on.

The Federal Reserve as Chief Manager

We argued in chapter 1 that the Federal Reserve System has become the stabilizer of last resort. Unlike in many other democratic countries, fiscal policy in the United States cannot be relied upon as a stabilizer because the fragmentation of political power makes action too slow and cumbersome. Without effective stabilizing action by government fiscal policy, the Federal Reserve is left as the only organization with both the power to substantially influence aggregate demand and with the capability of acting promptly. Therefore, it is now the chief manager of aggregate demand–the stabilizer of last resort. No matter what errors are made in fiscal policy, international trade, antitrust enforcement, labor negotiations, or other areas, the Federal Reserve must stand ready with a policy to prevent both accelerating inflation and deep depression. It cannot totally eliminate small recessions, although wise management and a little bit of luck can keep them to a minimum.

One of the most common cliches heard on Wall Street is that we have not repealed the business cycle. No, we have not repealed the business cycle, but we have, in truth, changed it into the "Federal Reserve cycle." The changing economic convictions of Federal Reserve governors now make a world of difference as to the characteristics of the cycle.

The Transmission Mechanism of Monetary Policy

What is the transmission mechanism by which the Federal Reserve controls (1) the level of business activity and (2) wages and prices? We shall now review briefly some of the material introduced in chapter 1.

The level of business activity. By well–established techniques, the Federal Reserve eases or tightens money, changing the availability of loanable funds, the rate of interest borrowers must pay, and the supply of money available for spending. This monetary manipulation encourages or discourages spending for goods and services by consumers, businesses, and sometimes governments. In turn, the changing spending (demand) for goods and services calls forth additional or lesser production of goods and services, and, therefore, determines the level of business activity.

The power held by the Federal Reserve to affect the aggregate demand for goods and services is substantial except in times of deep depression like the 1930s, when even very easy money failed to adequately stimulate demand.

Wages and prices. As pointed out in chapter 1, the Federal Reserve influences wages and prices by changing the intensity of competition. The mechanism is simple. By changing the level of business activity (as just described), the Federal Reserve determines how far below capacity the economy will operate. Thus, it changes the intensity of competition as the economy moves closer to or farther away from full–capacity output. The changing intensity of competition, in turn, changes the inflation rate.

A number of people apparently believe that the price level can be controlled by some mechanism outside the process just described. They believe we can have a restrictive policy for wages and prices and an expansive policy for output at the same time. But there is no way that monetary policy (or fiscal policy) can influence prices significantly other than through changing the level of business activity with its subsequent impact on below–capacity competition.

In summary, the Federal Reserve controls inflation by changing the intensity of competition. As stated in chapter 1, economists are well aware of the changing degree of competition as we move closer to or further away from full–capacity operation. But this awareness of the changing intensity of competition often gets lost when it comes to an explanation of the transmission mechanism by which monetary policy affects wages and prices.

Past Tests of Business Cycle Management

Some argue that business cycle management has not been properly tested, so we do not know for sure whether or not we can prevent deep depression. Business cycle management has not been tested by every conceivable event or combination of events, but it has been tested by the following events of the type that have been major causes of deep depression in the past:

- Bank and saving–and–loan failures. Waves of bank failures stand at the head of the list of factors that caused deep depression in the United States in the century–and–a–half prior to World War II. Depressions used to be called "panics" because they generally began with waves of bank failures precipitated by panic runs on banks.

  That is not likely to happen again. We now have the protection of federal deposit insurance and federal government backing of deposit insurance. And that insurance system has been thoroughly tested. In recent years we have had a great many failures of savings and loans and a number of bank failures. But the FSLIC and the FDIC have stepped in to prevent widespread losses to avoid runs on solvent banks and generally to sustain confidence in the banking system. And then when the FSLIC became overextended, the U.S. government stepped in to maintain its solvency. Indeed, the full faith and credit of the United States government is in a practical sense behind the deposit insurance system. Without that system we surely would have had a massive wave of runs on banks and savings and loans in recent years, and probably would have gone through a very serious depression.

- Heavy stock speculation followed by a major decline in the stock market in 1973–74. This decline was nearly as deep as the 1929–32 collapse when adjusted for changes in the Consumer Price Index which affects the *purchasing power* of stocks. And everyone remembers the crash of October, 1987, that produced barely a ripple in economic activity.

- The end of a major war—World War II. It did not produce a postwar depression as major wars had often done in the past.

- A major bout of inflation that was brought under control without producing deep depression.

- Irresponsible federal financing. It has been only partially corrected, but as yet has not produced deep depression.

Yes, the American (and the world) economic system has been well tested this past half century. It has survived without deep depression and even with relatively few moderate recessions. There is no reason it cannot continue to prosper as a managed economy, and management should improve.

We do not have to be fatalistic about the business cycle. It is not a natural law. The Federal Reserve has clearly demonstrated that it can modify the cycle by deliberate management. But we must be vigilant that we do not forget the mistakes of the past as they apply to the management of both recession and inflation.

Also, we need not be concerned that some longer *regular* cycle, such as the oft–resurrected Kondratief, is lying in wait to throw us into a long period of deep depression. The underlying economic structure has changed and will continue to change far too rapidly to allow much regularity in cycles to persist. There will be unanticipated shocks in our future, but not cycles with regular periodicity or magnitude.

CONTROLLING FACTORS IN A MANAGED BUSINESS CYCLE

The frequency, magnitude, and other characteristics of Federal Reserve managed cycles are determined largely by two aspects of competition:

- The changing effectiveness of structural competition.

- The promptness and vigor with which the Federal Reserve, as stabilizer of last resort, creates below–capacity competition to restrain inflation.

The interaction between these two types of competition over a business cycle can be illustrated by examining the two most important phases of the cycle—the peak and the trough.

The Peak: What Brings the Expansion Phase to an End?

Every downturn in business activity since the mid–1950s has been triggered by a tightening of monetary policy, and in each case monetary restraint was precipitated by accelerating inflation or the threat of accelerating inflation. Certainly some would dispute this statement, but it can be supported by an examination of the minutes of the Federal Open Market Committee and other economic data. How does the process work?

First, what causes inflation to accelerate? The culprit is declining competition.

As economic activity expands from the trough of the business cycle, we approach closer to full–capacity operation. Therefore, below–capacity competition declines.

An inverse relationship exists between the degree of competition and the inflation rate, but the two do not necessarily move proportionately. At first, the declining intensity of competition may have little effect on the inflation rate. However, as competition continues to decline, an "avalanche" point is finally reached when the decline causes inflation to accelerate. And this is the critical point of the expansion phase of the business cycle. It is the point that in the future will likely trigger Federal Reserve monetary restraint. Therefore, it is a kind of "stop sign" limiting the expansion of business activity on a short–term basis.

What determines the point at which declining below–capacity competition causes inflation to accelerate? *The point at which inflation accelerates is determined by the intensity of structural competition.* If structural competition is strong, inflation does not begin to accelerate until the unemployment rate is low and capacity utilization is high—that is, until below–capacity competition has weakened substantially. If, however, structural competition is weak, inflation begins to accelerate while unemployment is still high.

Second, what determines the exact timing and vigor of Federal Reserve restrictive action? The determining factor is the economic convictions that guide the members of the Federal Open Market Committee. If they respond quickly to accelerating inflation, containment can be achieved with a moderate degree of restraint, and even a small recession can be avoided. But if response is delayed until a norm of accelerating wage rates is established, then the subsequent therapy of below–capacity competition must be substantial.

On two occasions since the mid–1950s inflation began to accelerate from a very low level—in 1955 and 1966.

In the first case, the Federal Reserve promptly acted to restrict demand, accepting the hardship of recession in 1957–58 and again in 1960–61. Inflation was contained. The tradition of low wage and price gains was reinforced, a tradition that sustained a low inflation rate through the first half of the 1960s even in the face of substantial growth in the economy that brought the unemployment rate down to 4 percent.

In the second case, in 1966, as inflation accelerated, effective Federal Reserve restrictive action was postponed for four years. During this period a tradition of accelerating wage and price gains was established, and that tradition was not broken for a dozen years. Eventual costs were deep recessions, high unemployment, a slow growth rate, and many, many painful adjustments in various industries. Costs would have been minor if the Federal Reserve had acted earlier. This lack of quick Federal Reserve response to accelerating inflation has been the most serious mistake made in business cycle management in the postwar period.

Competition must be increased to curb inflation. The longer that steps to increase competition are postponed, the more serious is the medicine required.

The error of the Federal Reserve in the late 1960s was not simply a problem of lag between the time action was taken and the time it became effective. Minutes of the Federal Open Market Committee indicate that the committee was too afraid of the consequences of recession to take adequate restrictive action until conditions got so bad in 1969 that it had no choice.

In summary, the intensity of *structural* competition determines how soon inflation will begin to accelerate. The acceleration of inflation precipitates Federal Reserve restraint, slowing or even stopping growth in output. *Therefore, the intensity of structural competition largely determines the level of output and employment on a short–term basis, since it controls how closely we can approach full–capacity (full–employment) operation.* This point must be strongly emphasized.

Of course, the precise peak of the business cycle depends on the speed and vigor with which the Federal Reserve responds to the accelerating inflation, tightening money to create greater below–capacity competition. The promptness of Federal Reserve intervention depends upon the economic convictions of the governing bodies.

The Trough: What Brings the Contraction Phase to an End?

Federal Reserve authorities are quite properly scared to death of throwing the country into a 1930s–type depression. So as business activity declines, monetary ease is sure to follow–sometimes very quickly, but sometimes only after a few months of rising unemployment. Monetary ease will come even though the inflation rate is still high, although not accelerating.

Since World War II, starting a recovery in business activity has been very easy. There has never been more than a few months' lag between the time the Federal Reserve has decided to reverse the decline (as evidenced by the Federal Open Market Committee minutes) and the actual upturn in business activity.

Such quick response may not always be counted on to occur. The rapid build–up of debt, the weakened banking system, a possible slower response now that many markets are international, gross mismanagement of fiscal policy, enormous worldwide speculation—all are cause for concern. Future economic downturns will probably be contained by stimulative monetary policy.

In the unlikely event that gross mismanagement or some unforeseen event throws us into deep depression and stimulative monetary policy fails to bring recovery, then fiscal policy will once again become the stabilizer of last resort. The standard techniques of tax reduction and increased government spending will be used.

The Federal Reserve Cycle and Orthodox Business Cycle Analysis

For decades economists have endeavored to unravel the complex interacting forces that determine the characteristics of self–generating unmanaged business cycles. The following are a few of these forces:

The self–generating inventory cycle.

The investment multiplier.

The accelerator principle.

The automatic stabilizers.

The corporate profit cycle.

The consumer credit cycle.

All of these forces are still alive and well in our managed business cycles, but they have been somewhat overshadowed by the leading role now played by the Federal Reserve System.

The interrelationship between structural competition and changing below–capacity competition under Federal Reserve manipulation is the best organizing device available to understand the movements of the managed business cycle. There is no reason to expect regularity in the magnitude or frequency of managed business cycles since the two controlling factors—structural competition and the willingness of the Federal Reserve to create below–capacity competition to restrict inflation—are constantly changing.

TECHNIQUES OF MONETARY MANAGEMENT

The preceding analysis suggests that the Federal Reserve, acting as the stabilizer of last resort, should stabilize inflation in a fairly narrow range—say, somewhere between 0 and 4 percent. (A precise *practical* level cannot be theoretically determined.) Then, if unemployment remains at an unacceptably high level, greater efforts should be made to improve structural competition.

The actual *mechanics* to be used by the Federal Reserve to stabilize the inflation rate have been the subject of lengthy and intense debate. Recommended Federal Reserve policies fall into two categories—*automatic* and *judgmental*.

Automatic Policies

Automatic policies are those that tie Federal Reserve action firmly to a single indicator such as the supply of money, the price of gold or changes in the composite price of a basket of commodities. No judgment is required. Monetary policy could be conducted by a clerk.

The most prominent automatic system for stabilizing the inflation rate is the monetarist approach of maintaining a slow but constant rate of growth of a narrowly defined measure of the money supply—specifically, M1.

This policy has pretty well proven impractical because of the erratic relationship between the stock of money and the growth of the economy. If such a policy had been followed over the past five years, the American economy would probably have gone through a serious depression. The economy as represented by the GNP grew much more slowly during this period than it usually does in relation to the money supply as represented by M1. Consequently, if the Federal Reserve had maintained a slow, steady growth of the money supply, we probably would have experienced a long serious depression instead of the recession of 1982.[2] To repeat, the relationship between the stock of money and economic growth over short periods has been unreliable. At some times the economy needs more money to keep growing than it does at other times.

A second suggestion for an automatic policy is to stabilize the price of gold. The price of gold is considered by a few to be a proxy for the inflation rate for the entire economy. The record indicates, however, that there is considerable variation between changes in the price of gold and changes in the inflation rate. No economic reason exists why stabilizing the price of gold would stabilize the inflation rate. It would seem foolhardy to tie monetary policy to the price of gold, which can be affected dramatically by political events in the giant gold producers South Africa and the Soviet Union.

A third suggestion for an automatic policy has been to stabilize the price of a basket of commodities as a proxy for the inflation rate. This approach makes sense, *providing the basket of commodities is large enough to be an accurate proxy for the entire inflation rate.* But this is something of a tautology–stabilize the price of a very large basket of commodities that represents the inflation rate in order to stabilize the inflation rate. Why not just stabilize the inflation rate? But how to do that is the problem we set out to solve.

No *automatic* plan to stabilize the inflation rate is likely to be feasible in our rapidly changing economy, where relationships among economic variables change so much.

Judgmental Policies

A second approach is a judgmental policy for management of the monetary system. What does this mean? With a judgmental policy, in contrast to an automatic policy, the Federal Reserve examines a great many factors that influence the economy, rather than just relying on a single indicator such as the change in the money supply or the price of gold. Since different factors carry different weights over time, a judgment call is always necessary to dictate the amount of monetary stimulus or restraint that is required. No mechanical formula can dictate an answer under changing economic conditions.

The most serious problem with a judgmental policy is the lag between the implementation of a policy and the time it impacts the economy. Furthermore, the lag varies from one period to another. Therefore, the Federal Reserve has to *forecast* economic conditions to determine the amount of monetary restraint or stimulation necessary for stabilization. Forecasting is difficult and inevitably results in errors.

To minimize forecasting errors, the Federal Reserve must be willing and able to recognize its errors promptly. If corrected quickly, forecasting errors cause little damage. When allowed to continue, they become embodied in tradition and are difficult to correct. Forecasts by the Federal Reserve are included in Federal Open Market Committee minutes. The record shows that many errors have been made. But when those errors have been promptly recognized, little damage has been done.

The Roller Coaster Theory

It has often been argued that errors in monetary policy followed by an *overcorrection* of those errors results in a roller coaster economy, giving us alternating periods of boom and recession. A casual look at the business cycle record since the mid–1950s might lead one to believe that this is true. But it is not.

According to the roller coaster theory, in times of recession the impatience of monetary authorities causes them to overstimulate the economy because the effects of monetary stimulus take so long to be realized. Hence, as recovery proceeds, it is carried to an extreme resulting in inflation that must be corrected by monetary restraint. Again, because of impatience, the restraint is overdone, producing another recession. The new recession results again in overstimulation, and the cycle continues. The culprits in the roller coaster cycle are said to be, first, the unpredictable time lag between the implementation and impact of monetary policy; second, the inability of the Federal Reserve to forecast either the time lag or the amount of stimulus or restraint that is required; and third, the impatience of the Federal Reserve authorities anxious to see quick results from their policy decisions.

The key words in the roller coaster theory are *overstimulation* and *overrestraint*. The years since the mid–1950s have seen a few cases of overstimulation, but *no clear–cut cases of overrestraint*. They certainly have *not* presented a record of alternating periods of overstimulation and overrestraint.

At this point we must review briefly the record of the years since the mid–1950s outlined in chapter 1. (Refer again to chart 1.1.)

The acceleration of inflation in 1955–56 called forth sufficient monetary restraint to create enough below–capacity competition to slow inflation without throwing the country into a deep depression. It was *necessary* restraint—not *over restraint*. The recovery that followed was less inflationary than the 1955–56 recovery. If it was due to monetary overstimulation, it was only very mildly so. As indicated earlier, the restrictive monetary response that followed in 1959–60 may be considered excessive (unnecessary), but this call is debatable. In any event, the entire period 1955–60 was more one of a gradual dampening of inflationary forces than of a roller coaster. The result was the creation of the conditions necessary for the economic golden age of the early 1960s with stable prices and steady growth.

The inflation of the second half of the 1960s could not by any stretch of the imagination have been due to overstimulation from the tiny recession of 1960, five years earlier. It was due to the fact that the Federal Reserve changed goals, putting more importance on the goal of preventing recession than on the goal of curbing inflation.

The 1966–69 period was clearly a case of overstimulation by monetary authorities. But it was not followed by overrestraint. The monetary restraint that produced the 1970 recession was probably just about enough to curb the very serious inflation without throwing the country into a deep depression. It was *necessary* restraint, not *over* restraint. The error was in not holding to that restraint long enough to keep inflation under control.

The next decade (until 1982) consisted of periods of *necessary* restraint to slow inflation (without deep depression) alternating with periods of accelerating inflation. The periods of accelerating inflation were due to overstimulation in the sense that restraint was relaxed too soon to allow below–capacity competition to establish a tradition of low wage and price gains.

In the economic recovery since 1982, the Federal Reserve has twice acted to restrain overheating in the economy, once in 1983–84 and once in 1987. In both cases it has nipped slight inflationary tendencies in the bud without precipitating recession. This is an encouraging omen for the possibility of successful Federal Reserve management in the future. However, as this is written in late 1988, inflation has once again become a problem. And this time wages have begun to accelerate. The Federal Reserve has met this inflation challenge with a very gentle tightening of money. We are now in another test of monetary management, and it will be interesting to see how wise and courageous the Federal Reserve will be. Will it surrender long–term goals for short–term popularity?

It is, of course, often argued that the inflation of the late 1970s could have been broken more gradually with less pain and suffering. That is a claim that can never be proven or disproven. However, as for future policy, the Federal Reserve must never again allow inflation to get out of hand. Then, the painful decision between a quick or a gradual correction of a stubborn high inflation rate will not have to be made again.

In summary, a few observations should be made.

The roller coaster theory has been the major objection to the use of a judgmental approach to monetary management, and, therefore, its validity must be carefully examined.

The record of the years since the mid–1950s does not at all fit the description of a roller coaster with alternating periods of overstimulation and overrestraint.

Restrictive monetary policy covering the two periods of the late 1950s and the early 1980s effectively dampened inflation, resulting in substantial periods of noninflationary growth. In each case it took two recessions to do it. Furthermore, the recent inflation has not yet been completely contained.

The decade of the 1970s included two attempts to curb inflation by *necessary* monetary restraint. That necessary restraint was in each case relaxed before it could complete its task.

Some advocates of the roller coaster theory seem to have implied that mechanical maintenance of a steady growth of the money supply (as opposed to judgmental monetary management) would have brought inflation under control without recession. If they did, indeed, claim such a possibility, it represents a gross lack of understanding of the role of below–capacity competition as the transmission mechanism by which monetary policy influences wages and prices.

The Federal Reserve quite likely will be able to prevent a new norm of accelerating wage gains from developing. If so, the management of a judgmental monetary policy is likely to turn out to be surprisingly successful. Then, all the arguments for automatic stabilizers of recent years will find their place as a trivial skirmish in the history of economic thought.

THE POWER OF THE FEDERAL RESERVE

Much has been said in recent years about the extraordinary powers of the Federal Reserve. The chairman has been repeatedly referred to as the second most powerful man in Washington. The recent Greider book *Secrets of the Temple*, previously cited, has as its subtitle *How the Federal Reserve Runs the Country*.

This view of the power of the Federal Reserve is simply not correct when the Federal Reserve is doing its job properly. The decision–making power of the Federal Reserve is extremely limited when it abides by its primary role of preventing inflation from accelerating. Federal government decisions, as we shall see, dictate within a fairly narrow range the policies the Federal Reserve must follow.

When doing its job properly, the Federal Reserve has little freedom in determining the rate of interest. It must set the ease or tightness of money—and thereby the interest rate—at the level necessary to keep inflation from accelerating. And that level is basically determined by the size of the federal deficit plus all the actions of government that determine the intensity of structural competition. These are the many factors previously mentioned such as protectionism, antitrust enforcement, labor law, and tax and regulatory decisions that impact costs and prices. Failure to implement our prescribed policy #2 to reduce the budget deficit and policy #3 to support improved structural competition will result in high interest rates. The Federal Reserve cannot bring them down without abandoning its basic responsibility as it did in the late 1960s.

When doing its job properly, the Federal Reserve cannot choose between a little more inflation and a little less unemployment. As we have seen, that choice is a delusion. A little more inflation will ultimately lead to a lot *more* unemployment. Inflation control must come first.

When doing its job properly, the Federal Reserve has little choice of policy regarding the foreign exchange rate of the dollar. Policy must be conducted so as to prevent inflation from accelerating even though that policy produces a very strong dollar that reduces the competitiveness of American producers on international markets, as it did in 1984 and 1985. Again, it is legislative and executive actions that determine the rate of inflation that dictate Federal Reserve policy relative to foreign exchange rates.

What important policy decisions *can* the Federal Reserve make? Since Congress has not set specific guidelines, the Federal Reserve *does* have the power to choose the rate between, say, 0 and 4 percent at which it will hold the inflation rate steady. In this book we have studiously avoided the important question of what, precisely, the allowed inflation rate should be. It is a difficult practical problem that cannot be theoretically determined. It is extremely important that the inflation rate be held steady at a low rate. Whether it should be at, say, 1 percent or 2 percent is a much more difficult question to answer.

When past Federal Reserve policy has failed in its responsibility to prevent inflation from accelerating, and inflation is rampant, the Federal Reserve has the choice to correct that mistake quickly as was done in the period from 1979 to 1982, or to do it more slowly. This is a difficult and painful decision. We have argued earlier that the most important policy now is to prevent inflation from getting out of control, so that painful decision never has to be faced again.

The Federal Reserve, of course, makes many important decisions in connection with the administration of the banking system. But in its major role as stabilizer of last resort it should behave like a mid–echelon executive. It should find the best way to implement the basic policy—preventing inflation from accelerating—but it should not tamper with the basic policy.

In summary, then, the Federal Reserve has the power to abandon its responsibility of preventing the acceleration of inflation, as it did in the late 1960s, and thus get the country into heaps of trouble. If, however, it accepts its responsibility, its major decisions are dictated by conditions such as excessive demand that are largely determined by the policies of the government.

MONETARY MANAGEMENT BY FINANCIAL MARKETS

In this book we have consistently laid the responsibility for the management of aggregate demand upon the shoulders of the Federal Reserve, on the ground that it is the only stabilizing organization with the capability of acting swiftly. It may be that a little of that responsibility is being assumed by a more diffuse "organization"—the financial markets.

Three forces have combined to produce a quantum change in the nature of the financial markets just in the past few years.

- A host of new financial instruments, particularly futures and options markets, have been devised that allow traders to hold positions in bonds, stocks and currencies on very thin margins. Movements in and out of these markets are usually possible in huge quantities with low transaction costs. Both the long and short side of the markets are open to traders.

- An enormous shift has occurred in investment policies from long–term investment objectives to short–term market timing. Since on a short–term basis, emotion, ignorance, and news items are much more important in buy–sell decisions than are "value" considerations, markets have become much more volatile. This investment policy shift has not been just among individuals, but is prevalent also among a large part of the staid old institutions such as banks and insurance companies that manage hundreds of billions of dollars worth of pension funds.

- Financial markets are now worldwide, increasing the magnitude of funds moving in and out of markets, increasing the diversity of viewpoints from which trading decisions are made, and increasing the scope of news items that affect trading decisions.

Together, these three forces increase dramatically the volatility of markets and the quantity of funds sloshing around from one market to another. How does this affect the power of the Federal Reserve to manage aggregate demand? It reduces the choices the Federal Reserve has in managing the monetary system.

For example, a very small acceleration of inflation in 1987 produced a fantastic decline of about 25 percent in the price of U.S. Treasury bonds. The beginning of the decline in bond prices on the futures markets actually preceded the very slight tightening of money by the Federal Reserve as reflected by a mild rise in federal funds rates and a later half–point rise in the discount rate. Apparently the financial markets will, at times, raise interest rates themselves when the specter of accelerating inflation is even dimly perceived. Conversely, interest rates are likely to decline automatically when recession is anticipated. Changing interest rates are reflected in stock prices, currency exchange rates, residential construction, business expectations, plant and equipment spending, and other facets of the economy. So the financial markets themselves, in a crude sort of way, are now, in part, managing aggregate demand.

We would not want to argue that the Federal Reserve has been made obsolete, but a little of its power is being usurped by the financial markets. These markets are not likely in the future to let anyone ignore a budding acceleration of inflation. So if elected legislators and executives present us with a number of popular but inflationary policies, they will have a price to pay, and that price is rising interest rates with all their deleterious effects of higher unemployment and greater burdens on the marginal worker. How long will it take government officials to recognize this cost?

The influence of the financial markets on the management of the monetary system is gaining recognition on Wall Street. If, however, there is anyone who believes the financial markets can manage the monetary system without the aid of the Federal Reserve, he or she should review what happened on October 19, 1987. Without the powerful stabilizing impact of the Federal Reserve, the vivid manifestation of Wall Street hysteria exhibited that day would most likely have produced a series of catastrophic financial failures that would have had long–lasting repercussions around the world. Anyone familiar with the emotion and ignorance frequently displayed by the financial markets must be horrified at the thought of these markets running our monetary system. The best that can be expected from monetary management by the financial markets is an occasional prod if the Federal Reserve does not act promptly to restrain inflation.

CHANGING THEORIES OF BUSINESS CYCLE MANAGEMENT

For anyone growing up and studying economics in the Great Depression of the 1930s, a solution to the problem of depression had to become an all–consuming passion.

A study of the record of the previous sixty years or so was discouraging. Depressions had been frequent, long, and deep, and the severity of the 1930s depression seemed to indicate they were getting worse.

Some economists, and many others, viewed this record as proof that Marx was right that capitalism is fatally flawed, and they turned to communism. It is frightening to read the record of testimony delivered before Washington committees at that time, to see the willingness of eminent witnesses to give up on capitalism and even on much of democracy.

But to most, a solid hope came from another source, John Maynard Keynes, whose recommendations for managing aggregate demand and therefore the level of business activity by fiscal policy seemed to offer a simple solution for deep depression. Most young economists became ardent Keynesians. Business cycle management became widely accepted doctrine.

Those young economists are now old economists. Looking back at the record of the last half century of business cycle management, it doesn't look too bad, especially as contrasted with the previous century. Business cycle management has not been a thing of beauty, but *a deep depression has not occurred in half a century.* Although a great deal of argument has gone on as to *how* cycles should be managed, the notion that cycles need *no* management has never again become widespread.

The great mistake of the postwar period was the overstimulation of the economy in the late 1960s resulting in the inflation that is just now coming under control.

We can only speculate why that mistake was made. It may have been partly the product of another economic idea—the Phillips curve. The basic thesis was that you could get a little less unemployment by accepting a little more inflation, but it didn't work. Inflation got out of control.

A certain irony also resides in the development of stabilization theories. At the end of the Great Depression, monetary policy was in disrepute. It had failed to adequately stimulate the economy. Monetary stimulation was said to be "like pushing on a string."

But even though monetary policy as a stimulating device, was in disrepute among most economists it was used very effectively by the Federal Reserve, as a restraining device to stabilize the economy during the very critical times of the late 1950s when inflation otherwise would have gotten out of control. And the result was the economic golden age of the early 1960s.

By the late 1960s, interest was rekindled in monetary policy, largely due to the leadership of Milton Friedman. But as monetary policy came to be recognized by more and more economists as a useful stabilizing tool, the Federal Reserve neglected its use in the important area of inflation control.

We are now entering a new era. We have had the bad experiences of the Great Depression and serious inflation. We probably have learned from both of them. In the future, cyclical performance of the economy should be considerably better than ever before in history.

CONCLUSION

The major argument of this chapter has been that it is feasible, by a judgmental monetary policy, for the Federal Reserve to achieve policy #1 prescribed at the beginning of the book—to prevent the acceleration of inflation and keep the economy operating most of the time without recession.

Implementing the other two policies we prescribed in chapter 1 could vastly improve monetary policy as follows:

- Implementing policy #2—eliminate the federal budget deficit in four or five years, and then keep the deficit near zero except in times of recession—would eliminate the wide swings in fiscal policy that make monetary management difficult.

- Implementing policy #3—improve structural competition—would insure that when the Federal Reserve expands aggregate demand, production and employment would rise more and prices would rise less. Restrictive monetary policy would slow the growth of wages and prices, without a serious impact on production and employment. Monetary management would be much more effective and easier to administer.

CHAPTER 5

MANAGING COMPETITION TO REDUCE POVERTY

After examining the problems of managing structural competition in corporate and labor markets in chapters 2 and 3 and managing below–capacity competition in chapter 4, we are now ready to look at managing competition for two specific purposes—to reduce poverty and to improve productivity. We focus on the first purpose in this chapter and the second in chapter 6.

Poverty can be reduced in two basic ways. The first way is to tax those considered to be living above the poverty line and to use the tax revenues to provide funds or goods and services to those considered to be living in poverty. This is the welfare–state approach. The second way is to improve the effectiveness of competitive markets to provide a well–functioning economic system with better opportunities and incentives to work, save and invest.

The first approach has been used extensively in this country. We provide health care, food, low–cost housing, legal services, financial aid to dependent children, and a host of other services to those counted as living in poverty. Considering the tax revolts that have surfaced across the country, it seems unlikely that this approach can be extended much further. And we have not yet won the war on poverty.

This chapter describes several ways by which our three prescribed policies can help reduce the poverty problem in America, mainly by improving the effectiveness of competitive markets.

UNEMPLOYMENT AND MARGINAL WORKERS

As indicated in earlier chapters, weak structural competition (monopoly) tilts the millions of price–quantity decisions in the marketplace toward increased wages and prices, that is, toward accelerating inflation. Accelerating inflation, in turn, precipitates restrictive Federal Reserve monetary policy. The result is recession or at least slow economic growth—and increased unemployment. High unemployment has been to a considerable extent the consequence of monopoly in product and labor markets. These monopolies were unleashed by the permissive monetary policy of the Federal Reserve in the late 1960s.

Not surprisingly, unemployment impacts marginal workers more seriously than others. Who are the marginal workers? The marginal workers are low–paid workers. They are often insecure. They include the sick, the less talented, the unmotivated, the victims of discrimination. They are often poorly educated and poorly trained. They make up a large part of the poverty problem in America today.

Chart 5.1 shows the unemployment rate for blacks (a group containing a large proportion of marginal workers) compared to that for all workers. The five periods shown on the chart are the same as those described in chapter 1.

UNEMPLOYMENT RATES

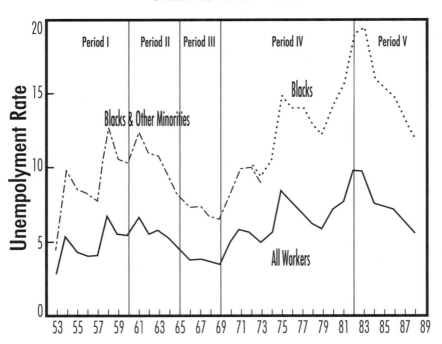

Chart 5.1 The unemployment rate for all workers, for blacks and other minorities (1953-73), and for blacks only (1972-88).[1]

As we have seen, in Periods I and IV inflationary forces, induced largely by weak structural competition, required restrictive monetary policy resulting in recessions and slow economic growth. In each of these periods, the unemployment rate for blacks grew faster than the unemployment rate for the total labor force. In Period IV, covering the 1970s and early 1980s, the spread between the rate of black unemployment and the rate of total unemployment was spectacular—almost tripling in size.

In Periods II and III, when growth was not interrupted by recession and unemployment was very low, the spread between the black unemployment rate and the total unemployment rate declined.

This data, of course, suggests that the obvious way to improve the relative unemployment situation of blacks is to maintain a high–employment economy. And the major thesis of this book is that the best way to maintain a high–employment economy is to continually work to intensify structural competition (reduce monopoly) in both product and labor markets. (Blacks are used as an example simply because data are available. The same principle applies to other groups—the less skilled, the chronically ill, the less talented, and so on.)

Of all the undesirable effects of monopoly, perhaps the cruelest is the negative impact on marginal workers. And heavy unemployment—often sporadic, sometimes long–lasting—is the vehicle carrying a major part of the pain inflicted by monopoly upon the marginal workers. Competition should be managed to reduce both monopoly and unemployment.

We have already made considerable progress. Long–term unemployment (fifteen weeks or longer) had dropped by the end of 1988 to less than half the average for the decade ending in 1984. The unemployment rate for all workers at the end of 1988 was at the lowest point in fourteen years, more than two percentage points below the average of that same decade. Proper management of competition will gradually reduce this unemployment. Extending the low unemployment rate for several years, and even reducing it further, should markedly ease the poverty problem. But it is not enough.

THE RELATIVE WAGES OF MARGINAL WORKERS

Besides bearing a disproportionate share of the increase in unemployment when economic growth is restricted, marginal workers experience a decline in *relative* wages. Let us consider the record of changing relative wage rates since the mid–1950s and the factors that have caused declines in relative wages of marginal workers.

Estimating Wage Rates of Marginal Workers

We have divided industries into quartiles based on wage rates (including fringes) paid by each industry. The top quartile consists mainly of strong union industries such as cigarettes, autos, steel and oil refining. The bottom quartile consists of nonunion and weak union industries such as eating places, retail stores, apparel and textile manufacturing. The *average* wage rates paid in the spring of 1988 in a few sample industries near the bottom of this fourth quartile were as follows:

Industry	Average Wage
Eating and drinking places	$4.50
Variety stores	4.91
Apparel—women's blouses	5.12
Misc. merchandise stores	5.33
Apparel—men's trousers	5.40

Of course, within these industries many individual workers receive wages below average and near the minimum wage. Many of these workers live in poverty, slipping in and out of even this meager employment. On the other hand, many of the workers in these industries are second–income earners, and the family is doing reasonably well. To many others, employment in these industries represents temporary entry–level work on the road to something better.

Nevertheless, we use changes in wage rates of this bottom quartile as representative of changes in the *relative* wage rates received by marginal workers.

How Have Relative Wages of Marginal Workers Changed?

Chart 5.2 shows the *relative* wages of production/nonsupervisory workers in the four quartiles for the period 1953 to 1987. We have charted three separate sets of data to allow us to go back to 1953 and also to include more industries plus data on fringe benefits as these data became available.

Measurement of the gap between high- and low–wage industries is misleading unless fringe benefits are included. Fringe benefits have become a very large part of the compensation package, especially to workers in the high- wage industries. Including fringe benefits widens the wage gap.

Over the thirty–five year period shown in chart 5.2, the spread between the relative wages of workers in the top and bottom quartiles increased by nearly two–thirds. Closing this wide gap will likely be, as we shall see, of paramount importance in solving the poverty problem in the coming years. The relative wages of workers in the two middle quartiles haven't changed much. They are now almost exactly where they were clear back in 1953.

In addition to changes in *relative* wages, it is instructive to look at the trend in *real* wages of workers in the bottom quartile. The compensation of bottom quartile workers in 1986, when adjusted for inflation, is significantly below

RELATIVE COMPENSATION

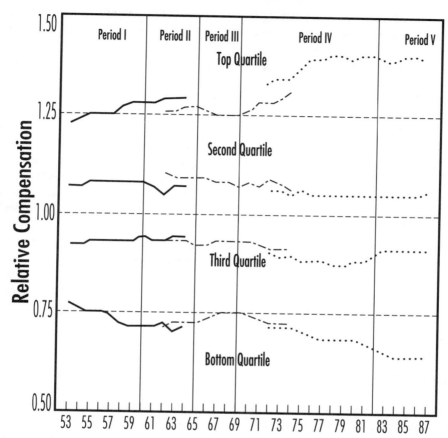

Chart 5.2 *Relative compensation for production/nonsupervisory workers by quartiles. The solid lines represent average wages for twenty-five Standard Industrial Classification (SIC) two-digit industries. The dashed lines represent average wages plus benefits for thirty-two SIC two-digit industries. The dotted lines represent average wages plus benefits for fifty SIC two-digit industries.[2]*

the level of 1971. That is, the standard of living—not just relative income—of this lower group has actually declined over the past fifteen years. Workers in the lower part of this fourth quartile must be a significant part of the poverty problem.

Factors Causing the Decline in Relative Wages of Marginal Workers

Referring again to chart 5.2, it is evident that most of the decline in the relative wages of workers in the bottom quartile came in Periods I and IV. In both of these periods, the Federal Reserve responded to accelerating inflation with restrictive monetary policy to slow the growth of business activity and thus create greater below–capacity competition. The only time in the entire thirty–five years that the wages of workers in the bottom quartile gained relative position was in the late 1960s, when we were pushing very close to full capacity, and below–capacity competition was very weak.

The evidence, then, is strong that the *relative* wages of marginal workers decline whenever it is necessary to slow the economy to create greater below–capacity competition. Why? The answer is simple. Below–capacity competition impinges more on wage rates in the nonunion and weak union industries than it does on wage rates in the strong union industries that have considerable monopolistic control over their markets.

Workers in the top quartile, consisting mainly of strong union industries, were able to advance their fortunes far above the rest of the wage earners, particularly in the first half of the 1970s. As argued in chapter 3, this advance was not due to difficulty in attracting new workers to those industries nor to dissatisfaction of workers sufficient to increase relative quit rates. It was due largely to the power that the unions had to control the markets in which the workers sell their services.

Besides the differential impact of below–capacity competition on wages of workers in the top and bottom quartiles, a second reason exists for the erosion of the relative position of marginal workers: demographics. The 1970s saw an unusually large number of new entrants into the labor force, young people of the baby–boom generation and older women with little training. These groups were competing for the entry–level jobs and thus kept downward pressure on wages in these bottom–quartile industries.

If relative wages of workers in the bottom quartile were to return to the 1961–65 average, the real income of these workers would improve by about 12 percent. A return to the 1953 relative position would bring an improvement of nearly 20 percent in real income. These improvements in relative income plus an extended period of low unemployment (compared to the last fifteen years) would go a long way toward alleviating the poverty problem.

IMPROVING THE INCOME POSITION OF MARGINAL WORKERS

As noted in chapters 2 and 3, considerable progress has already been made toward achieving markets more friendly to marginal workers. Both corporate and labor markets have become more competitive, mainly due to improved international competition. As a result, unemployment has been reduced. In addition, the relative wages of union workers have, since 1983, grown just a little more slowly than wages of nonunion workers. We are beginning to narrow the gap between high– and low–wage industries.

A great deal of emphasis is currently being placed on speeding the growth of productivity in the United States to improve the standard of living of everyone. This is right and proper. But the poverty problem in the United States cannot be solved *solely* by increasing productivity. Low–income workers must receive a larger proportion of our national income. They must recover the share of national income they have lost, particularly since 1969. If these marginal workers receive a larger part of our national income, some other group must receive a smaller part. And any shifts in these income streams must be made without harming incentives, and without causing inflation to accelerate.

We will examine two major approaches to shifting these income streams. First, we will look at the possibility of diverting income from property owners, mainly owners of stocks, bonds, bank accounts, and real estate, to low–wage groups. Second, we will examine the possibility of shifting part of the union wage premium in the high–wage sector to the low–wage sector. Neither of these methods involves the welfare–state approach. Rather, both center on improving competitive markets, and they will be natural products of our three prescribed policies.

Diverting Income from Property Owners

Our three prescribed policies act to divert income from property owners to lower–income groups by bringing down interest rates and by reducing monopoly in the corporate sector.

As indicated in earlier chapters, an elimination of the federal budget deficit, as called for by our prescribed policy #2, would allow the Federal Reserve to reduce interest rates substantially without causing inflation to accelerate. A reduction in interest rates would transfer income (or purchasing power) from creditors to debtors. Who are the creditors and who are the debtors?

As chart 5.3 indicates, in 1983 nearly half of all property income accrued to families receiving income over $50,000—the top 12.8 percent of families in terms of income. On the other hand, the bottom 22 percent of families—with incomes below $12,500—received less than 4 percent of all property income. Property income includes interest, dividends, rent and some miscellaneous items. We use property income as a kind of proxy for interest income for several reasons. It is the only available data that is at all compatible with studies of debtors. Interest makes up over two–thirds of total property

SHARES OF PROPERTY INCOME RECEIVED
AND SHARES OF CONSUMER DEBT
AND MORTGAGE DEBT OWED BY INCOME LEVELS

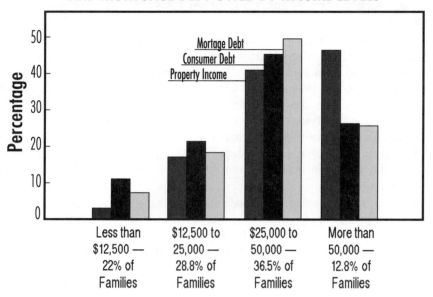

Chart 5.3   Shares of property income received and shares of mortgage debt and consumer debt owed by families for 1983, by annual income levels.[3]

income. And the yields from other types of property income tend to move in the same direction as interest rates but with a very considerable lag.

Looking at the debtor side, the share of all debt owed, and therefore the share of interest paid, by the low income group is far higher than the share of property income received. The opposite is true of the high–income group. Therefore, a major reduction in interest rates would shift income (or purchasing power) from the high–income group to the lower–income group. The two middle–income groups would remain about the same.

How great would this income shift be? Our estimates indicate that a one–third decline in interest rates would increase directly the purchasing power of the low–income workers by somewhere in the neighborhood of 1 to 2 percent by reducing the amount of interest they would have to pay. In addition, the cost of the things they buy would be reduced due to a decline in interest cost to business. Interest cost, of course, is part of the price of everything consumers buy. The total benefit to the low–income workers from a one–third reduction in interest rates could be in the neighborhood of a 4 to 7 percent improvement in purchasing power.

Our estimates of the impact of lower interest rates on low–income families should be regarded as only ball–park figures. The estimates are derived from two surveys that used somewhat different definitions of families. A number of other complications may also reduce the accuracy of the estimates. However, the estimates are probably sufficiently accurate to warrant the conclusion that a substantial reduction in interest rates would have a very beneficial impact on lower–income families, and that benefit would come at the expense of high–income families.

Shifting income or purchasing power from property owners to the low–income group would also result from implementation of our prescribed policy #3, improving structural competition to reduce or eliminate monopoly profits. A reduction in monopoly profits would undoubtedly redound to the benefit of lower–income families, who own virtually no common stocks, and would be mainly at the expense of the upper–income group. But how extensive would the impact be?

Again, estimates must be very tentative. If one–fourth of industries are monopolistic, and half of the profits in these industries are monopolistic profits, the elimination of monopoly would reduce corporate profit before taxes by about one–eighth, or in the neighborhood of $30 billion. This in turn would reduce the price of goods sold by that amount, and would increase real consumer purchasing power by around 1 percent. Any family not owning shares in monopolistic corporations would benefit.

This may not seem like a very important improvement to economic well–being, but it comes as a small bonus to the other advantages of eliminating monopoly discussed elsewhere in this book.

Diverting Income from Union Wage Premiums

Improving structural competition in labor markets, thereby reducing union wage premiums, would surely improve the lot of marginal workers. Few, if any, workers in lower–quartile industries have significant union wage premiums, so they would lose nothing as union wage premiums declined, but would gain as lower labor costs reduced the prices of the things they buy. How important would this shift be?

As we indicated in chapter 3, it is extremely difficult to estimate the precise magnitude of union wage premiums. But union wage premiums undoubtedly exist, meaning that unionized firms could hire qualified workers at lower wage rates if the union barriers did not prevent them from doing so.

Most of the industries in the top quartile are strongly unionized, and even some of those that do not have strong unions probably pay wages that are higher than are necessary to attract workers. This is because of either the threat of unionization or the union spillover effect. The union wage premium (including fringe benefits) for these top–quartile industries probably amounts to at least 20 to 25 percent.

If union barriers were eliminated and the union wage premium were to gradually disappear, the relative wages of workers in the top quartile would return to approximately the position they held in 1953 as shown in chart 5.2. Who would gain? Part of the lower labor cost would initially go to higher profits in some industries, but since most industries are subject to the convergence principle, eventually the lower labor costs would be passed on to the consumer in lower prices.

As chart 5.2 indicates, the relative wages of workers in the two middle quartiles have remained quite constant over the tumultuous years since 1953. This stability is probably a normal consequence of market action. If it persists, and if workers in the top quartile lose ground, workers in the lower quartile would improve their relative share, perhaps back to the 1953 position. An improved position for workers in the lower quartile would be made possible by changing demographics and by a decrease in inflationary pressure as the relative wages of workers in the top quartile declined. We could operate closer to full employment for extended periods, the only time when workers in the lower quartile gain relative position. A return to the 1953 relative position would mean an approximate 20 percent increase in real incom—a major improvement to the well–being of the poor.

Here we must distinguish between *absolute* and *relative* poverty. Absolute poverty involves the suffering due to the inability of low–income workers to buy the necessities of life. Relative poverty involves the discomfort to low–income workers who see others enjoying possessions they cannot afford. This differential can be especially galling when low–income workers perceive that some of those high–income workers are doing work no more difficult than their own.

If the effects of an elimination of the union wage premiums of the top quartile workers were to accrue entirely to the benefit of the low–income workers as we have indicated might happen automatically, and the wage gap returned to its 1953 relationship, the spread between wages of workers in the bottom quartile and workers in the top quartile would be cut about 40 percent.

The feelings of the low–income workers for the justice of the system and their place in society would be vastly improved, not to mention the substantial improvement in their absolute income. Add to this an improvement flowing to the low–income groups due to a substantial reduction in interest rates and profit margins and the United States would see a massive reduction in the problems of poverty and near–poverty.

Increasing competition to reduce the relative wages to top quartile workers would indeed be foolish if those wages were necessary as incentives to attract and retain qualified workers. However, much of these high wages represents union wage premiums. Qualified workers could probably be obtained at wages no more above average than those paid in 1953.

Narrowing the wide gap between high–paid and low–paid workers is not likely to be easy. The Federal Reserve will probably hold the increase in wage rates to 3 or 4 percent. If wage rates for lower–income groups rise faster than the 3 or 4 percent average, then wage rates of the higher wage groups must rise more slowly. Will the strongly unionized workers tolerate this below–average increase for many years?

In chapter 3 we argued that competition in strongly unionized industries must be increased to keep those industries from leading an acceleration of wage rates. Now we are requiring an even greater restraint. If the wage gap is to be closed, strong unions will have to submit to wage increases *less* than average. And it is not likely that we will make great progress toward solving the poverty problem until that wage gap is narrowed. The dollar amounts involved are very large.

The existing wide wage gap that we have inherited because of past union activity and other faulty economic policies may have still another serious consequence. It is probably incompatible with full employment. We may never achieve full employment for a prolonged period of time until that wage gap has been narrowed substantially. A clarification of this problem will be made in chapter 8.

CONCLUSION

In view of the analysis in this chapter, it is easy to understand the enormous build–up of the poverty problem during the inflationary era of the 1970s and during the two recessions of the early 1980s that were necessary to crush that inflation.

Marginal workers lost ground by suffering a disproportionate share of very high unemployment rates. They also lost ground due to a substantial decline in relative wage rates. They lost a substantial amount of purchasing power due to sharply higher interest rates.

And the tragic part of this whole episode is that most of it could have been avoided if the Federal Reserve had tightened money in the mid–1960s when inflation began to accelerate, accepting a small recession and keeping monopolistic wages and prices under better control. Members of the Federal

Reserve Board thought they were "compassionate" by avoiding recession. In reality they caused serious hardship to those least able to bear it.

All three of our prescribed policies are necessary to alleviate the poverty problem in the United States. Policy #1 requires the Federal Reserve to keep inflation from accelerating. Implementation of this policy over several years would gradually establish a strong norm of low wage gains. A low wage–gain norm combined with policy #3, improving structural competition, would enable us to operate much closer to full employment than we have since the late 1960s. Marginal workers would be the greatest beneficiaries by sharply reduced unemployment and by an improvement in relative wages.

But policy #3 also provides a large bonus—a direct diversion of a substantial amount of income or purchasing power from workers with large union wage premiums and from monopolistic corporations mainly to low–income, marginal workers.

Prescribed policy #2, eliminate the federal budget deficit, would enable the Federal Reserve to bring down interest rates (and profit margins). The reduction in interest rates would be beneficial in diverting substantial income from owners of stocks, bonds, bank accounts, and real estate to the lower–income groups whose debt is high in relation to their income.

These three policies should receive the support of both liberals and conservatives. Liberals should recognize that the poverty problem will never be solved simply by taxing those above the poverty line to help the poor. Conservatives should recognize that there will always be great pressure for increased taxes for welfare spending unless the poverty problem is alleviated by improving the working of the competitive market. The support of both liberals and conservatives should make possible the adoption of the three prescribed policies.

For many years the "compassionate" way to help the poor has been for governments to spend tax dollars to provide cash and various services for the unfortunate. The amount of *additional* support that can be provided by this approach is positively trivial compared with the possible gain through improving the operation of competitive markets. Hundreds of billions of dollars can eventually be made available for low income groups by eliminating monopoly in product and labor markets, by eliminating the budget deficit, and by following a rigorous anti–inflation monetary policy. Furthermore, the additional purchasing power made available to low–income groups will be received as pay for work performed and not as degrading welfare payments.

The weak are particular victims of monopoly whether that monopoly is in business, labor, the professions or government. An advocacy of free–market economics does not suggest that the weak should be turned over to the tender mercies of the strong. *The arguments that justify a free competitive market also demand that the weak have the right to live in a relatively monopoly–free environment.* This is not Robin Hood stuff. It's not charity. Purchasing power diverted to the weak from monopolies in product and labor markets would not reduce incentives since monopolistic income serves no economic function.

The weak should also have the right to live under a government that does not engage in irresponsible deficit financing, driving interest rates to unnecessary heights. High interest rates distress the weak especially when it comes to renting or buying suitable homes. Interest is a major part of the cost and price of a home since housing is very capital intensive.

The implementation of the three policies would go a long way toward relieving our welfare system of intolerable burdens, and would make America a more comfortable place for all of us. But these policies cannot totally replace the welfare system or private philanthropy. Help will always be needed for those who just cannot cope, or who are victims of accidents, or failures who deserve a second chance.

CHAPTER 6

MANAGING COMPETITION TO IMPROVE PRODUCTIVITY

So far in this book competition has been portrayed mainly as a disciplinarian preventing undue increases in wages and prices. In this chapter it has a grander role. Besides being a disciplinarian, it may also be important as a motivator, a whip to generate improved productivity. Productivity is now in the limelight of national debate. How can we improve our productivity, our efficiency, our output per man–hour, to be able to compete in the world economy and speed improvements in our standard of living?

A review of related literature reveals two important facts about existing economic studies of the productivity problem in America.

First, economists are not sure what has caused the decline in the productivity growth rate since the mid–1960s. Several factors are suspect, and undoubtedly the causes are complex. The same lack of certainty applies to possible remedies for improving productivity.

Second, little analysis has been done to estimate what effect the changing intensity of competition has on productivity. A single important exception has been the work of Burton Klein discussed in this chapter.

The proposition that the changing intensity of competition is an important determinant of productivity is not easy to test. But in this chapter we have assembled several pieces of evidence that seem to indicate that increased competition is a spur to productivity. If this positive relationship between competition and productivity does, in fact, exist, expanded competition will provide another important benefit in addition to reducing unemployment and moderating the burden of the marginal worker as discussed in the previous chapter.

THE NATURE OF THE PRODUCTIVITY GROWTH PROCESS

One fact stands out clearly in an examination of the productivity growth process. Growth in productivity is very difficult to achieve. It involves serious risks, the magnitude of which cannot be calculated, and it often requires unpleasant reorganizations including dismissing, reassigning, and demoting employees. The rocky path toward improved productivity is not likely to be followed for long without considerable outside pressure. In our economy, that pressure most often comes from competition.

In 1935, J. R. Hicks wrote, "The best of all monopoly profits is a quiet life."[1] But the quiet life is neither conducive to taking great risks nor is it conducive to sweeping reorganizations to clean out arthritic bureaucracies.

The Necessity of Cleansing the Bureaucracies

Large human organizations—now known as bureaucracies—tend over time to find the goals of the organization subordinated to the personal interests of the members of the organization—that is, to their job security, their advancement, their perquisites, their relaxed way of life. This statement applies not just to top management, but to the thousands of little lords presiding over the tiny fiefdoms that grow up in a bureaucracy, ranging from the dispatcher at the motor pool to the dispenser of paper clips.

Consequently, the tendency of bureaucracy is toward inefficiency. Individuals in a bureaucracy have such enormous power to perpetuate their personal interests at the expense of the organization that only extreme pressures can accomplish a cleansing of that bureaucracy. In the business world, the necessary pressure comes from competition, and often only extreme competition that threatens survival can accomplish the task. The "quiet life" of the monopolist is not conducive to the cleansing of bureaucracies.

We have seen many remarkable examples of bureaucracy cleansing in recent years. It is now (combined with other more controversial features) often called restructuring. Under extraordinary increases in competitive pressure (or fear of loss of control to a corporate raider), companies such as Caterpillar Tractor, International Harvester, Chrysler, and Union Carbide have found that they could dispense with tens of thousands of production and administrative personnel and still produce the same or greater output. Whole layers of administrators have been eliminated. The next question is obvious. Why did they wait so long? Why didn't they get rid of those inefficiencies sooner? Because it was an unpleasant and dangerous task. They put it off until competition forced them to act.

In a similar vein, reading thousands of corporate reports over the years has indicated to us what seems to be a reliable and very interesting pattern of corporate behavior. When corporations lose some control over their markets as evidenced by serious earnings disappointments, they will respond most of the time with cost–cutting programs (among other things). Less market control is, by definition, an increase in competition. Briefly, then, an increase in competition leads to cost cutting, increasing productivity.

The Necessity of Taking Risks

Increased productivity is not triggered by a cold, precise, profit–maximizing calculation on the part of business executives. Rather, it is a venture into worlds of frightening risk and uncertainty. Efforts to improve productivity usually involve research and development spending that often ends up as a dead–end venture. Productivity growth requires *new* machinery, *new* products, *new* plants, *new* markets, *new* relations with unions. Any of these may fail, and often do. Serious risk is the hallmark of rapid productivity growth, and the probabilities of success are not easily calculated. Without the whip of competition those risks may appear so daunting that innovation will not be undertaken. Competitors must innovate to survive.

IDENTIFYING RELATIONSHIPS BETWEEN COMPETITION AND PRODUCTIVITY

Four somewhat disparate pieces of evidence that indicate a relationship between the intensity of competition and productivity are included in this section. The first deals with the relationship between below–capacity competition and productivity while the other three deal with the relationships between various aspects of structural competition and productivity.

The Complacency Cycle

Conventional wisdom has it that recessions slow the growth of productivity. Evidence seems to indicate otherwise, at least on a short–term basis.

Chart 6.1 shows that every recession since the mid–1950s has been accompanied by an upsurge in productivity, beginning *not* at the bottom of the cycle, but very early in the contraction phase. Why? Probably because increasing below–capacity competition forces firms to cut costs in a mild "cleansing of the bureaucracies."

As the chart shows, capacity utilization usually peaks well in advance of the peak in business activity. That means that below–capacity competition begins to rise. At first this actually reduces productivity as companies horde workers, and as overhead costs are spread out over a smaller output.

Employers are waiting to see if the business slowdown is just temporary. But as recession deepens and profits decline, cost cutting begins and productivity rises.

CAPACITY UTILIZATION
AND CHANGES IN PRODUCTIVITY

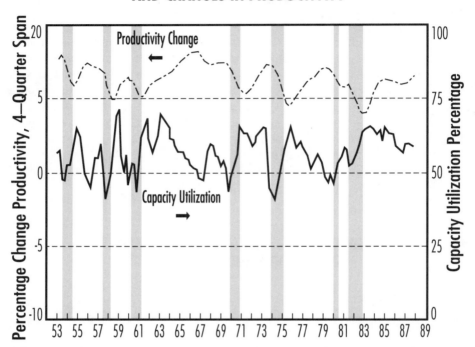

Chart 6.1 Manufacturing capacity utilization and percentage change in manufacturing productivity (four-quarter moving average). The shaded areas indicate periods of business contraction.[2]

The effect of increasing below–capacity competition on productivity has been dependable. Even the small "growth recession" of 1966–67 caused an upsurge in productivity.

On the other side of the recession, productivity usually begins to slow very early in a period of recovery. Why? Because capacity utilization begins to rise (below–capacity competition declines) right from the bottom of the cycle. The declining competition allows the growth of inefficiencies that proliferate like weeds in any bureaucracy not under continued pressure to cleanse itself. As chart 6.1 indicates, the longer the expansion lasts, the more slowly productivity grows.

Wesley C. Mitchell in 1913 was the first economist to describe the cost cutting prevalent in recession and the creeping inefficiencies in prosperity.[3]

He considered these items important in self–generating business cycles. But he did not explicitly designate the change in the intensity of competition over the business cycle as the operative force that produced those results.

The behavior of productivity over the business cycle could be described as a "complacency cycle." When business is good in a period of recovery, firms become complacent about their outlook and about their competitive position. They become careless about costs. Spending becomes extravagant. Consequently, productivity growth suffers. Then, when the onset of recession increases competition and brings them back to reality, they become very conscious about costs. Complacency disappears and productivity improves.

Anyone familiar with the volatile securities industry will surely recognize this complacency cycle. Strong business calls forth almost frenzied expansion and extravagance. Slow business produces stern frugality. To some degree this complacency cycle must prevail throughout most of the economy.

Even though the rising competitiveness of recession apparently stimulates sharp upsurges of productivity, recessions also have long–term negative effects on productivity. They usually slow spending for capital goods and research and development, both of which are essential for long–term productivity growth. Hence, in the subsequent periods of business recovery it is more difficult to keep productivity growing.

To repeat, virtually every major upsurge of productivity since the mid–1950s has apparently been triggered by rising competitiveness due to increasing below–capacity competition beginning near the onset of recession. Does this mean that we must have more frequent recessions to spur productivity growth? Probably not. The same stimulus to improved productivity can be achieved by improving *structural* competition, eliminating barriers to free competition in both product and labor markets.

We have, then, another possible trade–off between the use of structural competition and below–capacity competition—this time to improve productivity.

The Burton Klein Study

Surprisingly, only one economist has made a comprehensive study of the relationship between competition and productivity: Burton Klein of the California Institute of Technology, now retired. (See appendix B, "Competition and Productivity.") His studies have been presented in three publications, in 1977, 1984, and 1988.[4] His 1988 paper, presented at a meeting of the Schumpeter Society, foreshadows a soon–to–be–published book.

Klein has developed a model showing how competition improves productivity. He emphasizes two factors: "opportunistic risk taking" and "dynamic flexibility," the ability to make speedy adjustments to changing circumstances. Both of these factors, he argues, are products of competition, and they both speed the growth of productivity.

Testing for a relationship between competition and productivity is difficult at best. Klein obtained productivity and price restraint data for 387 separate manufacturing industries and conducted statistical tests for a relationship between price restraint and productivity. He argues that a high level of price restraint provides evidence of a high degree of competition. Similarly, a *changing* degree of price restraint provides evidence of a *changing* degree of competition. Thus, a positive relationship between price restraint (and/or changes in the degree of price restraint) and productivity is evidence of a positive relationship between competition and productivity. Klein's empirical results show just such a positive relationship.

One possible problem with this test, of course, is that we don't know which way causation runs. Did greater price restraint (increased competition) cause productivity improvements in the industries studied, or did productivity improvements cause the greater price restraint? Klein recognizes this possible weakness in his study but argues that for causation to run from improved productivity to greater price restraint we must be prepared to accept one very improbable assumption. Specifically, we must assume that corporations are altruistic enough to pass along improvements in productivity by restraining price increases no matter what level of competition they face. Klein points out that firms, acting in their own self–interest, will charge the highest prices the market will tolerate. Assuming that corporations are altruistic, acting in the interest not of their shareholders or management but in the interest of society, is indeed a naive assumption.

Klein's arguments are further buttressed by his observation that those industries exhibiting strong price restraint tendencies were primarily those facing stiff import competition; while those industries exhibiting weak price restraint tendencies were primarily industries that were for one reason or another shielded from import competition. Klein has not published any statistical work on import competition and productivity. But his observation at first glance appears to be correct, and it substantially strengthens his empirical results.

All in all, Klein's work is provocative and opens the door for a great deal of fruitful work on an industry–by–industry basis relating competition to productivity.

Productivity Growth in Increasingly Competitive Industries

As we compiled the data on the forty–two industries in appendix A, we were surprised to see recent sharp upsurges in productivity in a few of the industries. We noticed they were the industries that had faced the greatest increases in competition in the early 1980s, due to the recessions and the increase in imports: aluminum, cement, copper, steel, and tires. (See productivity figures in appendix A.) Not all industries that fell into desperate financial straits due to sharply increased competition showed large increases in productivity. Farm machinery and machine tools did not.

To pursue this relationship between increased competition and increased productivity further, we examined the latest issue of *Productivity Measures for Selected Industries*, published annually by the Bureau of Labor Statistics. The great majority of the industries showing upward spikes in productivity (that is, well above trend–line) were industries that had undergone substantial increases in competition. The copper industry is a spectacular example. (See appendix A.)

Granted, this approach is "casual empiricism," yet our observations are consistent with the notion that increasing competition generally has a large positive effect on productivity. And it points to a possible direction for further more rigorous studies.

These casual observations also raise two interesting questions:

- Would a massive increase in productivity be realized if other organizations were put under such intense competitive pressure, particularly government and the large public–utility sector? And how could this be accomplished? (See chapter 8 for one suggestion.)

- How much of the productivity improvement in these beleaguered industries has been due to improved management decisions, and how much has been due to willingness of unions to modify restrictive work rules? Or, how much has been due to transient factors such as closing down inefficient plants while keeping efficient plants in operation?

No clear–cut answers to these questions are as yet available, but some imaginative economic research could bring some useful answers.

Productivity in Manufacturing vs. Nonmanufacturing Industries

Chart 6.2 shows the change in productivity in the manufacturing sector as compared with the nonmanufacturing sector of the economy since 1953.

From 1953 to the early 1980s productivity of the two sectors moved pretty much together. Since then productivity in the manufacturing sector has grown rapidly while productivity in the nonmanufacturing sector has lagged. This is consistent with the argument that structural competition is a major determinant of the growth of productivity. The recent increase in foreign competition has been the primary element in the improvement in structural competition—and foreign competition impacts mainly the manufacturing sector.

CHANGES IN PRODUCTIVITY

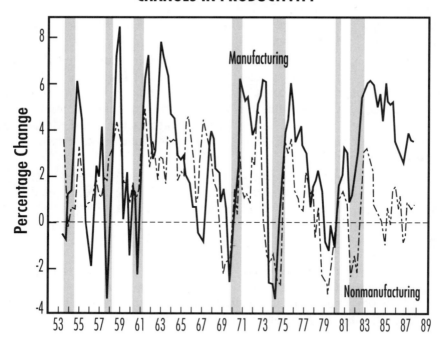

Chart 6.2 Quarterly productivity change for manufacturing and nonmanufacturing industries, four-quarter moving average. The shaded areas indicate periods of business contraction.[5]

A further inspection of chart 6.2 indicates that the growth of productivity in the manufacturing sector during the business expansion since 1982 has been superior to productivity growth in any period of expansion since the mid–1950s. Growth in the first three years of this expansion was as strong as or stronger than it had been in the first three years of any other period of expansion, and it has stayed high longer than it did in either of the other two long recoveries, 1961–69 and 1975–79. Surely this simple fact throws into doubt the many hand–wringing judgments that the United States is unable to compete on international markets and will eventually become a nation of "hamburger flippers." And surely the surge of competition in the manufacturing sector in recent years has been largely responsible for this delightful period of growing productivity. Might we now direct our attention to improving competition in some other sectors of the economy, including governments?

THE RELATIONSHIP BETWEEN MONOPOLY AND PRODUCTIVITY

So far we have examined a number of pieces of evidence that seem to indicate that the intensity of competition and the rate of growth of productivity are positively related. We should now look at the same phenomenon from the other side. How are *monopoly* and productivity related?

Monopoly and Innovation

Some have argued that bigness is necessary to finance and conduct successful research and development. The evidence does not bear out this assertion. A good deal of statistical work has been done to test the effect of firm size on innovational output. Frederic M. Scherer of Swarthmore College (see appendix B, "Market Structure and Innovation") sums it up. "A little bigness...is good for invention and innovation. But beyond the threshold further bigness adds little or nothing, and it carries the danger of diminishing the effectiveness of inventive and innovative performance.[6]

Arguments have also been advanced that high industry concentration (monopolistic market power) is necessary to provide high profits to finance inventive activity. Again, the evidence does not bear out this assertion. Scherer points out that the most favorable industrial environment for innovative performance probably includes a preponderance of medium–sized companies, pressed on one side by many small technology–oriented enterprises and on the other by a few large corporations with the capacity to undertake large projects.[7]

This arrangement looks like a near–perfect competitive environment for rapid improvement in productivity. Monopolistic market power is not necessary for innovation.

Union Effects on Productivity

Turning now from the corporate markets to labor markets, labor unions have a good deal of monopolistic power over some labor markets. Does this monopolistic control reduce productivity?

Until recently, union monopoly power was generally considered to be a hindrance to productivity. In the past decade, however, a group of studies—usually referred to as the Harvard studies—has argued that unions actually increase productivity. Richard Freeman and James Medoff go so far as to argue that the average union gain in productivity is sufficient to offset the substantial union wage premium.[8] These Harvard studies have been heavily criticized, and other studies with contrary findings have been published. The literature in total—what little there is of it—must be considered inconclusive.

More specific studies of the effect of *union work rules* on productivity have been directed largely at the construction industry, and in that industry, the few studies that have been done indicate that union work rules add little to total construction costs—that is, they reduce productivity only slightly.

But surprisingly, few studies in the professional economic literature have focused on the effect of union work rules on productivity in the *industrial* sector. And this is the area in which the popular press has so frequently cited "horror stories" of corporations forced to pay for redundant labor, or unable to modernize or cut costs because of union work rules.

In summary, then, existing economic research on the productivity–work rule relationship must also be considered inadequate. A brief survey of the economic literature analyzing union effects on productivity is presented in appendix B.

We cannot get definitive answers on the union–productivity relationship from existing economic research. What does the market tell us? One fact is clear. Unions generally have been losing market share as indicated by the loss of union membership. The Linneman and Wachter study previously cited documents the union decline. This fact does not support the notion that unions improve productivity sufficiently to offset the union wage premium as is sometimes claimed. In fact, the loss of union share has been so dramatic that one might suspect that the union competitive position has been burdened by both a substantial wage premium and lower productivity.

Noninflationary Wage Gains

A long time ago, in those innocent days of the late fifties and early sixties, frequent references were made in the economic literature and in the public press to something called a noninflationary wage gain for the entire economy. This was an average wage gain for American workers equal to the average improvement in their productivity. If the two were equal, unit labor costs would remain unchanged. Since labor (in the broadest sense) makes up almost two–thirds of the cost of production, there would generally be no need for price increases.

After inflation took off in the late sixties and average annual wage increases eventually approached 10 percent, the goal of limiting wage increases to productivity increases seemed to be an impossible dream. References to noninflationary wage increases pretty much dropped from sight.

But the concept of the noninflationary wage gain should now return to front stage center. It may be a realizable goal, or at least a goal that has an impact on policy even though results are always near–misses. The concept is understandable. It emphasizes the necessity of improving productivity if we want to improve our real income.

We cannot improve our standard of living by raising wages (including salaries), unless those wage gains are matched by gains in productivity. Any group that receives a wage gain greater than the average increase in productivity for the entire economy must be offset by another group receiving a lesser wage gain than the increase in productivity, or we will face rising prices.

IMPROVING PRODUCTIVITY

We have throughout this book pointed out areas where special effort is needed to preserve and promote competition, all of which will also help to improve productivity. At this time we should also emphasize additional factors especially related to productivity improvement.

Managing Interest Rates to Improve Productivity

Can productivity be improved by keeping interest rates low? Capital spending for modernization is undoubtedly necessary for improvements in productivity, but can low interest rates spur such modernization expenditures?

Economic studies have been inconclusive, but apparently, low interest rates do have some stimulative effect on capital spending by reducing risk.[9] Considerable spending for plant and equipment is financed by borrowing. Borrowing requires a commitment to make fixed interest payments far into an uncertain future. The risk of being unable to meet those payments is, of course, less at low rates of interest than at high rates of interest.

In addition, low interest rates reduce the cost of borrowing to state and local governments, thereby making possible improvements in America's infrastructure. An improved infrastructure also increases productivity.

But how can we keep interest rates low to improve productivity? The Federal Reserve shouldn't even consider the possibility of using its power to keep interest rates low just to improve productivity. As argued earlier, its objective should be purely and simply to prevent inflation from accelerating and to keep the economy growing as rapidly as possible without the accelerating of inflation.

The federal government should, however, seriously consider the problem of productivity—among many other things—in the preparation of the budget. Interest rates are lower with low deficits than with high deficits, and, therefore, productivity grows faster. Greater productivity, then, will be one of the benefits of prescribed policy #2—eliminate the federal budget deficit.

Human Factors in Productivity

A great deal has been written in recent years about the human element in productivity. Not surprisingly, the writing concentrates on such things as education, employee motivation, better business management, improved communications between workers and management, linking of pay to performance, and employee involvement in decision making. The literature on this subject is extensive and important. In this connection, we would like to make three observations:

- The human factors, such as education and training, that influence productivity are very important because in a market–managed economy devoid of serious monopoly, wage and salary rates tend to reflect the productivity of the individual. Therefore, if wage rates of low–income individuals are to rise, their productivity must also rise. Monopoly also raises *some* wage rates, but it has the other adverse consequences we have discussed elsewhere in this book.

- There has probably never been a time when so many people—both professionals and novices—have taken it upon themselves to lecture American business managers about their faults and failings. But increased competition is now rapidly improving business management. Rigorous competition concentrates the minds of managers. It overcomes arrogance. It opens the mind to new ideas. It gives managers courage to experiment with the new. Many revolutions in managerial policy are going on in this country under the extreme pressure of foreign competition. Those revolutions will continue as more and more foreign producers set up shop in this country and compete on our own turf. It will be fascinating to watch. Most American producers will likely make the necessary adjustments to survive and prosper.

- Improved education is always advanced as one answer to productivity problems, and usually the suggestion is to add more money to the system. Perhaps more money will solve the problem, but a lingering suspicion must exist in the minds of most observers that we need bolder, more radical approaches to the improvement of our educational system.

Anyone who is convinced of the efficacy of competition in motivating and disciplining human activity has to be intrigued with the possibility of using the frequently recommended voucher system in elementary and secondary education. Under this system local governments would provide vouchers to parents allowing them to send their children to private or public schools of their choice. Freedom of choice and competition are two parts of the same package. *Whenever consumers have a choice among suppliers, those suppliers are in competition with one another.*

Hence, schools would be competing with one another for students. Teachers would be paid on the basis of performance. Students would be expelled from the school of their choice if they didn't behave. Schools would be accredited on the basis of students' performance on tests covering core curriculum, not on the basis of the number of degrees held by teachers or the elegance of the physical plant. Core curriculum would be extensive at lower grades, covering the basics such as reading, writing, arithmetic, history, and geography. The required core curriculum would shrink at the higher levels, providing more variety for parents and students to choose between preparation for college and preparation for vocations. A greater variety of schools would be available with different educational philosophies in regard to such items as discipline.

But most of all, the parents would be in command, and the teachers and school administrators would be under the motivation and discipline of competition.

Would new and better techniques of teaching be developed under this decentralization of the educational establishment? Would the increased flexibility allow for greater innovation? The voucher system has never received much support from the education profession. We will not know if competition could produce in our educational establishment the same wonders it has produced in other sectors of human society until some such system is thoroughly tested over a period of years in a number of school districts across the nation.

Press reports indicate that a few school districts are now going part way by allowing parents and students a limited choice among public schools. If school administrations are given considerable freedom in designing school policies, competition among public schools may achieve part of the benefits a fully competitive system might produce.

Creative Destruction

The term "creative destruction" has survived in the economic lexicon for many years. It was coined by Joseph Schumpeter in his writings of the 1940s.[10] It is a very useful phrase because it emphasizes two important aspects of the competitive process by which progress is made toward improvements in our standard of living: creativity and destruction.

Economic progress (productivity) is made by *creating* new products, new processes, and new jobs. But such progress automatically means the *destruction* of old products, old processes, and old jobs. They are replaced by the new.

Destruction of the old is painful, especially to the employees who find their customary jobs obsolete, and to investors who find their old investments

119

worthless. *And this is the critical point in determining the future growth rate of productivity and our standard of living.* If we choose to alleviate that pain by preventing adoption of the new to preserve the old jobs and the value of the old investments, we automatically put on hold the improvements in productivity necessary to improve our living standards. On the other hand, if we choose to mitigate the pain by easing the movement of employees from old jobs to new, by retraining and other devices, our standard of living will continue to improve.

Politically, it is often easier to protect the employee in the old job, because the pain of movement to a new job is seldom completely alleviated. Furthermore, the small gains in living standards to millions of consumers is not easily recognized.

The new replaces the old when the new is better or less expensive. In the United States, many jobs could be performed at a lower cost. If all barriers to free and open competition were suddenly to disappear (structural competition were to increase), less–efficient, high–cost jobs would disappear, and our productivity and standard of living would rise sharply.

What are some of the jobs in the United States that could be performed at a lower cost if no barriers to open competition existed?

The largest group is the one protected by import barriers. Many products can be produced more efficiently abroad than in the United States. Unfortunately many people still believe that if import barriers were removed, jobs in the United States would be destroyed and new ones would not be created. As argued throughout this book, such fears are simply not warranted. But those fears must be alleviated to gain support for free–trade policies, and the steps necessary to do so are discussed in the final chapter of this book.

Most jobs performed by labor union members with their substantial wage premiums could be done at a lower cost by nonunion workers. Barriers protect the high–cost workers from competition from nonunion workers. If legal supports that buttress union bargaining power were sharply reduced, union wage premiums would also come down. Initially, corporate profits would rise, but since most industries are subject to the convergence principle, profit margins would be driven back down to the all–industry average, and so the benefits of reduced union wage premiums would be passed on to consumers in lower prices.

Other sources of inefficient production are corporations in industries not subject to rigorous competition, which are generally selling their products at excessive prices; and governments and public utilities, producing services that could be contracted out at lower costs.

To repeat, monopolistic or government–mandated barriers to creative destruction may temporarily reduce the pain of the high–cost producers by

120

protecting jobs, but those barriers increase the pain of everyone by holding back improvement in living standards.

No corporation, industry, union, occupation, association, cooperative, profession, or even government should have the power to exclude any person or any organization from undertaking any task when he, she, or it can perform that task better or at a lower cost than those already performing that task. Until we diligently pursue the implementation of that policy, we will not achieve a full measure of increased productivity or improved living standards. That policy, of course, is just a restatement of our prescribed policy #3—improve structural competition.

CONCLUSION

We began this chapter with a look at the high–risk and often unpleasant features of the productivity growth process. We will end it with a brief look at the nature of human competitiveness.

The ironman triathlon conducted each year in Hawaii illustrates as vividly as can be done the spectacular, almost unbelievable, things that can be achieved by human beings under the spur of competition. To swim 2.4 miles in an open sea, cycle 112 miles, and then run a marathon beneath a tropical sun, all in ten to twelve hours, to most of us seems like an absolute impossibility. But in competition a few can do it. Competition works equally well throughout most fields of human endeavor. Accomplishments in the sciences, arts, and industry as well as in athletics evoke a daily sense of wonder at what human beings can do.

Most people seem to have a strong desire to excel and to achieve the adulation that comes to those who do excel. Whether it is a genetic or cultural trait doesn't matter. The trait is widespread. And that inevitably means competition.

The whip of competition is the necessary motivation to overcome the dangers and difficulties of the productivity growth process. Many participants with the desire to excel, each with access to opportunities to compete and an economic and political environment that encourages free and open competition, will certainly overcome the problems of the productivity growth process. Improved competition is not the only answer to better productivity, but it is an important factor.

We would not want to argue that we have presented an unassailable case for the proposition that competition improves productivity. But it is unlikely that one could present even this convincing a case for the opposing proposition—that monopoly improves productivity—or even for the case that competition has no effect on productivity.

A sweeping overview of the years since the mid–1950s suggests that the sharp relaxation of below–capacity competition in the last half of the 1960s ushered in a period of low growth in productivity. It probably began with the establishment of a norm of accelerating wage gains, both union and nonunion. As this norm became established, higher wages and salaries had to be passed regularly through to consumers in higher prices. This habit spread to all costs, and there developed what some writers of the time referred to as a "pass through" mentality. Instead of fighting to hold down costs, management became hooked on passing rising expenses through to the consumer in higher prices. Everyone was doing it. It was the expected thing to do. And so productivity lagged.

In the early 1980s, the dramatic increase in below–capacity competition and foreign competition broke that "pass through" mentality, at least in manufacturing, where competition became so intense. Productivity growth in manufacturing returned to its earlier level. The increase in competition of the early 1980s may have been a watershed event that will keep the growth of productivity in manufacturing fairly high even in the face of some decline in foreign competition as the trade gap closes, and some decline in below–capacity competition as we operate closer to full employment for extended periods.

CHAPTER 7

A SPECIAL KIND OF
COMPETITION AMONG COUNTRIES

As previous chapters have made clear, one of the best ways to maintain and improve structural competition in the United States is to make sure our economy is tied closely to a well–functioning global economy. In searching for ways to improve this global integration we read economic reports from over one hundred less–developed countries (LDCs). We were fascinated to find among these LDCs a new and special kind of competition: *a competition to attract foreign capital and technology*. This new competition bears the promise of an astonishing period of worldwide economic development over the coming decades. How has this new competition come about, and why is it so promising?

A BRIEF HISTORY OF THE NEW COMPETITION

The new competition among LDCs has developed in the single generation since World War II. It is the more surprising because it represents a complete turnabout from earlier doctrines. Let us focus briefly on how it has come about.

The Old Doctrines

After World War II and the dismantling of Western colonialism, two convictions dominated most of the less–developed countries of the world. First, a great fear of control and exploitation by outside countries and corporations existed. Second, most people in these countries had a profound bias toward socialism and against capitalism. Both of these convictions are understandable. Colonialism had not been a pleasant experience to the colonies, and blame for their problems was generally heaped upon the imperialists. Capitalism had a bad reputation. It had gone through a terrible depression just prior to the war, and many felt that frequent deep depressions were an inevitable part of capitalism. Furthermore, an idealistic socialism had become the preferred economic system to a very large part of the intellectual community around the world.

It is not surprising, then, that most LDCs established rigid, government–controlled economic systems, nationalized foreign holdings, and attempted to become self–sufficient.

The Upset

Two things happened to upset the old doctrines. Socialism (defined in the traditional sense as government ownership and control of the means of production) failed wherever it was tried. In most cases it failed miserably. On the other hand, in several cases capitalism succeeded brilliantly. Among less–developed countries, some capitalist countries on the western Pacific Rim made spectacular progress, approaching the status of developed nations in a single generation. Among more advanced capitalist countries, Japan turned in an outstanding performance. And the advanced capitalist countries of Europe and North America turned in good performances. Since the thirties no deep depression has occurred, and in the last few years most of the developed countries have demonstrated they can conquer inflation—not without some pain, but without tearing apart the fabric of society.

The failure of socialism and the success of capitalism will likely prove to be watershed events that will be paramount in molding the shape of the world for decades to come. Already a majority of the LDCs are shifting toward market–managed economies, and the effects of this shift will be profound.

The New Competition

As the capitalist revolution began to take hold among more and more countries, a new problem arose. How could they obtain the capital and the technological expertise to become modern market–oriented economies?

At this point, the new competition began to develop. LDCs discovered that available capital and its related technology are extremely limited. And they discovered that they are in competition with one another to obtain this scarce capital and technological expertise. The evidence is simply overwhelming that more and more LDCs understand that they are under growing competitive pressure from other LDCs in the race to attract precious capital and its related technology. (See appendix B, "Competition for Foreign Investment Among Developing Countries.") And how do the LDCs compete? By improving their economic and political environments.

Their first efforts were directed specifically toward the obvious programs intimately related to foreign investment: eliminating discriminatory taxation, assuring against nationalization, allowing repatriation of profits, providing tax holidays to investors, reducing local content requirements, eliminating requirements for local control or even local participation, and placing fewer restrictions on the need to hire local administrators. In sum, these programs add up to less government regulation, greater respect for contracts, and more reliance on free markets. The detailed study in appendix B indicates the extent and momentum this type of activity has already achieved.

Those specific programs are the easy ones. The hard ones are much more important. The best business environment is one where peace with both neighbors and citizenry is assured. No investor likes to build a plant that may be involved in a war or revolution. A government that is legitimized by genuine support of the people is preferred. A motivated low–cost labor force is important. This means that workers should be able to keep most of what they earn. They should be able to accumulate property. They should be able to see a better future for themselves and for their children. All the features of a stable, peaceful, improving economy are desirable to attract investment.

It is difficult to envision a more promising climate for social development than competitive pressure directing human effort toward these elements of a proper business environment. This is not just ordinary commercial competition. It is a new and very special kind of competition. *It is a far cry from the militarism that has dominated competition among countries over the centuries.*

The creation of such an idealistic economic environment, of course, is often very difficult. Roadblocks include the following:

- The pervasive inherited notion that exploitation at the hands of international corporations has been the cause of most of the problems of the LDCs.

- A cadre of civil servants whose very jobs depend on the continued policy of government regulation of business affairs.

- A large, powerful group of domestic monopolistic producers—often inefficient—fearful of facing competition.

- Governments laced with corrupt officials requiring payoffs from business as a price of getting things done.

- Revolutionary minorities that throw doubt on the stability of government and the safety of private property.

The list goes on. But the LDCs have examples to follow. They now know the tremendous benefits that can be realized. And most of all, they are under the whip of competition to perform. Competition in many fields of human endeavor has produced astonishing results. Why can it not perform equally well in the race to build attractive environments to obtain the tools and expertise necessary to modernize?

RESULTS OF THE NEW COMPETITION AMONG THE LDCS

Looking at the present state of the Third World with its little wars, its inefficient governments, its poverty, one could be excused for being less than optimistic about rapid modernization in the foreseeable future. But the possibilities are really substantial, because Third World countries have successful examples to follow.

To know that something can be done is a powerful stimulus to action. The success of some Asian Rim countries that have developed relatively modern economies in just a single generation is known to most people around the world. Several other countries are on the same road to successful modernization. Pressure will build on laggard countries to improve their business environments as more of their neighbors move along the path of economic growth.

All Third World countries will not follow identical paths to modernization. Policies will have to be adapted to the conditions in each country. But improvement of the business environment to attract capital and technology is likely to be at the core of successful modernization plans.

Those countries unable or unwilling to provide an acceptable environment to acquire the modern technology will rapidly find themselves in the backwater of civilization. Modernization will grow at a geometric rate. The more countries that participate, the greater will be the pressure on others to provide the climate for development, difficult though it may be. South Korea and Taiwan are well on their way—like Japan—to becoming high cost producers. They will import and consume much more; and they will provide more investment funds for countries farther behind in the development race.

Mexico is one of the countries most likely to benefit as Japan, South Korea, and Taiwan become high–cost producers, limiting their exports and increasing their imports. Mexico has abundant, low–cost energy, a low–cost motivated labor force, and proximity to one of the world's largest markets. Its economic development in the coming years should be spectacular if it will continue to dismantle its restrictive regulations and improve its business climate. If it does not, the new investment will go to other countries, especially Asian countries that are rapidly improving their business environments.

Besides the material improvements to the people of the Third World countries through modernization, and besides the important nonmaterial advantages that will come through efforts of these countries to improve their business climates, additional benefits will accrue to the world from the new competition.

Many new viable participants added to several industries should substantially improve the global economy. To the United States, global competition is important because it is virtually impossible for labor unions to take wages out of competition when several transnational corporations in each industry have productive facilities in several countries. It is also difficult under these circumstances for corporations to maintain monopolistic profit margins for any length of time. More participants added continually to the global economy should help insure the improvement of structural competition.

But the new competition has an even more significant implication. Peter L. Berger, in his book *The Capitalist Revolution* argues that successful capitalism generates pressures toward democracy. "Capitalism creates a highly dynamic zone that is relatively autonomous vis-a-vis the state."[1] Within this autonomous zone many individuals are trained to make decisions—in business and in other related groups, such as cooperatives, labor unions, occupational groups, and voluntary associations. Soon these successful individuals who have learned to make decisions affecting their lives begin to demand and get greater influence in the political arena, and this produces movement toward democracy. Democracy, in turn, usually tends to expand human rights.

(This description of just one of Berger's important theses is a meager presentation. His book is an excellent combination of empirical and theoretical analysis. It should be carefully read by anyone who wishes to understand the many remarkable ways in which the capitalist revolution is changing the world. This book is one of the best books on economics published in the past quarter century—written by a sociologist.)

In summary, then, this is the likely sequence of events:

- To break the bonds of economic stagnation—that is, to modernize—LDCs are beginning to compete with one another to attract foreign capital and its related technology.

- Competition for foreign investment requires them to liberalize their economic and political environments to make possible the operation of the market mechanism—that is, capitalism.

- Successful capitalism in turn leads to substantial improvements in living standards and to democracy and personal freedom.

The movement is still in its infancy but is gaining momentum. There are many false starts, and many mistakes are being made. Conditions in many of the LDCs are very bad. Some of them seem hopeless. But with the example of others to follow, and under the driving force of competition, they will eventually find a way.

THE RESPONSIBILITY OF DEVELOPED COUNTRIES

Governments of developed countries need not pour huge *additional* quantities of money into the modernization of the LDCs. What they need to do is get out of the way and let modernization happen. How have governments of developed countries been standing in the way? By irresponsible deficit financing that has kept interest rates high and has absorbed large amounts of loanable funds that would otherwise have gone to investment, including investment in the LDCs. Several advanced countries have been at fault, but the United States in recent years has been among the worst. The United States government has been absorbing huge amounts of funds from the precious international pool of capital. The United States, through private channels, should have been *supplying* funds to that international pool of capital. Fortunately most advanced countries have been reducing their deficits, at least as a percent of their GNP. The trend is encouraging, but in the United States the movement has been painfully slow.

As argued earlier, a major reduction in the federal deficit would cause interest rates to decline substantially and make larger amounts of loanable funds available for investment, including investment in the LDCs. And, as argued in chapter 2, lower interest rates would lead to lower profit margins in the United States, stimulating the search for higher profits on investments in the developing countries.

Several channels are already open by which nongovernmental investment funds and the related technology can flow to the LDCs:

- Less–developed countries are competing to get multinational companies to build plants in their countries. This is the simplest approach. Technology, capital, and management capability are acquired in one package.

- Many less–developed nations are improving their financial markets to encourage foreign investors to invest directly in their local business firms. Stock markets are springing up in many places. Companies in LDCs are listing shares of their stock on foreign stock exchanges. With this approach, foreign capital is used to buy modern technology, but it is

128

developed under the control of home–grown management. This approach has great potential as Third World countries improve their business climates and overcome their fears of foreign investors' control of their domestic industries. The surface has barely been scratched.

- Another approach is to use local capital from local savings to buy modern equipment. Dozens of construction firms will come in and build the most modern plants on a turnkey basis and teach local people how to run them. Capital is raised locally, but initially needed technology is imported. Local capital will inevitably be required to finance the bulk of modernization for most countries.

- An increasingly popular channel for acquiring capital and technology is the joint venture. A local company with knowledge of local conditions teams up with a foreign company that has the necessary technology and capital.

These channels for investment in the LDCs are not just for projects aimed mainly for export. They are also for production of goods and services to be consumed largely within the LDCs. This is important because there is a limit to how many imports the developed countries will be willing to absorb, although that amount probably should be increased.

The channels for financing the modernization of the Third World are rapidly opening up. But the amount of capital required is enormous—trillions of dollars. And that is why it is necessary for governments of developed countries to quit absorbing such a large chunk of the world's savings, allowing interest rates to drop. Modernization of the world will happen even under present government obstruction, but it can be speeded dramatically if governments will get out of the way and quit siphoning off those huge amounts of investment capital. The proper management of competition requires the implementation of our prescribed policy #2—eliminate the budget deficit—to speed the development of the global economy.

ECONOMIC COMPETITION IS REPLACING MILITARISM

So far in this chapter we have concentrated on competition among LDCs to attract capital and modern technology. We now enlarge the focus to include a brief examination of competition among developed countries to see how it has changed from past rivalries.

Militarism has been the primary form of competition among countries throughout the centuries. Most of our modern nation–states are products of successful military excursions or military revolts. But in the twentieth century militarism has not performed so well. Attempts at empire building have generally been unsuccessful. The one large empire put together by military force—the Soviet Empire—seems now to be in grave danger of breaking apart. This century has pretty well demonstrated that seeking power and prestige by economic development has a much greater chance of success than seeking power and prestige by military means. Japan and West Germany are the spectacular examples.

Competition among countries is probably as intense as ever, but now it more often takes nonmilitary forms. *Economic* competition lies at the heart of present–day rivalry among countries.

Economic development requires countries to devote a large part of their production to capital goods. Therefore, great pressure arises to reduce expenditures on the military. And in order to safely cut military spending, tensions with other countries must be reduced. Of all the major countries in the world the Soviet Union is most subject to this pressure. It devotes a very large part of its output to the military—probably around 10 to 20 percent. This vast military complex is supported by a meager, failing socialist economy.

The United States stands second in line of major countries in the proportion of its total output devoted to the military. At the same time the United States is coming under great competitive pressure to increase its capital stock and improve its technology. This competitive pressure will certainly reflect itself in the need to reduce military spending.

Both the USSR and the United States, then, are being driven by economic competition to reduce expenditures on the military. To do so safely, they must reduce the many tensions around the world that make disarmament difficult. Conditions, at the moment, appear to be right for these countries to push the proper buttons to achieve a major reduction in tensions. Economic competition will likely force them to do so.

The dominant factor in international relations since World War II has been an expansionist Marxist socialism going up against a policy of containment by the United States. With the ongoing collapse of Marxist socialism, economic competition among nations is rapidly taking center stage as the major element in international affairs. As a result, militarism gradually will give away to a world–wide surge in economic development.

A great deal of economic competition among countries now exists among both advanced and developing countries. No nation is insulated from its pressures. We are all aware of the need for the Soviet Union to pull back from its empire, to reduce military spending and to move toward a market–managed economy. But competitive pressures are also impacting the United States. That competition is forcing the United States to reexamine its educational system, the quality of its business management, its commitment to research and its productivity failures. It most likely will require many more soul–searching evaluations over the years.

Peace is breaking out around the world, not simply due to the accession of new leaders or to an outburst of kindness among human beings. Economic competition is *driving* countries to reduce tensions. And so we believe that the twenty–first century will record another triumph for the efficacy of competition, this time in helping to bring peace, prosperity, and democracy to much of the world.

CHAPTER 8

BRINGING IT ALL TOGETHER

This book has emphasized the importance of competition in its twin roles as motivator and disciplinarian. It has also emphasized the many ways in which government has mismanaged competition, aggravating the problems of recession, inflation, poverty and slow productivity growth.

If we are to alleviate these problems by improving the management of competition we must find a way to make governments more efficient and more responsible. We will begin this summary chapter by undertaking that difficult task. Then we will review the status of the three prescribed policies for improving the management of competition. And finally we will take a look at the economic prospects for the coming decades.

MAKING GOVERNMENT MORE RESPONSIBLE

Federal, state and local governments are now absorbing by taxation about 40 percent of our entire national income. By mandating and regulating many private expenditures, governments control a substantial additional share of income. Altogether, probably half our nation's income falls under at least some government control. Are we getting our money's worth?

To make government more efficient and more responsible, we must limit the resources that can be commandeered by government spending and regulation. Constitutional amendments limiting taxes and requiring balanced budgets have been proposed. They may be impossible to ratify. In any event, they leave a gigantic loophole—the ability of government to mandate and regulate private spending and other activities.

Four constraints will help considerably to make government more responsible. The first is already in place and the third is nearly in place. These four constraints are:

- Tax revolts.

- A balanced–budget tradition.

- An ironclad Federal Reserve anti–inflation policy.

- Continuing aggressive effort to illuminate the linkages among government policies, inflation, and monetary restraint.

With these four constraints in place most government programs can be enacted only at a cost—the pain of additional unpopular taxes, the necessity of reducing other spending programs, or, finally, the unpleasant consequences of restrictive monetary policy. Government activity should be more responsible when benefits of a program must be balanced against its cost. How do these constraints work?

Tax Revolts

We live in a time of tax revolts. Government spending is clearly being restrained by difficulty in raising taxes. As chart 8.1 shows, state and local

STATE & LOCAL TAXES AS A PERCENTAGE OF NATIONAL INCOME

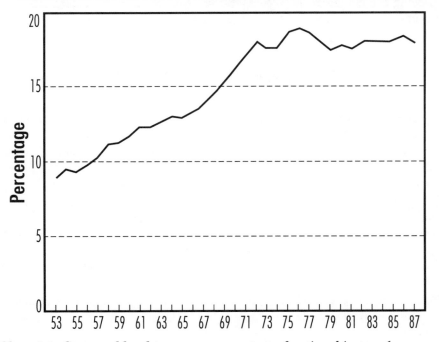

Chart 8.1 State and local taxes as a percentage of national income.[1]

taxes rose sharply from 1953 to the early 1970s, but since then have remained nearly constant as a percentage of national income. Tax revolts were apparently underway even before the highly publicized Proposition 13 revolt in California in the late 1970s.

As chart 8.2 indicates, federal government receipts rose moderately as a percentage of national income from the early 1950s to the late 1980s. This increase in revenues was not to support increased federal purchases of goods and services; on the contrary, federal purchases of goods and services as a percentage of national income declined over this period. The increase in federal taxes was mainly due to social security programs. Federal taxation is probably approaching a limit, evidenced by the emphasis on the tax issue in recent federal elections. Tax revolts are alive and well at all levels of government.

Irresponsible expansion of government will *not* come about through spending financed by taxation. Because any new tax increases will intensify tax revolts, tax increases are self–limiting. On the other hand, irresponsible government expansion may come about through spending financed by borrowing and through government mandating of private spending. Those are the gaping holes that must be closed.

FEDERAL RECEIPTS AS A PERCENTAGE OF NATIONAL INCOME

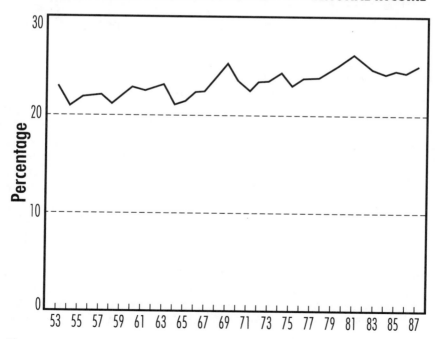

Chart 8.2   Federal government receipts as a percentage of national income·2

The Tradition of a Balanced Budget

State and local spending financed by borrowing is limited by credit ratings. Excessive borrowing destroys favorable credit ratings making continued borrowing more difficult. The federal government has not faced this limitation because it has the ultimate power to print money to pay its debts.

In the past, the strongest limitation on federal spending financed by borrowing has been the tradition of a balanced budget. This tradition stood up well for many years, although it was severely compromised in every major war and was slightly weakened by abandonment of the notion that the budget should be balanced in times of recession.

Still, in most of the last half century the tradition survived as a goal. Even though the goal was seldom met, misses were generally near–misses. As chart 8.3 shows, from 1953 to the mid 1970s, a period that included four recessions, the deficit averaged about 1 percent of national income. That wasn't perfect, but during that period the national debt was reduced from about 60 percent of GNP to about 25 percent of GNP—not a bad performance.

Under the Carter administration, the balanced—budget tradition began to fall apart; it then suffered a severe blow under the two–headed government represented by the Reagan administration and the mostly Democratic Congress. Can the balanced–budget tradition be revived? Without it, we are missing one of the major constraints on government spending. Few things are more attractive to lawmakers than spending without the necessity of increasing taxes.

The balanced–budget tradition will be revived only when the evils of past deficit financing are fully recognized. Those evils have been described throughout this book and are generally recognized by most, though not all, economists.

The deficits of recent years have added around $100 billion to our government's annual interest cost. They have absorbed a major part of total private savings, helping to make ours a low–savings, high–consumption economy. The deficits have held interest rates higher than they otherwise would have been, thus exacerbating the trade deficit and the trend toward protectionism. They have also intensified the savings and loan crisis, the LDC debt problem, and poverty. Many of these problems will continue to fester. An increasing awareness of the involvement of the deficit in these problems should help to break the political stalemate and reduce the deficit.

However, any prolongation of heavy deficit financing will further weaken the balanced–budget tradition. If it becomes impossible to get the genie of heavy deficit financing back into the bottle and to revive the balanced–budget tradition, the deficit financing of the 1980s will have been a tragic event from the standpoint of making government more responsible.

136

FEDERAL SURPLUS AND DEFICIT AS A PERCENTAGE OF NATIONAL INCOME

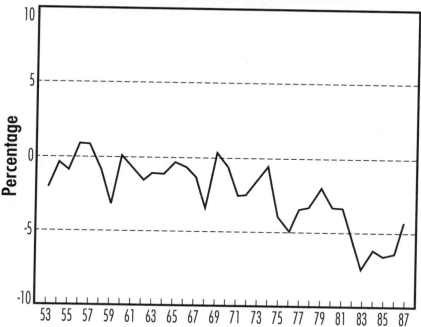

Chart 8.3   Federal deficit as a percentage of national income.[3]

One of the more startling developments of recent years has occurred in part of the conservative community. This group, which used to be so adamantly opposed to deficit financing, is now excusing the present large deficit mainly on the grounds that it is forcing government to hold down spending. Sometimes proponents of this stance refer to the deficit as harmless; occasionally they call it a blessing. This approach to limiting government spending is shortsighted and terribly dangerous. It will work only as long as deficits are considered to be bad. If the notion ever becomes widespread that deficits are not harmful or that they are blessings, then a wide, wide door for irresponsible government spending without the restraint of tax revolts will open. The view that large deficits are acceptable because they discourage government spending is self–destructive.

The constraints of tax revolts and a balanced–budget tradition are still not enough to assure government responsibility. The ability to mandate private expenditures and to regulate private markets is still unrestrained. And these government activities are the hardest to control. In fact, the more taxes and borrowing are limited, the more likely government is to mandate private spending. Therefore, we need the next two constraints, which must be used together.

An Ironclad Federal Reserve Anti–Inflation Policy

An ironclad anti–inflation policy requires the Federal Reserve to drive the inflation rate back down to some low level, say 1 or 2 percent, and hold it there. It must be made absolutely clear by word and deed that any acceleration of inflation above this level will be met by more–restrictive monetary policy. In chapter 4 we argued that it is possible to maintain a relatively steady low inflation rate by monetary management.

Then any time government undertakes actions that are inflationary, those actions will be met by monetary restraint with all its unpleasant consequences. *Most of the unwise economic policies of government are inflationary*, and with an ironclad anti–inflation policy in place, they could be enacted only at the cost of painful monetary restraint. Four types of policies that are often tempting to elected officials but that are clearly inflationary are the following:

- Fiscal policy that is excessively stimulating. Excessively stimulating fiscal policy is a policy of spending increases or tax cuts that produces too–rapid economic growth. Too–rapid growth is growth that accelerates (or threatens to accelerate) inflation.

- Increases in government spending financed by hidden taxes. Elected officials get credit for spending programs but are not blamed for the tax hikes that are hidden in the prices of the things consumers buy. All or part of many taxes such as the value–added tax, indirect business taxes, and the corporate income tax fall into the category of hidden taxes. Moderate increases in spending matched by tax increases generally do not appreciably affect total demand, and therefore do not affect the rate of growth of the economy. However, the hidden taxes affect prices through a different channel. Since they are ultimately shifted to the consumer in higher prices, they directly drive up the cost of living index, thus adding to the pressure for Federal Reserve restraint.

- Policies that subvert structural competition. Many policies fall into this category: protectionism, strengthening of monopolistic labor unions, faulty antitrust policy, business regulation that limits competition, and so on.

- Government requirements that business firms provide additional benefits or services to their employees or to the general public. Health insurance, day–care centers, pollution controls, and minimum wages are examples of this type of government program. The cost of these programs is, of course, largely passed on to the consumer in higher prices.

Not *all* of these government programs are bad, but many of them are. And to have to balance their enactment against the cost of painful monetary restraint should help weed out the worst.

No mushy monetary policy will do. An ironclad policy is required, administered by courageous people who are willing to suffer small immediate pain for far greater long–term benefits. As we have seen, such a monetary policy will provide enormous benefits in the proper management of below–capacity competition in the private sector. Making government more responsible is a very valuable side effect.

But an ironclad Federal Reserve policy is not sufficient. It must be accompanied by our fourth and final constraint on government activity.

Linking Government Policies, Inflation, and Monetary Restraint

An ironclad monetary policy will not restrain irresponsible government policies unless the linkage among these policies, inflation, and monetary restraint is evident. Herein lies a dual problem. First, the linkage is not often widely understood. And second, inflation is often significantly affected only by the cumulative impact of a number of programs, each of which has only a modest inflationary effect.

The great challenge before us, then, is to illuminate the linkage involved. We should require an inflationary impact statement to accompany every bill introduced into Congress. In a formal sense, that is not likely to occur, but responsible economic organizations should keep a running tab on the inflationary impact of pending bills as they move through the legislative process, and their impact should be added to an estimate of the inflationary forces usually near the surface in the private sector. This "inflation budget" would highlight the *cumulative* threat of inflationary government programs that would trigger restrictive monetary policy. We desperately need an inflation budget that receives as much attention as the fiscal budget.

An inflation budget would estimate the inflation impact of every government proposal and would identify the channel through which that proposal would affect the inflation rate. The four major channels are the ones described above–excessively stimulating fiscal policy, hidden taxes that accelerate the consumer price index, government–mandated activities of private business that increase costs, and weakened structural competition that tilts business decisions away from increasing output toward increasing wages and prices.

Those who keep running tabs on the inflation impact of *proposed* government initiatives also should keep a list of the many *existing* government programs whose elimination would reduce inflationary pressures. If any proposed program is of special merit, but is inflationary, existing programs could be eliminated to offset the new inflationary program and avoid the pain of

139

greater Federal Reserve restraint. If possible, an offsetting program should be selected that affects inflation through the same channel as does the new program to be adopted.

An inflation budget would be difficult to prepare. The precise inflationary impact of a government activity—existing or proposed—is always controversial. Yet, some kind of tabulation is necessary to accomplish three goals.

- Focus attention on the inflationary impact of each and every government program and describe the channel by which the inflation rate is impacted.

- Emphasize the *cumulative* impact on inflation of all government programs.

- Highlight the required Federal Reserve restraint to cumulative inflationary programs.

Even in rudimentary form an inflation budget would be invaluable. Over the years it could be developed to be an extremely beneficial adjunct to an ironclad Federal Reserve anti–inflation policy.

Wonderful things might happen if lawmakers came to recognize the cumulative inflationary impact of, and the predictable Federal Reserve response to, legislative action. For instance, suppose lawmakers have a terribly desirable, but inflationary project in view—say, some costly business requirement to protect the environment. To offset the inflationary impact and negate the restrictive Federal Reserve response, they might turn finally toward dismantling some of the many existing inflationary programs such as the infamous import quotas on sugar, or the Davis–Bacon Act that adds to construction costs, or gross inefficiencies in the federal establishment due to regulatory difficulties in firing incompetent employees, and so on. The result could be a continuing cleansing of the federal bureaucracies. When counter–inflation trade–offs of this sort become common, better government will be realized. Only the threat of painful monetary restraint can force such trade–offs.

Summary

The term "making government more responsible" means causing government to become less wasteful and to keep out of or get out of activities better conducted by the private sector. The four constraints just proposed would limit the resources subject to taxation, spending, and regulation, thus *establishing limits within which government would have to operate.* Only then would more attention be paid to priorities, and choices be made to eliminate the least desirable activities so that the more desirable activities could go forward. Efficiency would become a more important goal, to extend limited resources as far as possible. Advocates of new programs would be under pressure either to find other projects that could be eliminated or else face the undesirable consequences of higher taxes or monetary restraint.

These constraints for making government more responsible should appeal to both those who want far less government activity and those who want a great deal of government intervention but also want to get more value for their money. They will not appeal to those whose ideology calls for bigger and bigger government.

In a time of tax revolts, it is easy to speak against tax increases. That is the popular thing to do. But who has the courage and the wisdom to fight to return to a balanced–budget tradition and to demand an ironclad Federal Reserve policy that will often require some immediate pain to achieve far greater long–term benefits? *That is where the real battle against irresponsible government is being fought.*

Anyone seriously interested in limiting government would, of course, prefer to see the present budget deficit eliminated by reduced spending. But if a divided government makes that impossible, a moderate tax increase may be more desirable than a prolongation of the deficit. Tax increases are self–limiting since they intensify tax revolts. The public will prevent tax increases from going much farther. But on the other hand, a prolongation of the deficit weakens the balanced–budget tradition making more likely the future abuse of that avenue of government expansion.

The four constraints on government irresponsibility have been brought together and placed at the head of this final chapter for one single reason. The United States cannot be made more prosperous unless government (including the Federal Reserve) behaves more responsibly than it has in the past. The impact of government taxation, spending, monetary policy, and regulation is enormous. If government is not responsible, the whole economy suffers—and indeed, most of our present economic problems can be traced to past government mismanagement. Any topic as important as this must come at the head of a summary chapter.

Nothing that has been written here implies that government should not have an important place in economic affairs. But surely government can be made more efficient. The necessity of balancing the benefits of programs against the costs of unpopular taxes and inflation–induced monetary restraint should aid in improving efficiency. That will happen when government has to operate within limits.

The three policies prescribed at the beginning of this book relate closely to the four proposed constraints on government irresponsibility. Policy #1 represents the ironclad Federal Reserve monetary policy. Policy #2 represents the balanced–budget tradition. Policy #3, requiring the enhancement of structural competition, makes an ironclad Federal Reserve policy workable. We should now review the status of and outlook for each of the three policies.

THE STATUS OF POLICY #1

The Federal Reserve System should drive the inflation rate back down to a low level around 1 or 2 percent and then maintain as top priority the prevention of the acceleration of inflation. The second priority should be to keep demand, production, and employment growing as rapidly as possible without the acceleration of inflation.

This policy is apparently nearly in place, and excellent results are already evident. Since 1982 we have had economic recovery without recession, and the unemployment rate has dropped to its lowest level since 1974. Two episodes of mildly accelerating inflation (in 1983–84 and again in 1987) have been brought under control by restrictive monetary policy without precipitating recession. The major reason for this success is that the accelerating inflation was, in each case, recognized and attacked quickly.

(As this book is being completed in early 1989, inflation is again accelerating. The Federal Reserve has responded by a substantial tightening of monetary policy. Since wages have begun to accelerate, this period will provide the sternest test of Federal Reserve resolve that we have had for several years.)

What about the future? As long as this Federal Reserve policy remains in place, we will not have to go through another long, frightening inflationary binge like the 1970s, when we felt helpless because we knew inflation was eating away at the foundations of the economy and threatening to get out of control; and yet we were afraid to take serious restraining action for fear of throwing the country into a long and deep depression. Also, we will not have to go through recessions as serious as the back–to–back recessions of 1980 and 1982 that were required to break a long–standing period of accelerating inflation.

In another vein, the present Federal Reserve policy is gradually establishing a new norm of low wage gains. Employees do not expect to receive, nor do employers expect to grant, the 9 to 10 percent wage gains that were customary in the late 1970s. In a few years, an average annual wage or salary increase of around 2 to 4 percent should be customary and generally accepted. When firmly established, this norm will be something of a disciplining force and should allow us to operate closer to the goal of 4 to 4.5 percent unemployment for extended periods without causing inflation to accelerate.

Inflation is to a considerable extent a habit, especially as related to wage gains. And once the habit has been established, maintaining a 1–percent inflation rate will probably be as easy as a 4–percent inflation rate.

The simple lesson that accelerating inflation must be curbed early is one great benefit salvaged from our experience with the inflationary ills of the 1970s and the painful recessionary cure we took in the early 1980s.

To repeat, the greatest danger to an effective Federal Reserve anti–inflation policy is misguided compassion. Sometimes the Federal Reserve fails to tighten money when inflation threatens, or fails to hold money tight until inflation is brought under control, because its compassion will not allow it to risk the hardships of recession. It postpones monetary restraint until inflation gets so bad something has to be done. Then the recession cure is much worse.

That is exactly what happened following 1965. The result was more than a decade of severe inflation, punctuated by very serious recessions when monetary restraint was necessary to bring dangerous inflation under control. Surely Federal Reserve policy in the late 1960s was misguided compassion.

As a matter of emphasis, another point should be repeated at this time. Policy #1 does not allow the Federal Reserve to choose between a little more inflation or a little more unemployment. *Inflation control comes first*, even if it results in slow economic growth, increased unemployment, or recession. If the economy grows too slowly or recessions are too frequent under this policy, efforts must be redoubled to improve structural competition to hold wages and prices down, rather than following the seductive policy of allowing a little acceleration of inflation. We cannot tolerate a Federal Reserve Board that belongs to the "prevent recession at any cost" school.

We do not quite have an ironclad anti–inflation policy yet, but we have been moving in that direction since 1979. The reestablishment of a vigorous anti–inflation monetary policy should not be lightly dismissed. It is a major landmark in American economic history. If maintained, it will by itself do wonders for the improvement of the American economy as compared to the years since 1965. But it needs a lot of help from prescribed policies #2 and #3 to achieve all the goals we are aiming for.

THE STATUS OF POLICY #2

The federal government should speed the movement toward balancing its fiscal budget and complete that balance within three to four years. Then it should hold the deficit near zero except in times of recession.

143

The tradition of a balanced budget has been seriously wounded. But the wounds are probably not yet fatal and should heal gradually, judging by the following signs:

- Almost all the arguments in Washington about the deficit are directed at *how* the deficit should be reduced, not *whether* it should be reduced. The deficit is constantly listed among urgent problems to be solved.

- As the failure of socialism in the Soviet Union forces that nation to help reduce tensions around the world in order to cut back on its heavy military spending, defense spending in the United States will also be reduced. Defense spending may return to the same percentage of GNP that prevailed in 1978–79: less than 5 percent. This could reduce the deficit by a third.

- Significant reductions in the deficit will make possible less–restrictive monetary policy and thus reduce interest payments on the debt, further reducing the deficit. Perhaps as much as a third of the deficit may be eliminated by lower interest rates.

- Most economists are still convinced of the dangers of large deficits, and the general public is apparently still concerned about deficit financing. More effort is being devoted to relating the deficit to its adverse consequences.

However, one important item of confusion regarding the deficit deserves special attention. A few writers have questioned the present method of computing the deficit. Some alternate measures show larger deficits than those officially reported and some show smaller deficits or even surpluses for the past few years. If the deficit is measured incorrectly, can it really be so important? Most of this confusion, however, disappears when we realize that *each of the measures of the deficit is for a different purpose.*

One complaint is that all government *investment* spending is included in the budget as a current expense. If the purpose of measuring the deficit were to distinguish between the dollar amount spent to satisfy immediate desires (consumption) and the dollar amount spent to satisfy future desires (investment), then the deficit as measured by the difference between income and consumption would be much smaller. But how do you distinguish between government consumption and government investment?

Bridges, schools, parks and highways are certainly investments. But what about military spending? If the hundreds of billions of dollars we have spent on defense have helped to contain Soviet expansion and have helped to persuade the Soviet leaders that their future lies in economic development rather than in military competition, then that military spending will have been the most dramatic investment we could have made for future satisfaction. Counting military spending as investment and measuring the deficit as the difference between income and consumption would produce a substantial surplus every year instead of a deficit. But the arguments as to what consumption is and what investment is would be never–ending.

Another purpose of measuring the deficit is to document the total future obligations that the government is accruing each year, including future social security payments. Using this measurement, the deficit is far greater than has been reported.

But the most important purpose of measuring the deficit is to estimate its impact on current aggregate spending, income, prices, production, employment, and interest rates. For this particular purpose the existing measure of the deficit is reasonably satisfactory, although somewhat understated due to the fact that a number of government projects are kept off the budget. Certainly, the problems of measurement are not sufficient to induce us to forget the dangers of the deficit.

THE STATUS OF POLICY #3

Governments should take steps to improve the intensity of structural competition (reduce monopoly power) in both product and labor markets.

No simple grand design exists for making markets more competitive. The design of necessary improvements in each market is difficult and must ultimately rest largely in the hands of specialists. But the attitude toward the need for vigorously competitive markets is extremely important and should be of great concern to everyone.

The Effectiveness of Antitrust Enforcement

Almost every day brings a report of a new merger or acquisition. Simultaneously, the antitrust laws are being relaxed and persistent calls for further relaxation are being heard. It is enough to strike terror into the heart of anyone concerned with the preservation of competition. Does all this mean that we are experiencing a disastrous loss of competition in corporate product markets? To put the whole thing in perspective, we should look at three areas of concern.

First, what is happening to antitrust policy toward *price fixing* among sellers? Price fixing is still proscribed by antitrust law. No significant change in policy is evident, and very little call for abandonment of this policy is heard, although a few representatives of the Chicago school believe that it is unnecessary. Price–fixing agreements, they claim, will quickly crumble. In any event, in this extremely important area no significant weakening of antitrust policy has occurred.

Second, what is the status of *conglomerate mergers*—that is, mergers between companies in different industries? Antitrust enforcement has never been seriously directed against conglomerate mergers, although occasionally the authorities have flirted with that approach, especially in dealing with mergers between very large companies.

Once in a while the claim is heard that conglomerate mergers have concentrated too much economic power in the hands of a few large companies. What is the trend? From 1960 to about 1970, the percentage of all assets of manufacturing and mining firms in the United States held by the 500 largest industrial firms (the Fortune 500) rose slightly. Then that percentage held steady for several years before beginning a decline. By 1984 the percentage had dropped below the level prevailing in 1960. The trend in the percentage of employees working for the Fortune 500 has shown a similar pattern, but the percentage employed is still well above the 1960 number.

In summary, no important change in antitrust policy has been made regarding conglomerate mergers. Antitrust law has never seriously restrained conglomerate mergers. Conglomerate mergers make up a very large proportion of the mergers involved in the current consolidation boom.

Third and finally, most argument currently revolves around *horizontal mergers* of firms in the same industry. In contrast to the two other areas of antitrust concern, in this area enforcement has been relaxed. Concentration in some industries such as the airline industry is certainly increasing, and that concentration is cause for serious concern. However, weaker antitrust enforcement is not the major cause of the wave of mergers and acquisitions. Those mergers have been most prevalent in the conglomerate sector.

If relaxation of antitrust enforcement has not been the main cause of the merger boom, what have been the causes?

The consolidation movement began several years ago when stocks were grossly underpriced. Companies could be purchased at prices well below their intrinsic values. The acquisition movement accelerated when lending institutions became willing to put up most of the acquisition money—especially via junk bonds—in return for high rates of interest. Furthermore, high leverage saves on corporate taxes because interest is deductible. And finally, the movement was accelerated by foreign buying of American companies as the dollar became cheap on foreign exchange markets.

The undervaluation of common stocks is rapidly disappearing as an incentive for acquisition as stocks become fully priced. But the other forces will remain for some time. Foreign companies own large amounts of dollars and are interested in acquiring American companies for many reasons. Two other factors—the willingness of lending institutions to assume high risks for high

146

interest returns and the tax benefits gained by shifting equity capital to debt capital—are probably the most powerful forces behind the current merger mania. The movement will likely continue until the tax laws are changed, lending institutions are more limited in their risk–assuming practices, stock prices become so high that the risks outweigh the other advantages, or several large failures increase the perception of risk in the financial community.

Experimenting with a relaxation of antitrust enforcement is very dangerous while these pressures for business consolidation remain high and while foreign competition is declining as we close the trade gap.

The American economy is generally very competitive. Few industries have sufficient control over markets to keep their profit margins much above the all–industry average for any appreciable period of time. *Average* profit margins for all industries are momentarily high, but will likely be substantially reduced as the economy slows and as interest rates decline. Competition increased after the 1960s primarily as a result of sharply increased foreign competition and because we operated during the 1970s and the first part of the 1980s well below full capacity, that is, with a substantial amount of amplifying below–capacity competition. In the coming decade we will test the effectiveness of competition under conditions closer to full employment and more balanced international trade.

The one large area of the corporate sector with the market power to keep profit margins above the all–industry average for long periods is the marketing conglomerate area. Antitrust enforcement should be intensified in this area to prevent further consolidation.

Bringing Competition to Public Utilities

Public utilities have been viewed as natural monopolies. Competition has not been considered a feasible means to regulate them. For example, competition might require several uneconomic power lines running down every street. Therefore, utilities have been regulated by government. But even utilities can, in part, be brought under the motivating and disciplining power of competition.

The key to bringing competition to public utilities lies in two points: First, it is not feasible to rely on competition to regulate a public utility *as a whole.* Second, many *individual segments* of a public utility service can be regulated by competition.

Already segmentation has begun. The most notable example is the division of the telephone company into long–distance and regional service, bringing competition, more efficiency, and lower prices to long–distance service. Large–area electric power grids are beginning to make possible competition in power generation. Power generation, transmission, and distribution are becoming segmented functions that can in some cases be handled by separate and often competing companies.

To really introduce competition into the life of the utilities, segmentation, or the threat of segmentation, will have to go much farther. Virtually every department in the utility should be thrown open to competition, whether it be line maintenance, meter reading, data processing, construction, back–office administration, janitorial service, or power plant management.

Service industries in the United States—specialists in managing data processing facilities, managing hospitals, providing janitorial services, running clinical labs, even managing entire offices—have seen phenomenal growth in recent years. If public utility segments were explicitly thrown open to competition from bidders, a whole service industry of competing firms would eventually grow up around the utilities. Not all public utility segments would be operated by outside service industries, but some of them would, and the competition of outside bidders would bring much–needed improvements in efficiency to the industry and hold down excessive wage demands.

Public service commissions should demand that utilities produce their services at the lowest possible cost. If a utility can perform any function more cheaply by contracting it out, or in any other way, it should be obligated by law to do so. As the number of service industries expands, the operation will become nearly self–enforcing. Service industries excluded from bidding on the performance of some utility function will complain to the public service commission—and to the press. Action will probably be forthcoming.

A change in labor law will likely be necessary, making it an unfair labor practice for a union to bargain to prevent contracting out or any other practice such as hiring temporary help that would enable the utility to produce its service at a lower cost.

Public service commissions have long regulated utility profits, restricting them to the level necessary to attract capital to the industry. From the consumer's point of view, restricting wages to the level necessary to attract workers to the industry is equally important. Such restriction can likely be accomplished far more easily by open competition in various segments of the utility service than by direct public service commission regulation of wages.

As we discussed in chapter 6, competition is probably an important determinant of productivity. A whiff of competition might bring astonishing results to many sectors of the utility industry. Consumers have a lot to gain. When competition is not the disciplinarian, government must be. But generally it is better for government to improve the effectiveness of competition than to directly regulate business activity.

Bringing Competition to Governments

Even many government functions can be brought under the motivation and discipline of competition. Many local governments have already begun the process of segmentation that we have just suggested for public utilities.

The most common method of bringing competition to government services is by contracting out. This is now being done for a very wide variety of government functions, such as solid waste collection, utility billing, meter reading, vehicle towing, day–care facility operation, delinquent tax collection, animal shelter operation, and data processing management. Another approach has been the voucher system, whereby qualified recipients of government services are given vouchers that entitle them to receive certain goods or services from firms in the private sector, rather than having the government provide those services itself.

These techniques of privatization are not always successful. If government functions end up in a highly competitive part of the private sector, efficiency will likely improve. If, however, the market environment—both corporate and labor—is not competitive, efficiency may actually decline.

An exhaustive survey done in 1987 by Touche Ross in conjunction with the International City Management Association and the Privatization Council highlights the many benefits and problems of privatization.[4] The major conclusions are as follows:

- The primary purpose of privatization has been to cut costs, and in most cases—but not all—substantial savings have been realized.

- The most important impediments to privatization plans are a concern about loss of control, a belief that cost savings will not materialize, and union or employee resistance.

- Substantial numbers of public services and facilities have been privatized, and the trend seems to be strongly upward.

Improving Competition in Labor Markets

In 1935, with the passage of the National Labor Relations Act, the United States provided extensive legal support of workers to organize and bargain collectively as labor unions. Part of the act dictated a powerful adversarial relationship between unions and corporations. The stated purpose of the act was to equalize bargaining power between workers and management, ostensibly to enable workers to demand and get a larger share of corporate revenues that were previously going to the corporations as profits.

But as pointed out in chapters 3 and 5, it didn't work out quite that way. The bargaining power of unions allowed them to gain substantial monopolistic wage premiums for their members over and above the wage necessary for employers to attract and retain qualified workers. A very large part of that premium was passed on to consumers through higher prices. Higher prices affected low–income workers most, exacerbating the poverty problem. An effort to improve workers' income, then, turned out to hurt the weakest of the labor force. Was that not another case of misguided compassion?

The labor union movement reached its peak, as measured by the percentage of workers organized, shortly after the Korean War. It probably reached its peak (more like a plateau) as measured by the size of union wage premiums in the late 1970s or very early 1980s. Both union membership as a percentage of the labor force and the average union wage premium have since declined, and some are predicting further declines. This result, however, is far from certain, and unions still play a powerful role in determining wage rates. The Bureau of Labor Statistics estimates that union compensation still makes up about one–quarter of the entire employment cost index. In addition, a spillover effect from high union wages impacts other wages.

Regardless of what happens to union membership, past union activity has left an extremely important legacy. That legacy is the very wide gap between high–wage industries, mostly unionized, and low–wage industries, mostly nonunion or weak–union. This wage gap will have a profoundly negative effect on the American economy for years to come, for two reasons.

First, as described in chapter 5, the wide spread between high–wage and low–wage workers is a major cause of the important poverty problem in the United States. That poverty problem is not likely to be solved until the wage gap has been narrowed substantially. Second, *a large wage gap is not compatible with prolonged full employment.* Why not?

The wage gap arose mainly during periods of recession or slow growth when the economy was operating well below full capacity. At such times below–capacity competition was intense, preventing wages in weak–union and nonunion industries from matching the wages gained by the strong unions that were more resistant to the restraint of below–capacity competition. But now as the economy expands, approaching full employment, the intensity of below–capacity competition diminishes, and workers in weak–union and nonunion industries try to catch up with higher–paid workers. Low–paid workers move to higher paid jobs as those jobs become available. Employers in low–paying industries have to raise wages substantially to attract and retain workers.

As wages in low–paying industries accelerate, the inflation rate also accelerates unless wages in the strong–union industries slow their rate of growth. If wage gains of high–paid workers slow, the wage gap will narrow. If they do not slow, inflation will accelerate, and the Federal Reserve will restrain growth, keeping output from approaching capacity. Consequently, a very wide wage gap is incompatible with full employment.

Put another way, as we approach full employment, *relative* wages of high–wage industries must decline if *relative* wages of low–wage industries are to rise without causing inflation to accelerate. An acceleration of inflation will trigger Federal Reserve restraint, and full employment will not be reached. A large wage gap is an imbalance that must be corrected before prolonged full employment can be realized.

A narrowing of the wage gap, allowing us to move closer to full employment and to ease the poverty problem, will be extremely difficult to achieve. Four possibilities should be considered:

- Competition may restrain union wage increases, particularly where unions have gone a long way toward pricing their workers out of the market.

- The percentage of workers unionized may decline farther.

- Unions may show extraordinary restraint, allowing relative wages to gradually decline.

- Labor laws may be modified to bring union wage determination more under the discipline of competitive markets.

The first three of these restraining factors should have some impact in keeping the wage gap from widening and may even narrow it somewhat. However, unions most likely will need to be brought more under the discipline of competitive markets. How can that be done?

If unions are to face a competitive market, employers must have alternatives to paying high union wage premiums obtained under strike duress. Only when alternatives exist is competition present. The alternatives now available are contracting work out to other firms, automating, relocating plants, and hiring part–time or temporary workers. These alternatives should be guaranteed to employers by modifications to labor law that make it an unfair labor practice for unions to bargain to prohibit any of these employer alternatives to high union wages. As pointed out in chapter 3, union workers would then be competing with nonunion workers, but they would be competing as a group. Nonunion workers compete with each other as individuals.

Critics may respond that such legislation would leave union workers at the mercy of employers. That simply is not true. Workers would still have the protections that the other 80 percent of the labor force now have. The most important protection is the necessity for employers to provide adequate compensation and satisfactory working conditions to attract, retain, and motivate workers. The ability to do this is becoming more and more a factor in the successful operation of a business. From a slightly different point of view, workers have the protection of their ability and willingness to work, which usually (but not always) gives them the opportunity to shift jobs.

Furthermore, governments are providing employees with many new protections, some of which have previously been the responsibility of unions: prohibiting discrimination, protecting against arbitrary discharge, promoting safety in the work place, and working to preserve employee rights to private pensions.

Many programs can likely be devised to bring union workers more under the discipline of competitive markets, and thus reduce the size of the monopolistic union wage premium. But only when the realization is common that these premiums are paid largely by the consumer and rest most heavily upon the poor will action be taken.

The strict adversarial relationship between unions and management created by the NLRA is an archaic system that sets the stage for economic combat where consumers, especially the poor, are the chief casualties. This system ought to be speedily dismantled. Monopolies in the labor market, like corporate monopolies, are devices to plunder the weak.

Improving the Global Economy

One of the most important supports of effective structural competition is the existence of a global economy in which goods, investment capital, and managerial talent move across international boundaries with a minimum of government interference. In a global economy unions find it virtually impossible to take wages out of competition on a worldwide basis. Multinational companies producing in several countries with different cost structures find it difficult, though certainly not impossible, to establish strong monopolies. What, then, is the future of the global economy?

It is almost universally recognized that the Smoot–Hawley tariff bill was a mistake and that it contributed substantially to the depth of the Great Depression that followed. For over half a century after that legislation was passed, our country moved back toward free trade by a series of tariff reductions. The great majority of both liberals and conservatives supported free trade.

But in the 1980s things began to change. The volume of trade–restrictive bills introduced in Congress increased sharply. The number of executive–arranged restrictions such as "orderly marketing agreements" and "voluntary export restraint agreements" rose substantially. Why has the attitude toward free trade been changing? The change has to be due largely to the loss of preeminence of U.S. industries in the world economy, culminating dramatically in the huge trade deficit that arose in 1983. Many people became convinced that the United States could no longer compete on open international markets. So they began to demand protection from foreign competition by various kinds of restrictions on imports.

The lesson is simple. Explaining the benefits of free trade is not enough. *To gain public support to eliminate the remaining trade barriers, government policy must create the conditions that make the explanation of the benefits of free trade believable.* And by far the most important condition that must be achieved is a reduction in the trade deficit. It is positively mystifying how some economists can view the trade deficit with great equanimity and at the same time rail against the trend toward protectionism.

Implementation of prescribed policy #2—eliminate the federal budget deficit—would go a long way toward closing the trade gap. It would slow domestic consumption of goods, releasing productive capacity to replace imports and to increase exports. The Federal Reserve could stimulate the economy by easing money and bringing down interest rates. The dollar could find whatever level is necessary to eliminate the trade deficit.

We also need substantially full employment most of the time, so that workers who lose jobs in any industry impacted by imports can find alternative employment elsewhere. The best way to maintain full employment is by enhancing all the factors we have discussed that improve structural competition. Adequate retraining of workers who lose their jobs due to foreign competition is also needed.

Wide swings in exchange rates cause unnecessary turmoil and tend to turn victims of that turmoil against free international trade. For example, the sharp run–up in the value of the dollar in 1984 and 1985 made American goods so expensive on the international markets that their competitive position became untenable. Foreign producers stepped in, took control over many markets, and earned vast profits that allowed them to develop new products, establish new marketing channels, and take over productive facilities around the world. No one could really expect American producers to compete under such circumstances. Many companies and even industries were nearly destroyed. Now that the value of the dollar has declined, many American companies that cut way back to survive do not have adequate productive capacity to meet their markets demands.

We can avoid wide swings in foreign exchange rates by greater steadiness in fiscal policy, which, in turn, allows greater steadiness in monetary policy. Eliminating the uncertainties and dislocations caused by wide swings in exchange rates should aid in gaining support for free–trade policies.

A few special comments should be made about the jobs issue. Protectionism and many other political programs are promoted on the grounds that they will create or protect jobs. Why is there so much fuss about creating jobs? Jobs are easy to create. All the Federal Reserve has to do to create more jobs is to create more demand by making money more readily available through the banking system. Except in times of deep depression, the Federal Reserve has almost unlimited power to do so.

Why, then, doesn't the Federal Reserve stimulate the economy to create new jobs? It is limited only by the danger of inflation. And what keeps inflation under control? Competition! If structural competition is strong, the Federal Reserve can move aggressively, increasing demand and jobs close to the physical limits of production. If, on the other hand, monopoly in corporate and labor markets is widespread, the Federal Reserve must restrain economic expansion to avoid inflation.

Unfortunately, political promises to create new jobs are not usually based on policies to improve the intensity of competition. Rather, they are based on dubious propositions such as protectionism.

If we address the problem of unemployment and the trade deficit by a protectionist movement, just as sure as night follows day, structural competition will be reduced, prices will rise, and the Federal Reserve will be forced to tighten money. Sooner or later we will end up even farther away from full employment. Foreign competition actually creates new jobs by increasing structural competition, allowing the Federal Reserve to bring us closer to full employment without triggering inflation.

The need to maintain effective structural competition cannot be escaped if we wish to maintain a high–employment economy.

MANAGING COMPETITION AS AN IDEOLOGY

This book has emphasized a middle–ground ideology between the left, which wants extensive government management of the details of economic activity, and the right, which wants the economy to operate substantially on automatic pilot with very little government interference. The ideology, however, is much closer to the right than to the left.

Considerable government intervention in economic activity is necessary, but that intervention can be minimized and is most effective when it is directed toward improving and preserving a viable competition. Nevertheless, under no circumstance should competition be considered an end in itself. It is just a tool—a wonderful tool—to motivate, discipline and organize the participants in economic activity.

A clear, explicit recognition of government's responsibility to manage competition is important for the following reasons:

An Activist Government Will Find Something to Manage

For over half a century we have had an activist government in Washington. That government has tasted the pleasure of exercising power over money and people. It is not likely to ever retreat to the restrained position of earlier years. An activist government is going to find something to manage. Better its attention be devoted to improving competitive markets than directly regulating the details of economic activity. The outstanding example at the moment is the poverty problem. In chapter 5 we argued that far better results can be achieved by improving competitive markets (and federal fiscal policy) than by direct transfer of money and services to the poor. Many other examples could be cited.

Put another way, if it becomes abundantly clear that the market itself will not heal a particular economic blemish, government should always look first to the possibility of improving the operation of the competitive market before even thinking of government regulation of the details of economic processes. That would be one of the effects of an acceptance of the "managing competition" ideology.

Competition Must Not Be a Victim of Unexpected Side Effects

Most government policies—budget deficits, import barriers, labor legislation, minimum wages, taxes, business regulation, and so on—affect the intensity of competition. Only if government recognizes the importance of competitive markets and recognizes its obligation to preserve and enhance viable competition, will it consider the possible side effects of legislation on competition. Otherwise, effective competition will continue to be an unintended victim of many government policies.

Managing Competition Emphasizes a Neglected Trade-Off

The managing–competition concept has extraordinary value in dealing with monetary policy.

As indicated in earlier chapters, monetary policy must be actively managed by the Federal Reserve. No one has yet come up with any automatic system that will obviate the necessity of active management. Again, as argued in earlier chapters, changing the intensity of below–capacity competition is the transmission mechanism by which monetary policy controls the inflation rate. And so the Federal Reserve is managing one very important kind of competition. Once this important fact is recognized, attention immediately turns to the possible substitution of increased *structural* competition for increased *below–capacity* competition to control inflation. This substitution is highly desirable in order to avoid the unpleasant side effects, including unemployment, that come when output is held below full capacity. So the inevitable

155

conclusion is that structural competition should also come under improved management.

In summary, then, active management of below–capacity competition is necessary, and this management effort directs attention to the need for improving (managing) structural competition, leading to a major improvement in the performance of the economy.

Effective Competition Does Not Automatically Happen

Almost everyone recognizes the need for government management of competition to the extent of preventing price collusion among sellers in product markets. A great many economists also recognize a need for government to limit horizontal mergers between firms in an industry. These views are simply a recognition that competition does not automatically happen in product markets. The major argument is *how* competition should be managed, not *whether* it should be managed.

Competition does not automatically happen in labor markets, either. The need to preserve and enhance effective competition in labor markets is every bit as important as in product markets.

A Free Competitive Market Cannot Do Everything

Management of competition in most cases involves the protection and enhancement of competition. But in a few cases, competition has an adverse impact and must be limited by deliberate government restraints.

The most obvious example is that of the impact of competition on the environment. Competition actually intensifies industrial damage to the environment unless government rules are in place. Competitive markets, for example, *force* firms to find the cheapest way to dispose of wastes, and often that means just dumping them into a river or the atmosphere. Government regulation requiring better but more expensive methods of waste disposal raises prices to the consumer, but it protects the environment. Free competition cannot, by itself, do so. It tends to aggravate the problem.

Another example deals with risk taking. In chapter 6 we pointed out the power of competition to force risk taking. In most business sectors the result is a needed improvement in productivity. But in the financial area, competitive stimulation of risk taking somehow becomes perverse. In the past competition has driven banks (and savings and loans) to make more and more risky loans in order to get higher yields. The result has been several waves of bank failures that have been major contributors to deep depression. Without deposit insurance and federal protection of deposit insurance, we would surely now be in a very serious banking crisis and perhaps on our way to deep depression. We simply cannot tolerate waves of bank failures. They bring far too much instability to the economy. And a few failures too often turn into waves of failures. Even if we had no deposit insurance, government would have to step in to prevent a few failures from causing runs on banks thereby creating many failures.

Since, in a practical sense, the full faith and credit of the United States government is behind the deposit insurance system, the government must insist on reasonably safe lending policies. It has failed in this responsibility.

The history of the United States is replete with periods of excessive lending at high risk. Just a few examples are the massive loans to developing countries, the loans on thin margins for stock speculation in the 1920s, the real estate loans during the inflationary 1970s, the loans to oil–related industries during the recent oil boom, and probably the current wave of high–risk junk bond and junk loan financing.

Excessive lending hurts both the lender and the borrower. We can tolerate substantial bankruptcies in the nonfinancial sector of the economy. An industrial plant or retail chain will usually stay in business even though stockholders are nearly wiped out in bankruptcy. But the financial sector is a different story. A few bank failures can create a wave of bank failures that can destroy a large part of the money supply, dry up the source of credit, and precipitate major depression. In this area, excessive risk taking, often driven by competition, must be restrained by government regulation such as substantial minimum capital requirements or deposit insurance premiums based on a bank's risk exposure.

We have described here two ways in which competition has a perverse influence on the operation of the American economy. Over enthusiastic advocates of free enterprise sometimes damage public support for a free market economic system by claiming that competitive markets can do more than they are capable of doing. Effective competition is surely being under utilized as a disciplinarian and motivator, but it can't do everything. As valuable as it is, competition is not an end in itself. It is but a tool to achieve valuable social goals. In those few cases where it clearly fails, it needs to be modified or replaced.

Of course, argument as to what aspects of the economy can best be managed by government and what can best be managed by a competitive market will never end. At the moment, management by competitive markets is in the ascendancy, simply because it has been so much more successful.

THE ECONOMIC OUTLOOK FOR THE COMING DECADES

Optimism about the economic outlook grows out of two convictions. First, most of our economic troubles have been due to ignorance. Second, we have improved our understanding of the economic system and are continuing to learn.

Pessimism grows out of an awareness of the snail's pace at which we learn.

If our economic troubles have, indeed, been due to ignorance, and if the solution is learning (both formal and informal), then a forecast must be based on a judgment of our learning experience and our learning capability.

What Have We Learned?

We have learned that the business cycle can be managed sufficiently well to avoid deep depressions. We may even have learned that this can best be done by controlling aggregate demand without burdensome government interference in the detailed workings of the market system. (Of course, deposit insurance in our banking system and a number of other structural changes have helped.)

We probably have learned that to prevent serious inflation, incipient inflation must be quickly restrained before a norm of accelerating wage gains has been established. The Federal Reserve will likely stabilize the inflation rate at somewhere between 0 and 4 percent. Perhaps this can be done with no more than a single recession per decade resulting from the required application of monetary restraint to hold back wage and price acceleration, to adjust for the unpredictable shocks that are sure to come, or to compensate for errors in Federal Reserve management.

But even if the Federal Reserve does err and allow inflation to accelerate for a year or so, we should now know that it can be brought under control with painful but not catastrophic results by substantial application of monetary restraint to increase below–capacity competition.

Learning that inflation can be controlled is not a minor step. It is a major achievement. Just as many had given up on capitalism during the 1930s on the basis that it could not prevent deep depression, so in the 1970s many gave up on capitalism on the grounds that it could not eliminate destructive inflation. They gave up too soon. Capitalism is alive and well, spreading around the world, probably in an unstoppable revolution. Democracy and personal freedoms should follow not far behind.

Many Third World countries and several failing socialist countries have just begun to learn that they can tap a substantial, and growing, pool of capital and technology. They are also learning that they are competing with one another for that capital and technology. But the exciting part of this competition is that these countries compete mainly by improving their economic, social and political environments. This special kind of competition will likely chalk up another great victory for the effectiveness of competition. It carries the promise of one of the great eras in economic development in the history of the world.

158

After many years of widespread pessimism, the economic outlook has turned brighter, and rightfully so. But we are not out of the woods yet. Our unpleasant past experience with deep depressions and double–digit inflations can now, most likely, be traded in for new and potentially more serious problems. Some of these will certainly arise from burgeoning human pressure on the physical environment.

Even here, some help may come from the three policies recommended in this book. Population growth is the basic force putting pressure on the environment, and the problem of population growth in the developing countries is not likely to be solved without the modernization of those countries. The policies leading to low interest rates and improvements in the global economy can help appreciably in this modernization. Of course, modernization of developing countries puts additional pressure on the environment. But better they modernize now than when the population has doubled and redoubled.

What Have We Yet to Learn?

Too much to list! But within the limited confines of the analysis presented in this book, the next step is to learn how to improve structural competition (reduce monopoly power) so that we can ease the poverty problem, so that the economy can operate closer to full employment for extended periods without inflation, and so that we can increase productivity to improve our standard of living.

Considering the time it took us to learn how to prevent deep depression and serious inflation, we should not anticipate quick success. Many—especially those who now hold monopolistic positions, and those whose natural instincts drive them toward increasing government power—will give up on improving the market mechanism and will say it can't be done.

But the potential rewards are great: lower unemployment, greater productivity, a higher standard of living, and finally, better breaks for the long–suffering marginal worker.

APPENDIX A

INDUSTRY ANALYSES

161

SELECTION OF INDUSTRIES

When we began this study, we planned to include every industry for which data were readily available. We expected to have seventy–five to one hundred industries. But we quickly ran into the problem of industry classification.

In many industries the principal participants are heavily involved in two, three, or more industries, and thus classification becomes very difficult. Consequently, for a number of industries we could not find enough companies that clearly belonged in that industry to make up an adequate proportion of the total business done. Other problems involved very serious differences in accounting as in the insurance industry. Consequently, the number of industries in the study dwindled to the present forty–two.

Some of the problems can be solved with more time and resources. Corporate data for our forty–two industries can be improved and a number of other industries can be added, but the effort will have to await further publications.

DESCRIPTION OF DATA

For each of the forty–two industries, we present one page of descriptive material and one page of graphics, consisting of three charts:

The top chart presents corporate data. The middle chart presents labor data. The bottom chart presents productivity data, concentration ratios, and import data, (where available).

Corporate Data (Top Chart)

Relative return on equity: This is the most important variable. It represents the return on equity (profit margin) for the individual industry expressed as a percentage of the all–industry average. Return on equity of the Standard & Poor's 400 is used as the all–industry average.

Market price–to–book value ratio: The average market price of stocks of the companies in the industry is divided by the average equity of those same companies.

Debt to capital ratio: Long–term debt is expressed as a percentage of total capital for each industry.

(All corporate data are taken from the Standard & Poor's Compustat Services. All industry averages are weighted averages of the individual companies included therein.)

163

Labor Data (Middle Chart)

Relative wages: Relative wages for an industry are computed by dividing industry production (nonsupervisory) worker average hourly earnings by total private nonagricultural establishments production worker average hourly earnings. The source of data for the variable is the Bureau of Labor Statistics' *Supplement to Employment and Earnings.* (Data do not include fringe benefits.)

Employment: Employment for an industry is measured by the number of production workers in thousands. The source of data for this variable is the Bureau of Labor Statistics' *Supplement to Employment and Earnings.*

Relative quit rate: The relative quit rate is defined as industry quits per one hundred employees divided by manufacturing quits per one hundred employees. The source of data for this variable is the Bureau of Labor Statistics' *Supplement to Employment and Earnings.* Relative quit rate data are available only for manufacturing industries and were not collected past 1981.

Miscellaneous Data (Bottom Chart)

Productivity: Productivity is defined as output per hour of all employees. The source of published data for this variable is the Bureau of Labor Statistics' *Productivity Measures for Selected Industries.* Published productivity data were not available for several industries, so, where available, unpublished BLS productivity data were used.

Concentration: Concentration is defined as the percentage of industry value of shipments accounted for by the four largest firms. The source of data for this variable is the Census Bureau's *Census of Manufactures, Census of Retail Trade*, and *Census of Service Industries.* Concentration figures for SIC two– and three–digit manufacturing industries are weighted averages of the SIC four–digit industry concentration ratios.

Imports–to–new supply ratio: The import–to–new supply ratio is defined as value of imports divided by the value of shipments plus imports. The import numbers are from unpublished Census Bureau data. Value of shipments numbers were obtained from the Census Bureau's *Annual Survey of Manufactures.*

Data Included in Descriptive Material

Unionization: Unionization percentages were obtained from several sources. First, a paper by Edward Kokkelenberg and Donna Sockell contains data on the percentage of production workers that belong to labor unions by three–digit census industry classification code for the years 1973 to 1981 obtained from the Current Population Survey Tapes.[1] Second, we computed the percentage of production workers both covered by collective bargaining agreements and belonging to labor unions from the 1983 and 1984 Current Population Survey Earnings Tapes. Third, we called several of the major corporations in each industry to get a general impression of the dynamics of unionization in the industry.

Union Wage Premium: To estimate union wage premiums, data contained in the 1983 and 1984 Current Population Survey Earnings Tapes were used. A regression model similar to that employed by Gregg Lewis[2] controlling for various personal, industry, and demographic characteristics was used. Many, but not all, of the union wage premium estimates are considered unreliable and are not used in this study.

Fringe benefits: Fringe benefits data for the entire economy and for SIC two–digit industries are available in the Department of Commerce's National Income and Product Accounts. Fringe benefit data for all manufacturing industries are available in the Census Bureau's *Annual Survey of Manufactures*.

Employment compensation as a percentage of sales: The source of data on employment compensation and sales is the Standard & Poor's Compustat Services. Adequate data were not available for several industries.

Industry Description

This industry consists of about 130,000 stores employing about 2,000,000 nonsupervisory workers. Ownership varies from very large chains to regional chains to very small independent stores.

Competitive Classification

The industry has not had the market power to keep profit margins above the all–industry average for any appreciable period of time. Therefore, it is classified as long–term competitive. Profit margin data shown on the chart cover thirty–eight large and medium–size chains. Data are not available for the small chains and independents. Profit margins for the entire period averaged almost exactly the same as the all–industry average, and they have fluctuated around the all–industry average. Clearly, the convergence principle is at work in this industry. Sharply changing market shares indicate aggressive competition among the members of this loose oligopoly.

Labor Market

The major union in this industry is the United Food and Commercial Workers; the Teamsters and several other unions also represent some workers. Although the entire industry is only about 30 to 40 percent unionized, most of the large chains in urban areas are strongly unionized except in the Southeast. Dominant unionization among the large chains has effectively taken wages out of competition in most areas. Union wage premiums are high, apparently between 40 and 50 percent even without considering fringe benefits.

The relative wage data shown on the chart cover the entire industry including the tens of thousands of nonunion independents and small chains. The wage data are not representative of union contracts.

Who Pays the Union Wage Premium?

This industry (chains only) consists of very strong unions with high wage premiums arrayed against competitive corporations with average profit margins. In urban areas, wages have generally been taken out of competition by effective unionization.

Employee compensation is four to five times larger than pretax profits, making it virtually impossible for companies to absorb any appreciable wage premium via lower profit margins.

The evidence strongly suggests that most of the union wage premium is passed on to the consumer in higher prices.

Productivity

No productivity data are available for this industry.

GROCERY STORES

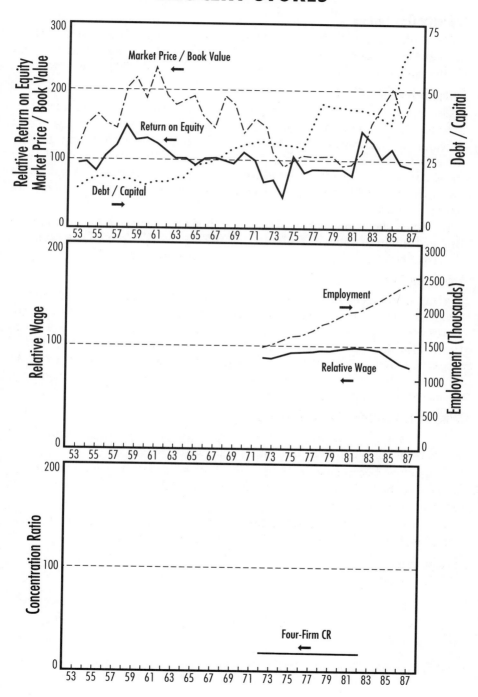

Industry Description

About 35,000 general merchandise stores in the United States employ about 1,800,000 nonsupervisory workers. Operators vary from the strong national chains like Sears and Penneys to the thousands of small independent stores.

Competitive Classification

General merchandise stores have not had market power to maintain profit margins much above the all–industry average for any appreciable period of time, and are, therefore, classed as long–term competitive. Profit margins for the entire period have been almost exactly equal to the all–industry average, indicating the effectiveness of the convergence principle. Aggressive competition among the large chains is demonstrated by major changes in market shares.

The chart shows the extraordinary valuations the stock market put on even the modest profit margin premiums in the 1960s, apparently not realizing that competition would soon eliminate even those premiums.

Labor Market

About 10 percent of nonsupervisory workers across the nation are union members. But in some large cities in the Northeast and on the West Coast the stores are strongly unionized. The major unions in this industry appear to be the United Food and Commercial Workers and the Retail, Wholesale and Department Store Union. Average union wage premiums do not appear to be as high as those of grocery stores. Information is not available on union wage premiums in highly unionized cities.

Who Pays the Union Wage Premium?

In a few highly unionized cities, wages have largely been taken out of competition. Strong unions face highly competitive employers.

Employment compensation is apparently three or four times pretax profits, making it virtually impossible for companies to absorb any significant wage premium through lower profits.

It appears, then, that in the highly unionized cities, most of the union wage premium is passed on to the consumer through higher prices.

Productivity

No productivity data are available.

GENERAL MERCHANDISE STORES

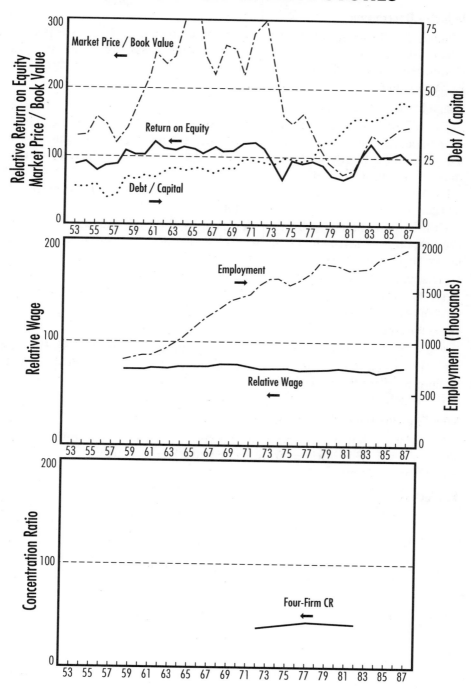

Industry Description

About 14,000 banks in the United States employ over 1,200,000 people. None, as yet, is of national scope, although a strong trend toward consolidation exists. Banks are generally classed as money center banks or regional banks.

Competitive Classification

The industry is clearly a long–term competitive industry. Profit margins over the entire period 1960–85 have averaged almost exactly the same as the all–industry average as should be expected under the influence of the convergence principle.

Even if we isolate the money center banks as a separate industry, profit margins clearly fall in the long–term competitive category.

With banking functions being undertaken by thrifts, brokerage firms, and even retailers, it seems highly unlikely that the industry will be able to gain monopolistic control over its markets any time in the foreseeable future.

(The sharp decline in bank profit margins in 1987 was due to massive write–offs due to the setting up of reserves for possible losses on loans to developing countries.)

Labor Market

The industry is very lightly unionized—apparently around 2 to 3 percent. As far as can be estimated, the union wage premium is also very small—less than 10 percent. Wages have been below average and lagged somewhat in the 1970s when most highly unionized industries achieved dramatic increases.

Who Pays the Union Wage Premium?

No information is available to determine who pays the union wage premium. If it is taken from corporate profits, it is taken from competitive—not monopolistic—profits.

Productivity

Productivity data show just a very modest rate of growth.

BANKS

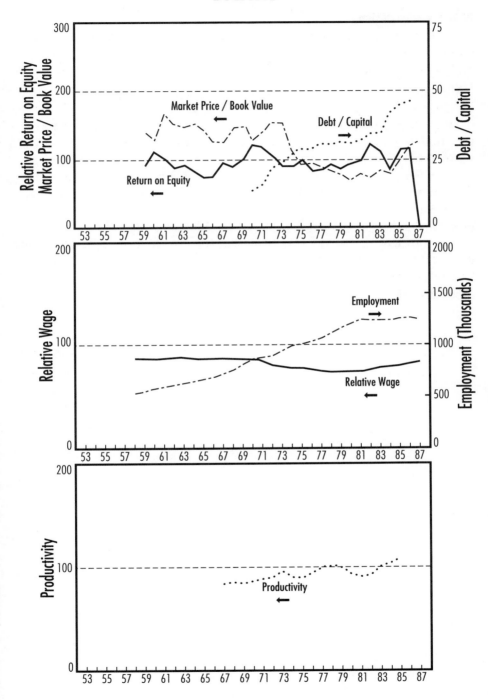

Industry Description

The industry consists of about 3,500 firms. The best known are the large California chains.

Competitive Classification

Market power to hold profit margins substantially above the all–industry average has not been available to this industry. Average profit margins over the past twenty years have been close to the all–industry average. Therefore, this industry must be classed as long–term competitive, subject to the convergence principle.

The corporate data shown in the chart are for only twenty–eight of the large firms for which data are readily available.

Competition with banks, brokerage firms and credit unions is growing more intense. The high profit margins shown for 1985 and 1986 were apparently due to transient economic forces related to the decline in interest rates and fees related to mortgage refinancing. These high profit margins will not be long sustained in the face of existing competitive pressure.

Labor Market

Unionization in the industry is almost nonexistent.

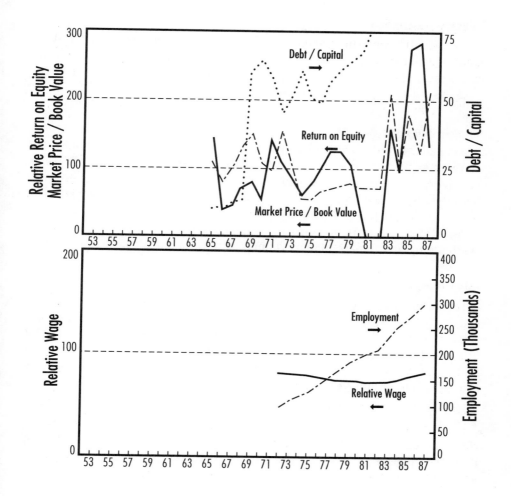

Industry Description

Over 35,000 hotels and motels in the United States employ about 1,200,000 nonsupervisory workers. The eight largest chains do approximately 18 percent of the business, and the fifty largest chains do about 34 percent of the business. Obviously there are many independents. The corporate data on the top chart on the opposite page cover a dozen of the publicly held companies.

Competitive Classification

The major firms in this industry have not had market power to hold profit margins above the all–industry average for any appreciable period of time. For the entire period the average profit margin has been nearly identical to the all–industry average. The industry, therefore, is long–term competitive, subject to the convergence principle.

Variations in profit margins have been created by alternate waves of overbuilding and underbuilding. We may now be in one of those overbuilding periods.

Labor Market

The industry as a whole is moderately unionized—about 15 to 20 percent. But in certain areas it is heavily unionized. Las Vegas and Atlantic City are strongly unionized. Some other cities such as San Francisco are also heavily unionized. One or two of the large hotel chains are apparently unionized across the country. A variety of unions represent the workers, the largest being the Hotel Employee and Restaurant Employee International Union.

Who Pays the Union Wage Premium?

In those highly unionized cities where wages have been taken out of competition, the strong unions face a highly competitive industry. The industry appears to be rather labor–intensive, and, therefore, union wage premiums are likely to be shifted on to the consumer.

Productivity

Productivity has grown moderately in the industry.

HOTELS AND MOTELS

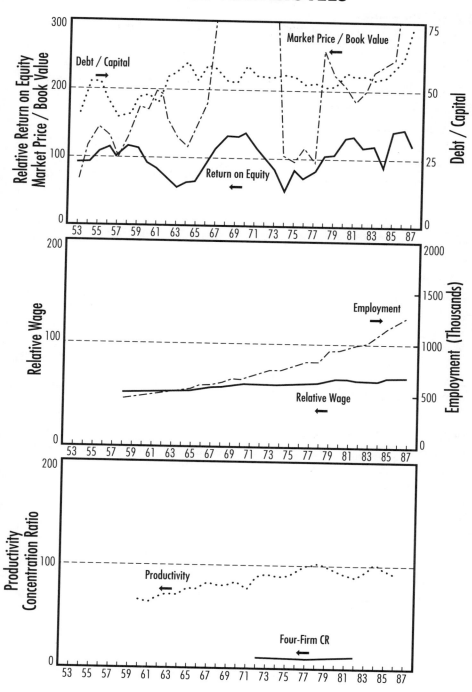

175

Industry Description

As is well known, this industry consists of a few major carriers such as United and American plus a number of smaller regional carriers such as Alaska Air and Southwest Airlines. Some of the regionals are disappearing through acquisition or bankruptcy. The industry has been growing rapidly.

Competitive Classification

We have classified this industry as long–term competitive.

Although the industry has been short–term endangered, it has always been able to borrow money on its marketable aircraft. Perhaps the term "accident prone" best describes the industry. Fuel costs, lengthy strikes, over–expansion, and fare wars have plagued the industry. Many of these problems are diminishing. The industry is gaining better control over its markets. In fact, considering the many mergers and the shortage of loading and landing slots that make new entry difficult, a possibility even exists that this industry could begin earning monopolistic profits.

Labor Market

The industry is heavily unionized mainly by the Machinists, the Air Line Pilots Association, and the Flight Attendants Association. The Bureau of Labor Statistics does not gather monthly data on airline wages. But other, less–comprehensive data show strongly rising relative wages in the 1970s when relative wages of most highly unionized industries were rising. Recently, relative wages in this industry have apparently declined, probably as a result of intense competition induced by the 1978 industry deregulation. Tax–free fringe benefits have been high.

Who Pays the Union Wage Premium?

Strong unions have been arrayed against highly competitive corporations. Until recently, the unions had organized sufficiently to take wages out of competition. In addition, government regulation prior to 1978 facilitated the pass through of all labor cost to the consumer.

The industry is labor–intensive.

In view of these facts, we conclude that most of the union wage premium has likely been passed on to the consumer in higher prices.

Productivity

Productivity has grown substantially in the industry. Deregulation does not appear to have had any significant impact on the rate of productivity growth.

AIR TRANSPORTATION

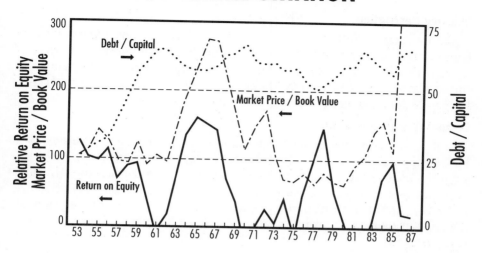

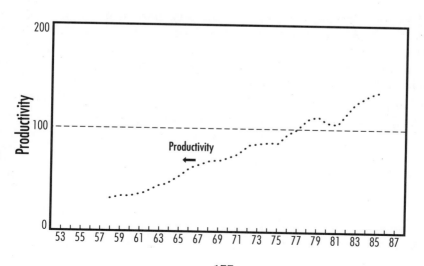

Industry Description

The industry consists of a number of large firms like Hartmarx and Levi Strauss, and a great many smaller firms producing an enormous variety of apparel products. The industry is declining slightly in the United States as imports grow, but still employs nearly 1,000,000 nonsupervisory workers. Corporate data include, of course, only publicly held firms.

Competitive Classification

Lack of market power to hold profit margins above the all–industry average for any appreciable time clearly makes this a long–term competitive industry, subject to the convergence principle. Over the entire period studied, profit margins have averaged close to the all–industry average. Like the shoe industry, apparel manufacturers are meeting foreign competition by manufacturing more abroad.

Labor Market

The industry is moderately unionized with unionization most heavily concentrated in women's, misses and junior outerwear, and second in men's and boys' outergarments. The two major apparel unions are the Amalgamated Clothing and Textile Workers and the International Ladies' Garment Workers. But even in these industry segments unionization is not nearly complete. The union wage premium is apparently rather small.

Who Pays the Union Wage Premium?

Weak unions that have failed to take wages out of competition face a highly competitive industry.

The industry is labor–intensive, with labor costs far higher than pretax profits.

Under these circumstances it has been very difficult for corporations to absorb the union wage premium through lower profits and also difficult to pass it on in higher prices. We cannot, therefore, say how much of the union wage premium has been passed through to the consumer and how much has been absorbed in lower profits.

Productivity

Productivity has grown substantially in this industry.

APPAREL

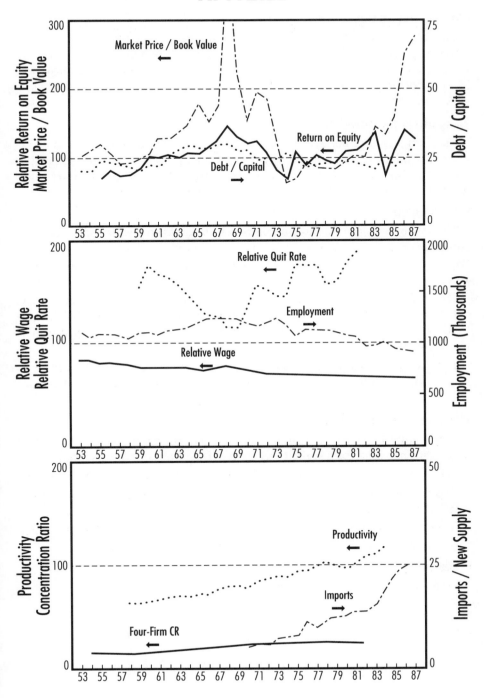

Industry Description

The heart of the industry consists of a few large companies that operate large pulp and paper mills. Most of these firms also produce various specialty paper products. Many smaller companies are engaged in making products from paper or paperboard they buy from the mills. The paper industry is a slow growth industry.

Competitive Classification

The industry has not had sufficient market power to hold profit margins above the all–industry average. It is clearly a long–term competitive industry, subject to the convergence principle. The corporate data in the chart cover most of the basic firms, but not the many smaller paper products companies.

Labor Market

The major mills are solidly unionized but many of the smaller paper product companies are nonunion. The major paper unions are the United Paperworkers International and the Association of Western Pulp and Paper Workers.

The nonunion sector probably accounts for about 40 to 50 percent of the entire industry, so the data on relative wages do not fully reflect the changes in union wage rates. As with most highly unionized industries, *relative* wages rose strongly in the 1970s.

Tax–free fringe benefits for the entire industry add nearly one–quarter to wages. For the union sector alone, benefits are substantially greater than that.

Who Pays the Union Wage Premium?

This is another case of a highly competitive industry facing a powerful union that has organized sufficiently to take wages out of competition.

Labor costs are in the neighborhood of 50 percent higher than pretax profits.

The rise in relative wages did not coincide with any significant drop in relative profit margins.

In view of these facts, we conclude that it is highly likely that the union wage premium has been shifted on to the consumer.

Productivity

Productivity has grown substantially in this industry.

PAPER

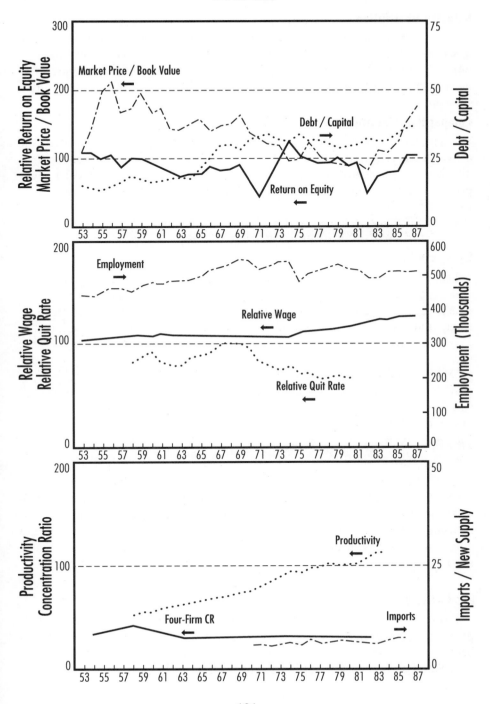

Industry Description

A half dozen very large international oil companies make up this industry. They are integrated from exploration clear down to marketing. The corporate data in the top chart cover all parts of the industry. The labor and productivity data cover only the oil *refining* sector of the industry, and only in the United States.

Competitive Classification

This very large industry is clearly long–term competitive, subject to the convergence principle. Profit margins for the entire period were only slightly above the all–industry average. The two oil shocks—1973 and 1979—sent profit margins up moderately, but competition quickly drove them back down to the all–industry average again. It will be interesting to see how long it takes profit margins to rise to the all–industry average after the 1986 decline due to the drop in crude oil prices of that year.

Labor Market

The oil *refining* industry is highly unionized mainly by the Oil, Chemical and Atomic Workers. As in most highly unionized industries, relative wages rose sharply in the 1970s although beginning a little later than most. Relative wages appear to have leveled off, but have not begun to decline. Since the 1986 oil price break, oil companies are under much greater competitive pressure. Following the example of other industries that have come under great financial pressure, relative wages are likely now to slow their rate of growth or even decline. This is especially true since modern refineries can be run for such a long time with just supervisory help. Tax–free fringe benefits are high, adding more than one–quarter to wages and salaries.

Who Pays the Union Wage Premium?

The oil *refining* industry has a strong union arrayed against competitive corporations. Wages have been taken out of competition. Labor costs are a very small percentage of sales—probably less than 3 percent. Pretax profits on sales *for the entire integrated industry* are in the 8 to 10 percent range. The oil refining industry is the only industry in our group where labor costs are appreciably less than pretax profits. The rise in *relative* wages came at the most prosperous period for the oil industry. It may have tempered the profit rise of the period.

Productivity

After each of the sharp oil price and profit surges in 1973 and 1979, productivity declined. Was this due to a relaxation in cost–control efforts because profits came so easily? If so, productivity should rise vigorously now that competitive pressure has become onerous with the collapse of oil prices.

OIL - INTERNATIONAL INTEGRATED

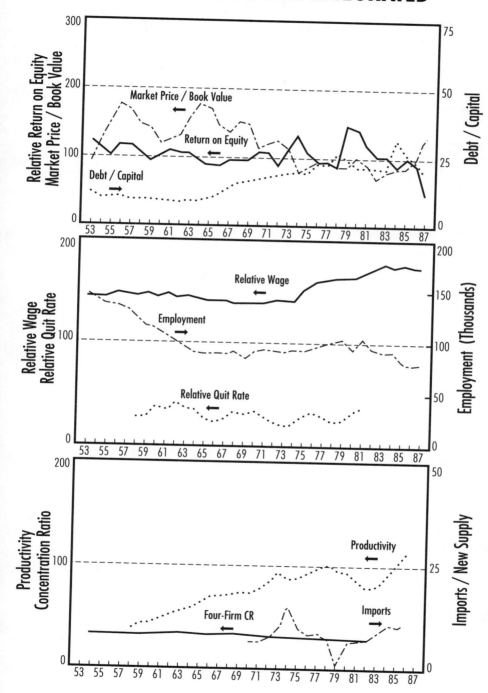

183

Industry Description

This industry includes twenty–four firms in our corporate data. These firms must compete not only with one another but also with the much larger internationals. Some of these firms, like Phillips Petroleum, have expanded abroad, but they are still counted as domestic firms in the literature.

The twenty largest firms (domestic and international) do about 76 percent of the refining done in the United States.

Competitive Classification

The industry is clearly long–term competitive, subject to the convergence principle. For the entire period, profit margins averaged just a bit above the all–industry average. Profit margins lagged behind those of the international oils in the 1950s and early 1960s but outdid them in the 1970s.

Labor and Productivity

All labor and productivity data shown are identical to those for the international oils. The data cover only the refining part of the oil industry. The refining activities of both the international and domestic oils are included.

OIL - DOMESTIC INTEGRATED

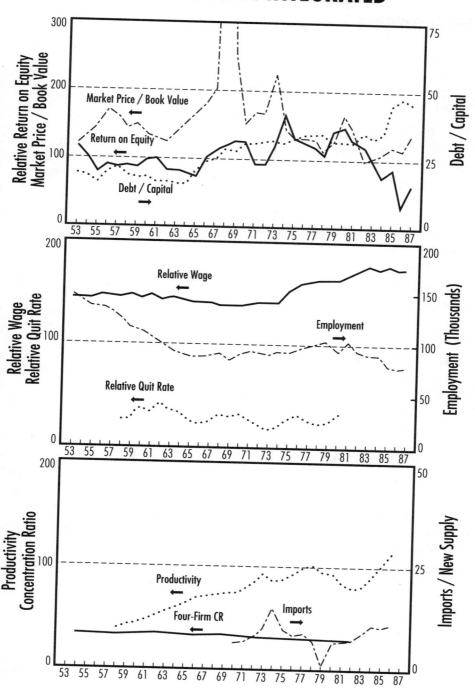

Industry Description

This industry is highly fragmented with a few large companies and thousands of smaller firms. It is a very old industry, beginning in the North but gradually moving south.

The industry includes wood, metal, and upholstered furniture, plus mattresses, bedsprings, and wood TV cabinets.

Industry Classification

This is undoubtedly a long–term competitive industry, subject to the convergence principle. Although our corporate data indicate high profit margins in the late 1960s, such high profit margins are due to the very low number of firms for which data are available.

The very large number of small firms, the ease of entry, and the marketing through furniture expositions guarantees the competitive nature of the industry.

Labor Market

Unionization is fairly substantial in the North but light in the South. Limited information indicates the union wage premium is small. Unions include a branch of the Carpenters' Union and the United Furniture Workers of America, among others.

Who Pays the Union Wage Premium?

A very weak union is arrayed against a highly competitive industry. Wages have not been taken out of competition.

The industry is labor–intensive, with labor costs double pretax profits even in the larger firms.

No perceptible change has occurred in relative wages over the period for which data are available.

In view of these conditions, it has been difficult for union firms to shift even the small union premium on to the consumer. The result has been at least part absorption by the employers. The net result has been a very substantial loss of market share by union firms, as evidenced by a shift in production from the union North to the nonunion South.

Productivity

Productivity has grown substantially and fairly regularly over the period studied.

FURNITURE (HOUSEHOLD)

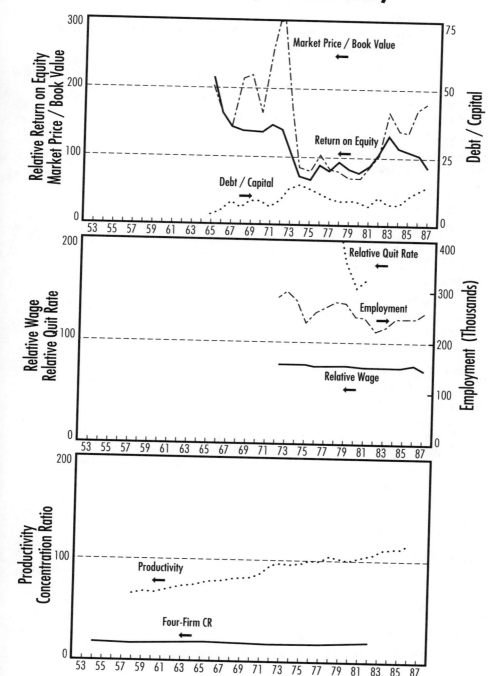

Industry Description

The corporate chart covers the basic industry of mining, milling, smelting, refining, and some fabrication. It starts out mainly with the majors—Kennecott, Anaconda, and Phelps Dodge. The industry, however, has been decimated, and the only major independent left is Phelps Dodge.

Labor data cover only copper ore mining, but much of the data is indicative of what has been happening in the rest of the industry. Productivity data cover the smelting and refining of copper.

Nationalization of Kennecott and Anaconda mines in Chile in 1971 caused a serious loss to those companies.

Competitive Classification

This industry has been highly competitive. Beginning in the 1970s competition got so severe the industry became endangered. The main driving force has been foreign competition plus a slowing in growth of demand for copper. In the last two years, the industry has staged a dramatic recovery.

Labor Market

The industry has been strongly unionized, mainly by the Steelworkers, although the union has recently lost representation in the well–known Phelps Dodge dispute and in the newly reopened Butte Copper Mine, formerly operated by Anaconda.

Who Pays the Union Wage Premium?

A very strong union was arrayed against an extremely weak, highly competitive industry. Wages in the domestic industry were taken out of competition. Labor costs in good years were probably slightly less than pretax profits in this capital intensive industry. But for most of the last fifteen years, virtually no profits have been earned in the industry.

The sharp rise of relative wages in the 1970s coincided with low and declining profits in the industry. The very low profit margins may have been partly due to the rising relative wages, but if that is true, the unions were taking away competitive profits—not monopolistic profits—and were partly responsible for the disaster that overtook the industry.

Productivity

One cannot overlook the remarkable surge in productivity in this mature industry as competition became intense and financial conditions became desperate. Surely this remarkable surge in productivity deserves a special study. How much was made possible by new technology; how much was achieved by elimination of union work rules; how much resulted from better management; and how much was due to closing down inefficient mines?

188

COPPER

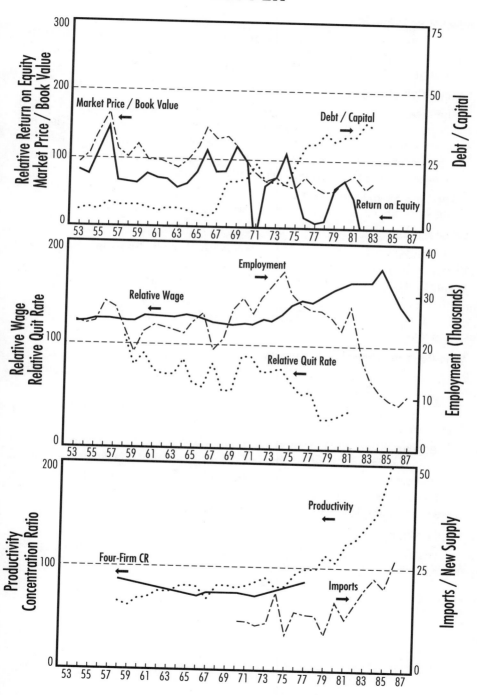

Industry Description

This industry includes the large well–known integrated steel companies plus a fringe of smaller companies. The eight–firm concentration ratio is 56 percent and the twenty–firm ratio is 76 percent.

Competitive Classification

The steel industry could easily be classed as long–term endangered, but it did have a few pretty good years in the 1950s. Since then, competition has increased, forcing profit margins down to disastrous levels, and the industry has for several years been critically endangered. Rising imports, of course, have been a major factor in the increased competition.

The upsurge in the market price–to–book value ratio in 1985 was not due to rising stock prices but rather to major write–down of book value.

Labor Market

This industry is very strongly unionized by the Steelworkers. As in most highly unionized industries, relative wages rose rapidly in the 1970s. They began to decline only after the industry got into extremely serious financial trouble.

Tax–free fringe benefits added substantially to the total compensation of steelworkers.

Who Pays the Union Wage Premium?

The union has been strong enough to take wages out of competition. The industry has been a weak, highly competitive industry.

Steel is a fairly labor–intensive industry. Labor costs are considerably higher than pretax margins, even in good years.

It appears, then, that much of the union wage premium was earlier shifted on to the consumer. To the extent that the wage premiums have been absorbed by the corporations in the more recent years of increased competition, the profits have been taken from competitive firms, not monopolistic firms, and have contributed to the disaster that overtook the industry.

Productivity

Once again we see an industry under great competitive stress come up with an extraordinary burst of increased productivity.

STEEL

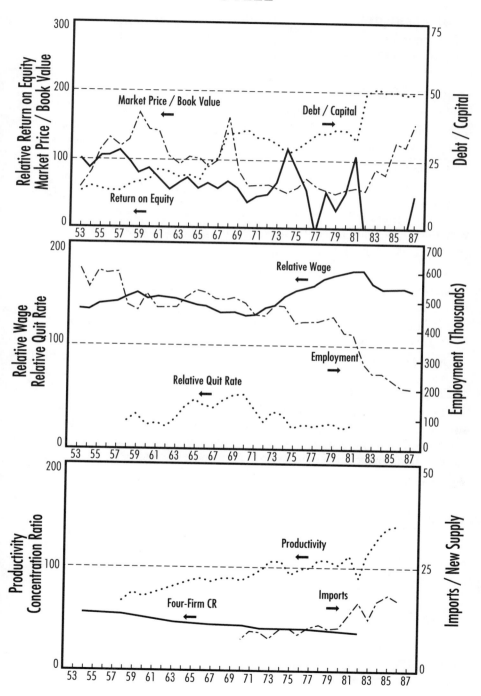

Industry Description

The industry comprises the large well known tire companies and just a few smaller producers. The four–firm concentration ratio is 66 percent and the eight–firm ratio is 86 percent.

Competitive Classification

The tire industry had a number of reasonably good years in the 1950s and 1960s, but competition has gradually increased, reducing profit margins and dropping the industry to endangered status in the late 1970s and early 1980s.

Labor Market

The industry is highly unionized by the United Rubber Workers (URW), but local unions in the URW have an unusual amount of autonomy. Although relative wages have leveled off in recent years as the industry has come under very severe financial pressure, they have not yet begun to decline.

Who Pays the Union Wage Premium?

Except for occasional rebellious local unions, organization has been strong enough to take wages out of competition. The industry has long been highly competitive.

The industry is labor–intensive, with labor costs more than double pretax profits even in good times.

The decline in relative profit margins is not closely related to rising relative wages. Relative profit margins have declined both when relative wages were falling and when they were rising.

In view of these facts, we conclude that the union wage premium has likely been largely passed on to the consumer. That part that has reduced corporate profits—since competition has become so onerous—has taken those profits away from a competitive industry, not a monopolistic industry.

Productivity

A sharp burst of productivity improvement has accompanied the severe competitive pressure of recent years.

TIRES

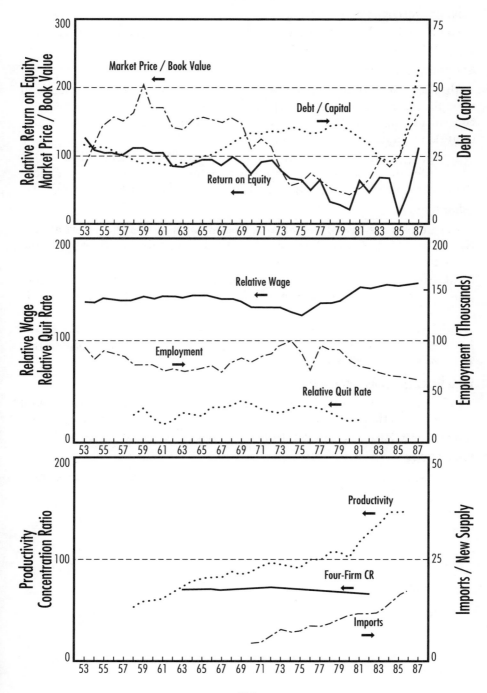

Industry Description

These are the electric utilities we all deal with. Their prices and profits are regulated by state public service commissions.

Competitive Classification

Although they are regional monopolies, their regulated profit margins tend to be close to the all–industry average. Because of regulation they do not have control of their markets, and thus are included along with long–term competitive industries.

Actually, our data show profit margins slightly above the all–industry average for the period studied. To the extent these margins have been above the level required to attract capital, it has been regulatory error.

Labor Market

The industry is heavily unionized. The major union is the International Brotherhood of Electrical Workers. We do not have satisfactory estimates of the union wage premium.

Nonsupervisory labor costs are apparently somewhat less than pretax profits, which are necessary payments to attract equity capital to this capital–intensive industry.

Relative wages increased in the late 1950s and from about 1974 to the present. In recent years that increase in relative wages has accelerated. Tax–free fringe benefits are also high.

Who Pays the Union Wage Premium?

Public service commissions do not regulate wages, which are considered part of production cost and are passed through to the consumer in higher prices. Therefore, the consumer bears the burden of any union wage premium.

Productivity

We have not yet discovered an explanation as to why productivity leveled off after 1977.

ELECTRIC SERVICE

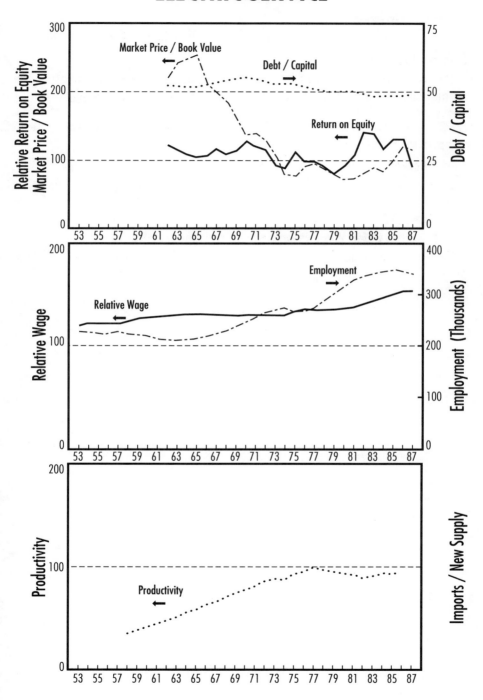

Industry Description

These are the natural gas companies that service homes and businesses.

Industry Classification

The industry consists of regional monopolies. Prices and profits are regulated. Profits have averaged modestly above the all–industry average for the entire period studied. Because of regulation, these companies do not have control over their markets, and are, therefore, classed along with long–term competitive industries.

Labor Market

The industry is quite strongly unionized. Relative wages grew in the 1950s and the 1970s and the rate of growth has recently accelerated. Tax–free fringe benefits are apparently high.

Who Pays the Union Wage Premium?

Under public utility regulation, all labor costs including any union wage premiums are passed through to the consumer in higher prices.

Productivity

No productivity data are available.

NATURAL GAS DISTRIBUTION

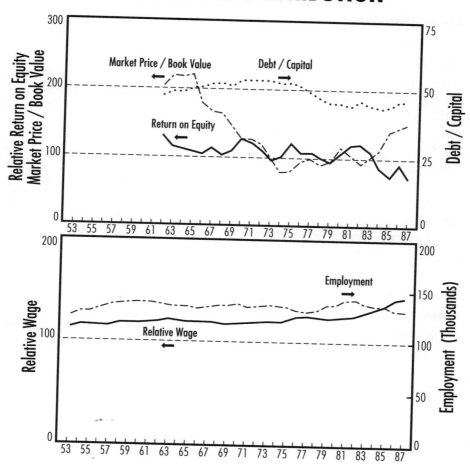

Industry Description

Telephone communication includes both local and long–distance service.

Competitive Classification

The industry is a regulated public utility. In this case, profit margins have averaged somewhat less than the all–industry average. Long–distance telephone service is now under some degree of competitive discipline.

Since regulation takes away industry control of markets, this industry must be classed along with the long–term competitive industries.

Labor Market

The industry is highly unionized, mainly by the Communication Workers of America, and is a labor–intensive industry. As in many highly unionized industries, relative wages rose sharply in the 1970s. They are still climbing. Tax–free fringe benefits are high.

Who Pays the Union Wage Premium?

As in other regulated utilities, union wage premiums are passed through to the consumer in higher prices.

Productivity

Productivity has had a spectacular gain, undoubtedly due in large part to the extraordinary advances in technology in the industry.

TELEPHONE COMMUNICATION

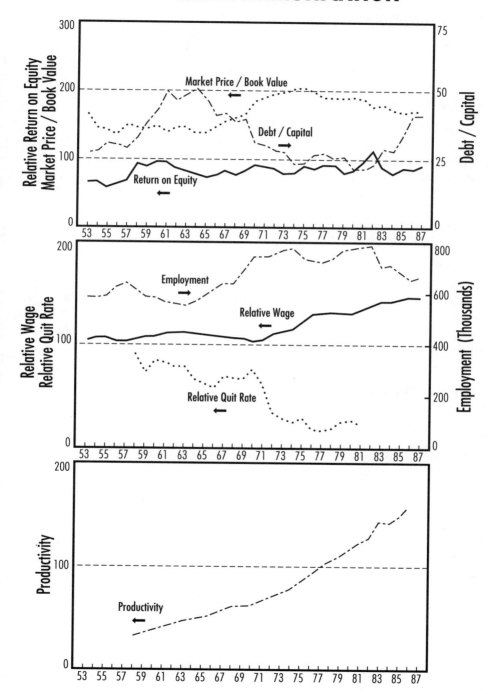

Industry Description

Corporate data cover the four majors—Alcoa, Alcan, Reynolds, and Kaiser—that are producers of primary aluminum plus many fabricated products. Labor and productivity data include the smaller producers of primary aluminum. Basic aluminum products trade on a world market.

Aluminum has become a slow–growth industry.

Competitive Classification

The aluminum industry is increasingly competitive. For a few brief years in the 1950s, the industry had the aura of a growth industry and the market power to hold profit margins well above the all–industry average. But that market power quickly disappeared. In the 1980s competition became so onerous as to make the industry short–term endangered.

Note how the four–firm concentration ratio has declined. Also note how long it took the stock market to recognize the loss of market control.

Labor Market

The industry is heavily unionized by two unions, the Aluminum, Brick and Glass Workers, and the Steelworkers. Relative wages rose rapidly in the 1970s even though profit margins were well below the all–industry average. Relative wages began to decline only in 1983 when the industry was in serious financial trouble.

Tax–free fringe benefits are very high, adding over a third to labor costs.

Who Pays the Union Wage Premium?

A very strong union has confronted a highly competitive industry. Wages have effectively been taken out of competition *among domestic producers*. The industry is of about average labor intensity. In good times, nonsupervisory labor costs have probably been fairly close to pretax profits.

The 1970s rise in relative wages coincided with low but irregularly flat profit margins in most of the period. Hence, some of the union wage premium may have come out of corporate profits. If so, it came at the expense of competitive profits, not monopolistic profits. For the corporations to have absorbed the entire increase in union wage premiums would have devastated profit margins even more.

Productivity

The industry showed a substantial spurt in productivity beginning in 1982 as it came under extreme pressure with the recession of 1982 and mounting foreign competition.

200

ALUMINUM

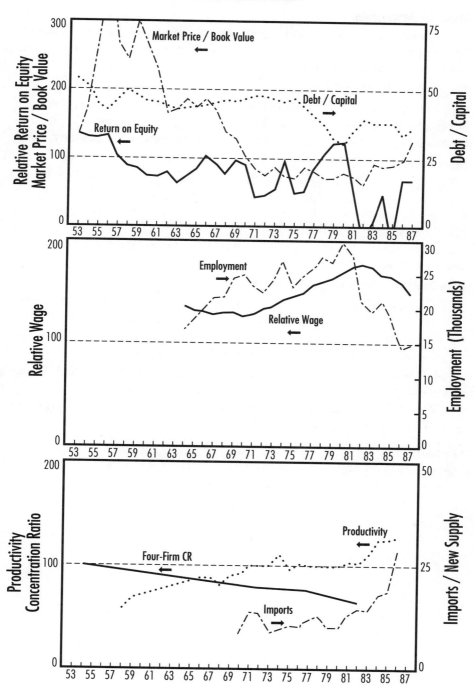

Industry Description

The large well–known cement companies are covered by the corporate data. Labor and productivity data include smaller firms as well. The eight–firm concentration ratio is 52 percent.

Competitive Classification

The industry could easily be classed as a long–term competitive industry, but since it has recently come under considerably greater competitive pressure from imports, we have placed it in the increasingly competitive category.

Labor Market

The industry is highly unionized. The major unions are the United Cement, Lime and Gypsum Workers, and the Steelworkers. Relative wages rose strongly in the 1970s, and turned down slightly only when the industry got into serious financial difficulty.

Tax–free fringe benefits add a good deal to the relative position of the cement workers.

Who Pays the Union Wage Premium?

Strong monopolistic unions have been arrayed against a highly competitive industry through most of the period studied. Union wages have been taken out of competition.

Labor costs have been somewhat higher than pretax profits.

Relative wages have risen most of the time in the period studied. Rising relative wages do not appear to be related to declines in profit margins.

In view of these facts, we conclude that most of the union wage premium has been passed through to the consumer.

Productivity

A substantial burst of improved productivity has followed the sharp increase in competitive pressure in recent years.

CEMENT

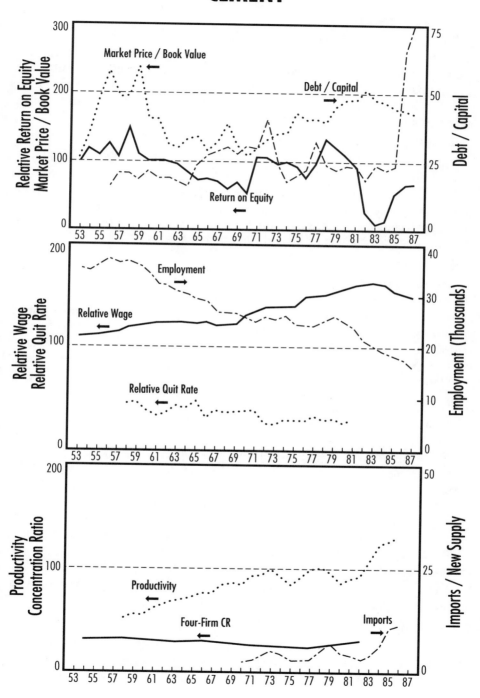

Industry Description

This is a very large industry, covering basic organic and inorganic chemicals, plastics, synthetic fibers, paints, and agricultural chemicals. The corporate data cover mainly the large firms such as Dow, DuPont, and Monsanto. The remaining data cover the large companies plus a very large number of smaller firms. Many products trade on international markets. Eight large firms cover 53 percent of the industry, and twenty firms have 73 percent.

Competitive Classification

Throughout the 1950s and early 1960s, the chemical industry was a premier growth industry with market power to hold profit margins safely above the all–industry average. Competition due to the ordinary workings of the markets finally destroyed that market power, and the chemical industry became a competitive industry. Note the many years it took the stock market to recognize the loss of market power in the industry.

Labor Market

Several parts of this highly diverse industry are strongly unionized. But unionization is spotty, with only about 30 percent of all workers belonging to unions. A large proportion of workers is represented by local independent unions. Several national unions represent other workers, including the Oil, Chemical and Atomic Workers, the Steelworkers, and the Teamsters, among others. Most bargaining is done on a plant–by–plant basis rather than a companywide basis.

Who Pays the Union Wage Premium?

Wages have not been taken out of competition. But telephone interviews seem to indicate that the unionization threat is a significant factor in wage–setting policies in at least part of the industry.

In this capital–intensive industry, nonsupervisory labor costs probably average about the same as or a little less than pretax corporate profits. In the 1960s when relative profit margins declined, relative wages were flat. Therefore, the decline in relative profits was not due to rising relative wages. In the 1970s and 1980s, relative profit margins declined as relative wages rose. However, preliminary information indicates that profit margins are now recovering nicely while relative wages are still rising.

These factors are inconclusive, but part of the rise in relative wages in recent years may have come at the expense of corporate profits.

Productivity

Productivity in this technical industry grew quite steadily until 1979. It is likely that the recent restructuring drive will significantly improve productivity again.

CHEMICALS

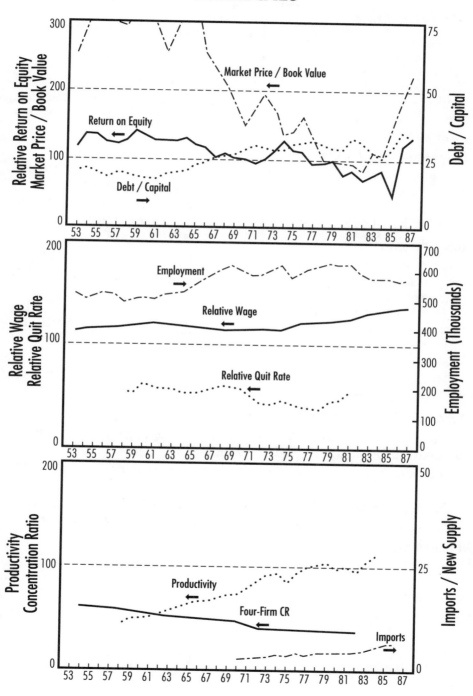

Industry Description

Lumber and wood products (except furniture) is a very broad industry including logging camps, sawmills, millwork, plywood, structural members, wood buildings, and mobile homes. There are a few large firms such as Weyerhaeuser and Georgia Pacific and many smaller firms. The top fifty firms have only about 56 percent of the industry. Corporate data shown on the chart cover only a few large firms, a subsector of the industry. Labor data cover the entire industry.

Competitive Classification

Limited available corporate data indicate increasing competition probably due to three factors: (1) the ordinary working of the market, (2) slow growth in construction, and (3) increased price pressure from Canada, although available data show no increase in imports as a percentage of new supply.

Labor Market

Large firms have been strongly unionized, but union wages in the South have been considerably lower than in the Northwest where unionization has been somewhat reduced in past years. Louisiana–Pacific has been successful in decertifying most of their union plants. Only about 20 percent of the workers in the entire industry are union members. Unions in the industry include an affiliate of the Carpenters and the International Woodworkers of America.

Data on relative wages do not properly reflect the union contracts because of the high proportion of nonunion workers.

Who Pays the Union Wage Premium?

Union organization has not been adequate to take wages completely out of competition. The industry is highly competitive.

The industry is labor–intensive, with labor costs running far above pretax profits.

Consequently, most of the union wage premium has likely been shifted on to the consumer, but part has probably been reflected in lower profit margins.

Productivity

No productivity data are available.

LUMBER

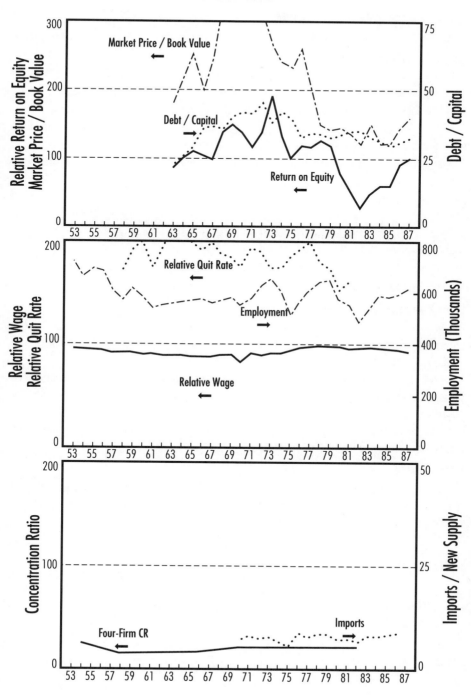

Industry Description

All data cover mainly the big three auto companies.

Competitive Classification

Until the late 1960s this industry was clearly monopolistic. If not for imports, it would still be monopolistic. The surge in relative profit margins in 1983 to 1985 is probably temporary unless imports are seriously curbed.

Four–firm concentration ratios were still above 90 percent in 1982, but they will decline as foreign producers expand production in this country.

As usual, the stock market recognized only belatedly the loss of market power.

Labor Market

The industry is highly unionized by the United Auto Workers. The rise in *relative* wages has been persistent since 1970. Relative wages are not likely to turn down very much until the industry gets in serious financial difficulty—and, perhaps, until chief executive salaries are cut.

Tax–free fringe benefits are very high in this industry.

Who Pays the Union Wage Premium?

The union has been strong enough to take wages out of competition. Even though the industry farms out much of its parts production, labor costs are still somewhat above pretax profits.

The loss of monopolistic profit margins came *before* the sharp rise in relative wages in the 1970s, and therefore, was not caused by that rise in relative wages.

In view of these facts, we conclude that most of the rising labor costs have likely been passed on to the customer.

Productivity

Productivity has shown considerable improvement. Growth should accelerate as competition intensifies from foreign producers manufacturing in this country.

MOTOR VEHICLES

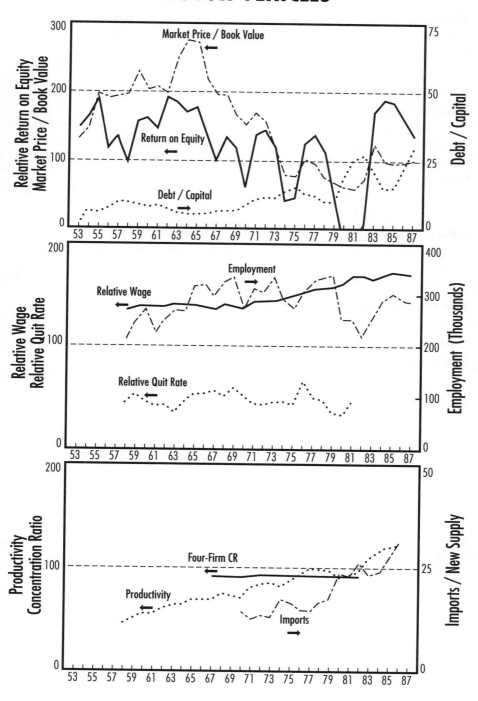

Industry Description

This rapidly growing industry consists of the well–known firms such as Intel, Texas Instruments, and Motorola, plus a number of smaller firms. The eight–firm concentration ratio is 57 percent, and the twenty–firm ratio is 77 percent. The industry has historically been highly cyclical.

Competitive Classification

Increased competition initially grew out of the rapidly changing technology, allowing leapfrogging by new firms. Then a rapid increase in imports added to the competitive environment. This has quite clearly gone from a moderately monopolistic industry to a competitive industry.

Stock prices have rather consistently appraised the industry as one that can generate monopolistic profits.

Labor Market

The industry is almost totally nonunion. Relative wages have risen slightly in recent years probably in response to the rising quit rates. It has been necessary to raise wages to keep employees.

Who Pays the Union Wage Premium?

No data are available to make a judgment. The light unionization rate makes the question pretty much irrelevant.

Productivity

As is well known, growth of productivity in the industry has been phenomenal.

SEMICONDUCTORS

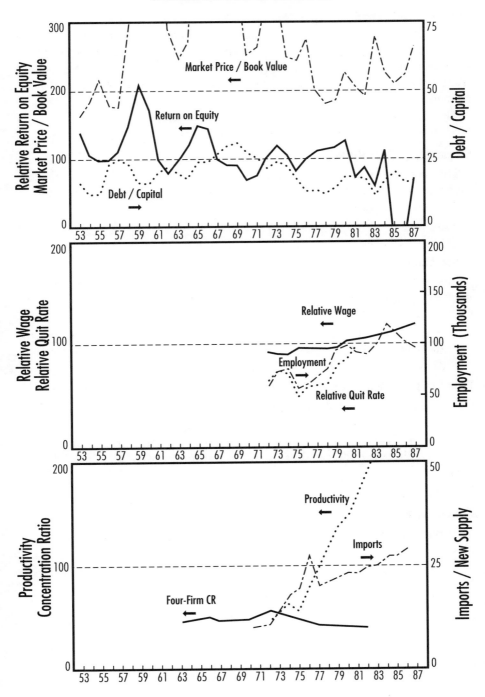

Industry Description

The contract trucking industry must be divided into two parts: (1) The less–than–truckload (LTL) carriers, which include the very large carriers that have terminals for assembling full truckloads, (they also carry a good deal of freight not assembled from less–than–truckload lots), and (2) full truckload carriers.

The corporate data shown in the chart cover mainly the less–than–truckload carriers. Labor data are for the entire industry.

Competitive Classification

The industry is clearly an increasingly competitive one. It apparently lost much of its early market power through the ordinary working of the market before the 1978 deregulation.

Many bankruptcies occurred in the industry following deregulation and the serious 1982 recession.

Labor Market

The large LTL carriers are strongly unionized by the Teamsters, and workers apparently receive union wage premiums far above nonunion drivers. The smaller truckload carriers are generally nonunion.

The small decline in relative wages began immediately following deregulation. Relative wage data shown in the chart do not fully reflect changes in union wages because the data include so many nonunion workers.

Who Pays the Union Wage Premium?

A strong union has taken wages out of competition among the large LTL carriers. The trucking industry is now highly competitive.

Nonsupervisory labor costs are several times pretax profits, making it inconceivable that profits could absorb any significant wage premium.

Therefore, union wage premiums are largely shifted on to the consumer in higher prices.

Productivity

Productivity data cover only long–distance trucking.

TRUCKING

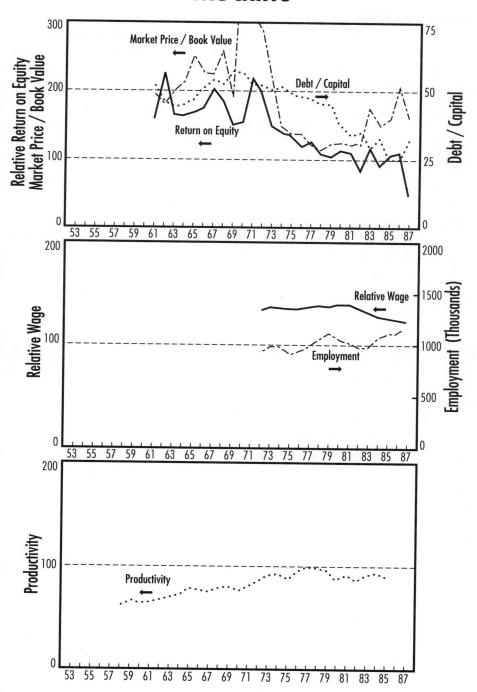

Industry Description

This industry has been decimated. Employment of nonsupervisory workers has dropped to about 50,000 in 1985 from nearly 110,000 in 1979. Only a couple of large and a few small producers remain.

Competitive Classification

This industry has had only two or three good years since 1953. In recent years, competition has become even more severe, creating a desperate financial situation for most firms in the industry.

Labor Market

The industry has been strongly unionized by the United Auto Workers Union.

Who Pays the Union Wage Premium?

A strong union has faced a very weak, highly competitive industry. Union organization has been complete enough to take wages out of competition.

Labor intensity has been moderately above–average.

Relative wage data go back only to 1972. It is interesting to note that the rise in relative wages in the 1970s coincided with some of the best profit years the industry has had.

In view of these facts, we conclude that a good deal of the union wage premium has likely been shifted to the consumer, but part of it may have served to destroy profits in this endangered industry.

Productivity

Intensified competition in this industry so far has failed to generate rising productivity as it has in so many industries.

FARM MACHINERY

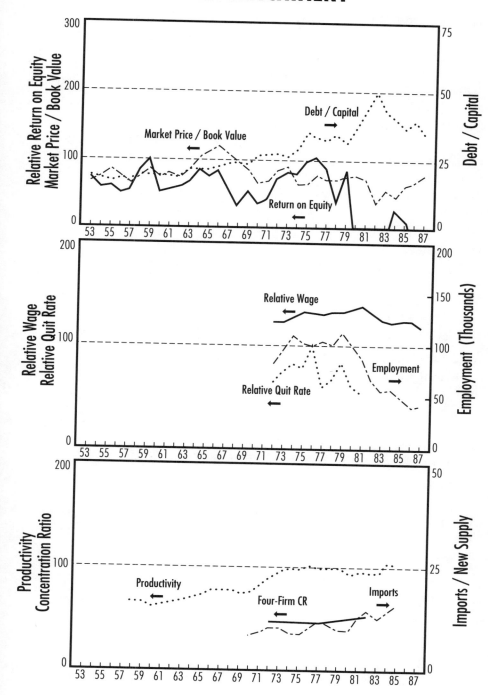

Industry Description

The domestic shoe *manufacturing* industry has been almost destroyed. A large proportion of the small firms have simply gone out of business. Imports have taken over a large part of the market. The eight largest of the remaining manufacturers have 47 percent of the market, and the twenty largest have 70 percent of the market.

Competitive Classification

Larger firms have survived by turning to importing and retailing. Consequently, the good profit margins shown on the corporate chart are due mainly to retailing rather than manufacturing.

The shoe *manufacturing* industry certainly has been a long–term endangered industry—critically endangered. The large firms have survived mainly by changing the nature of their business.

Labor Market

The industry is still moderately unionized by several unions, including the United Food and Commercial Workers, the Amalgamated Clothing and Textile Workers, and the Retail Clerks International, among others, but any union wage premium must be very small.

Relative wages have shown a steady but very slight downward trend.

Who Pays the Union Wage Premium?

Several weak unions face an extremely weak and highly competitive industry. Wages have not been taken out of competition.

This labor–intensive industry has labor costs far higher than pretax profits.

Therefore, it would be difficult to absorb any union wage premium out of profits. To the extent any union wage premium has reduced profits, those profits have certainly not been monopolistic profits.

Productivity

Productivity improvements have been almost nonexistent for many years. This may well be a very difficult industry in which to improve productivity. The incentive may be lacking with such an adequate supply of product from abroad.

FOOTWEAR (EXCEPT RUBBER)

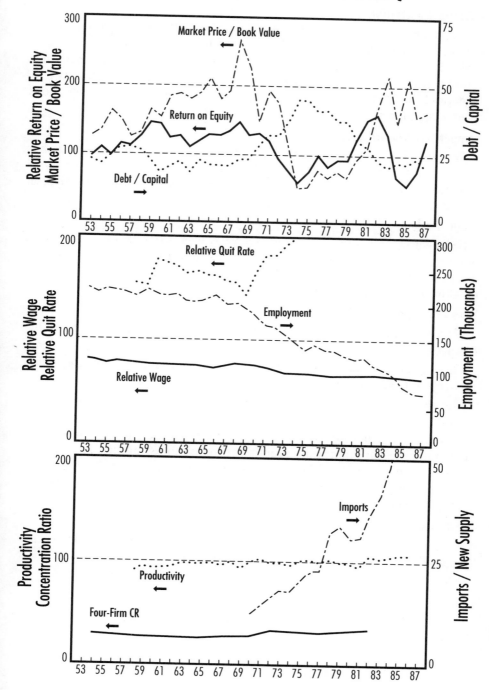

Industry Description

This industry produces large machines such as mills, lathes and presses for cutting and forming metal. It is not a highly concentrated industry. The eight–firm concentration ratio is only 42 percent, and the twenty–firm concentration ratio is only 63 percent. Until recently, the industry was only moderately endangered, but sharply rising imports in recent years have added a new sense of urgency to the endangered status.

Competitive Classification

We have classified this industry as long–term endangered because it has had so few good years over the past three decades. It could just as easily be classified as long–term competitive. The industry is now showing good signs of recovery.

Labor Market

Unionization in the industry is spotty. A few firms are fully unionized, some partly, and many not at all. A number of different unions are involved, including the Machinists and the Steelworkers. Bargaining is either on a plant or company basis. No industrywide pattern exists.

Who Pays the Union Wage Premium?

Wages have not been taken out of competition. The industry is highly competitive.

The industry is very labor–intensive. Labor costs run two to three times pretax profits even in good years.

The steady relative wages could not account for the substantial fluctuations in profit margins.

In summary, in an industry so labor–intensive, it has not been possible to absorb much of a union wage premium through lower profits. Most of any union wage premium has had to be passed on to the consumer. To the extent that union wage premiums have come at the expense of profits, they have not been monopolistic profits.

Productivity

We have not yet discovered why this industry, under great and increasing competitive pressure, has failed to improve productivity. It seems to be an anomaly.

MACHINE TOOLS

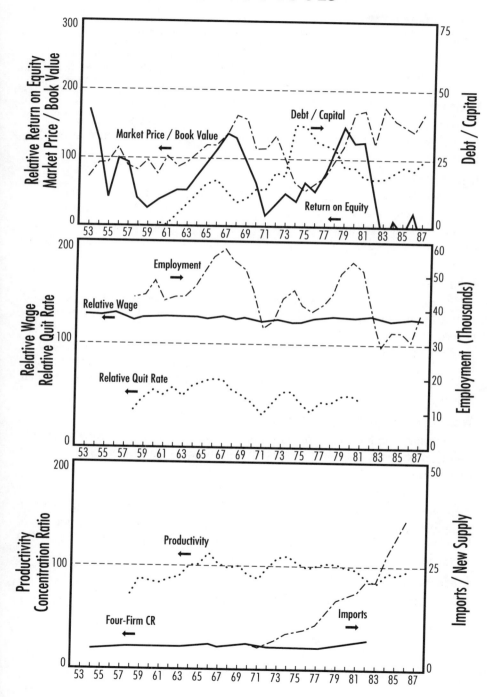

Industry Description

This industry includes slaughter facilities and meat packing.

Old–timers would not recognize the industry. Most of the good old firms have been reorganized, acquired by other firms, or have gone through bankruptcy. The largest beef packer is Iowa Beef Processors, partly owned by Occidental Petroleum, a relative newcomer on the block.

There are a few large producers, but the industry is fragmented. The 20 largest producers have only 61 percent of the industry, the fifty largest only 75 percent.

Competitive Classification

Meat packing has long been an endangered industry, reporting profit margins consistently below the all–industry average. The corporate chart shows a recent rise in profit margins. That is misleading because most of the firms had dropped out of the data due to reorganization, acquisition, and so on.

Labor Market

Unionization has long been strong in the beef and pork industries, the major union being the United Food and Commercial Workers. Master contracts covered most large producers. But the union was defeated in some Iowa Beef Processing plants, which set up processing in rural areas and specialized in producing boxed beef. In recent years, both beef and pork master contracts have been broken. As a result, relative wages in the industry have declined sharply.

Who Pays the Union Wage Premium?

For a long time strong unions faced a very weak industry. Now relatively weak unions face a highly competitive industry. Wages are not now out of competition.

Labor costs are considerably more than pretax profits.

In view of these facts, we conclude that in the past much of the union wage premium was likely passed on to the consumer, but also part of it may have been extracted from corporate profits, helping to keep the industry in the endangered status.

Productivity

Productivity has grown steadily in this industry.

MEAT PACKING

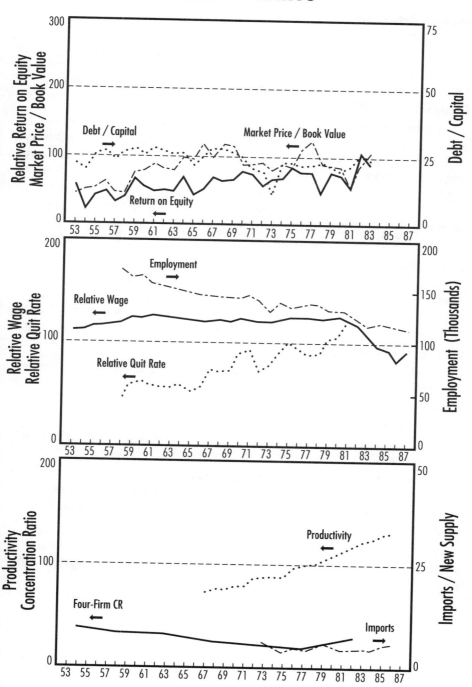

Industry Description

Manufacturers of woven and knitted fabrics of all kinds, carpets, and many miscellaneous items are included in this industry. It is a large but slowly growing industry. The industry is not highly concentrated. The eight–firm concentration ratio is 51 percent and the twenty–firm ratio is 69 percent.

Competitive Classification

Since 1953, the textile industry has not once earned a profit margin equal to or above the all–industry average. Because of this, we have classified it as a long–term endangered industry. Internally generated funds have been scarce, and debt has been high for this type of industry. But the problem of attracting capital has not reached the desperation point.

The textile industry has received considerable import protection. Imports have not surged in recent years to the extent they have in shoes, machine tools, steel, and some other industries.

Labor Market

The industry is about 10 to 20 percent unionized, mainly by the Amalgamated Clothing and Textile Workers. Unionization has declined over the past thirty years as the industry has relocated from the Northeast to the Southeast.

Who Pays the Union Wage Premium?

A weak union has faced a highly competitive industry. The union has not been able to take wages out of competition.

The industry is labor–intensive. Labor costs tend to average two to three times pretax profits.

Variations in relative profit margins cannot be explained by variations in relative wages.

It appears, therefore, that any wage premium would be difficult to absorb through lower profits. But to the extent that union wage premiums have reduced profits, they have been competitive, not monopolistic, profits.

Productivity

The industry has been a plucky survivor, funding—with difficulty—the necessary capital improvements to increase productivity regularly and substantially.

TEXTILES

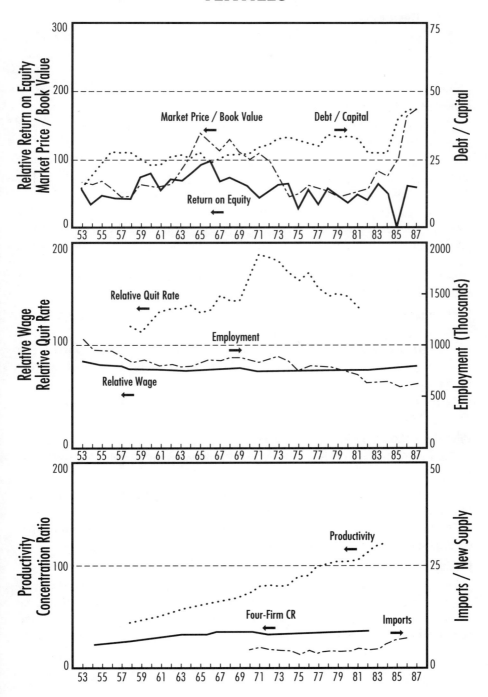

Industry Description

The brewing industry consists of a very few large brewers and a shrinking number of small independents. It is a rather small industry, employing only about 27,000 nonsupervisory workers. The industry is now a slow–growth industry.

Competitive Classification

This is one of only two of our forty–two industries that has the earmarks of a *decreasingly* competitive industry.

Numerous acquisitions of smaller firms by the larger firms have occurred. This is the only industry we have analyzed that shows a sharply rising four–firm concentration ratio. The eight–firm ratio is 94 percent.

Until recently, aggressive rivalry was present in the industry as Miller Brewing fought for and achieved greater market share at the expense of low profit margins. The industry now appears to be moving a bit more toward a "live–and–let–live" policy, with less emphasis on gaining market share. If so, this industry should join the ranks of our marketing conglomerates with substantial market control.

Labor Market

Almost the entire industry is unionized. (Coors is an exception.) Several unions are involved, but the Teamsters Union is dominant in the industry. The union wage premium is apparently very large, but difficult to estimate in this industry.

As in most highly unionized industries, relative wages rose rapidly in the 1970s. They show no sign of declining.

Who Pays the Union Wage Premium?

The unions have largely taken wages out of competition. The industry has, in the past, been vigorously competitive.

Labor costs are about average (around 10 percent) as a percentage of sales and about equal to pretax profits as a percentage of sales.

The industry, then, has likely shifted most of the union wage premium on to consumers rather than absorbing it via lower profits.

Productivity

The sharp rise in productivity may have been due to the consolidation of small producers, or perhaps to the strong competitive environment. It will be interesting to see if productivity continues to improve as less–aggressive competition settles in upon the industry.

MALT BEVERAGES

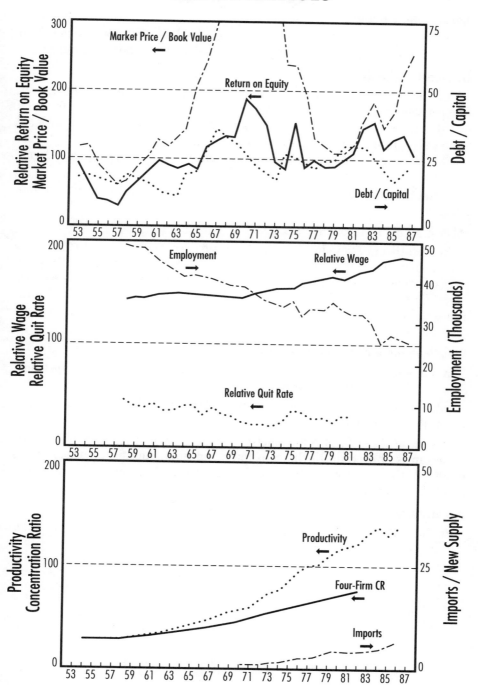

Industry Description

The corporate data show just a few publicly held newspapers, some of them very successful chains. Labor and productivity data cover the entire industry.

Competitive Classification

This is a rare industry that appears to have *decreasing* competition. Competition seems to be destroying itself. In many cities, fierce competition has driven all but one daily newspaper out of business, leaving a local monopoly. In other cities, two surviving papers have declared a truce, combining printing and other facilities and effectively eliminating most forms of competition.

As the chart shows, stock prices have rewarded the rising profit margins handsomely.

Labor Markets

Unionization in the industry as a whole is moderate. But in particular cities and in particular crafts within the industry, unions have organized sufficiently to take wages out of competition. Union wage premiums appear to be very high. One of the major unions in this industry is the International Typographical Union. The relative wage data do not fully reflect union wage rates because they include so many nonunion workers.

Who Pays the Union Wage Premium?

In many highly unionized cities, wages have been taken out of competition. Strong unions face monopolistic firms.

Labor costs are about 12 to 14 percent of revenues, but pretax profits are generally a little higher.

In view of these facts, we cannot determine how much of the union wage premium is shifted on to the consumer and how much is absorbed out of profits. If the union wage premium has been absorbed out of profits, it has surely left a handsome residue.

Productivity

Productivity has grown only moderately in the industry.

NEWSPAPERS

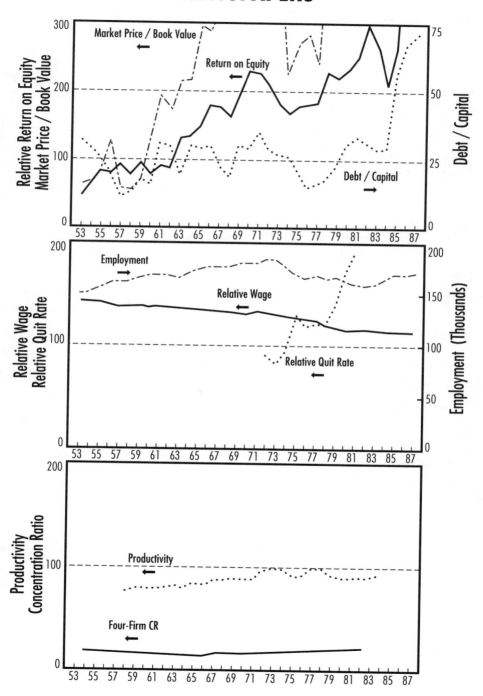

Industry Description

This industry is made up of a number of subindustries: cigarettes, household paper products, cosmetics, perfumes, personal care items, soaps, detergents, confectionery, soft drinks, packaged foods, and proprietary drugs. These are all small consumer goods sold mainly through grocery stores and drugstores. Skill in advertising and selling is as important as or more important than skill in design and manufacture. Most firms are active in several of these sub–categories. (Justification for lumping all these firms into a single industry was made in chapter 2.)

Competitive Classification

As the chart shows, the industry has had the market power to maintain profit margins persistently and substantially above the all–industry average. It must, therefore, be classed as long–term monopolistic. The market power that enables this industry to maintain high profit margins stems from consumers' brand loyalty, which serves as a barrier to new entrants.

Labor Markets

Unionization in this industry is spotty. Some firms are totally union. Some are totally nonunion. Most are partially union. A number of different unions are involved.

No estimate of a union wage premium is possible. Certainly it varies from one subcategory to another.

Who Pays the Union Wage Premium?

Insufficient information is available to make a judgment. But one thing seems clear: if union wage premiums have been partly absorbed through lower profits, a handsome residual has been left.

Productivity

Data are not available.

MARKETING CONGLOMERATES

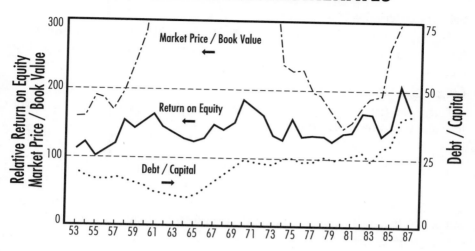

Industry Description

The industry consists of two large firms—Philip Morris and RJR Nabisco—and a very few smaller firms. This is a sub–industry of the marketing conglomerates.

Competitive Classification

This industry is clearly a long–term monopolistic industry. Control over markets might be expected of the only major industry that has the legal right to sell addictive materials almost indiscriminately. Perhaps the very fact that the cigarette health threat has thrown so much doubt on the future of the industry has helped protect its extraordinary monopolistic profit. Potential competitors have not been willing to make the necessary investment to break down the barriers to entry in view of the shadow on the long–term industry outlook. A ban on TV advertising reinforces the barriers against entry.

The chart shows relative profit margins averaging about 50 percent above the all–industry average. But this return on equity includes many major products other than cigarettes. Estimated return on equity for just the cigarette segment of these companies in U.S. markets shows profit margins three to four *times* the all–industry average in recent years.

The fact that the top four firms control nearly the entire industry doesn't hurt the profit position. Imports are irrelevant.

Labor Markets

Relative wages in this industry have gone from slightly below the all–industry average in 1953 to very near the highest existing relative wage at the present time. Tax–free fringe benefits are high in this industry.

Who Pays the Union Wage Premium?

A very strong union, the Bakery, Confectionery and Tobacco Workers, faces an extremely powerful industry. Wages have been taken out of competition by organization or threat of organization. (RJR–Nabisco is nonunion but apparently pays wages close to union scale, perhaps due to the threat of unionization.) Labor costs are only about 7 percent of sales, and are far less than pretax profits. The sharp rise in relative wages has been concurrent with a rise in relative profit margins.

This information suggests that the union wage premium *could* have been absorbed through lower profits, but has probably been passed through to the consumer in higher prices.

Productivity

Productivity growth has been moderate but regular.

CIGARETTES

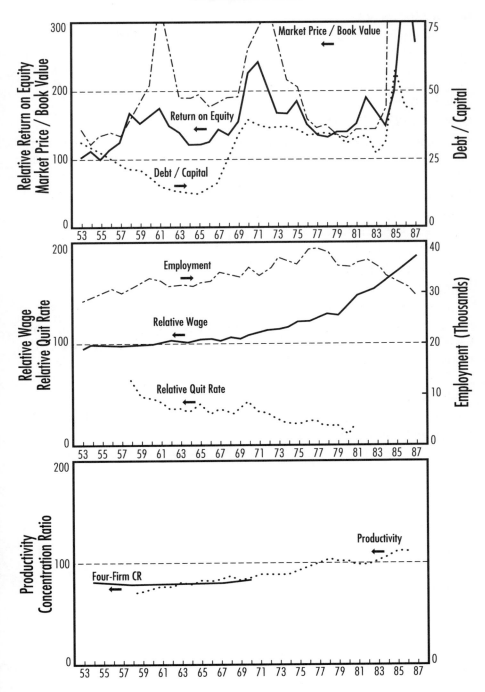

Industry Description

Revlon, Avon and Alberto–Culver are among the majors of the industry, but there are many smaller firms. The top eight–firms have about 50 percent of the industry, and the top twenty firms have about 80 percent of the industry. The industry is growing rapidly. This is a subindustry of the marketing conglomerates.

Competitive Classification

The long–term decline in relative profit margins indicates that the industry has lost some market power. However, it still has not reported a single year's profit margin at or below the all–industry average.

Labor Market

Unionization in the industry is spotty. Apparently it is only lightly organized by several unions.

Also, apparently the union wage premium is small.

Who Pays the Union Wage Premium?

Wages have not been taken out of competition.

Labor costs are considerably smaller than pretax profits.

Both of these factors indicate that any union wage premium *could* have been absorbed in lower profits. However, the monopolistic nature of the industry would indicate the *possibility* of passing union wage premiums on to the consumer.

Productivity

Productivity grew impressively until about 1978 and has since declined. No explanation is available.

PERFUMES AND COSMETICS

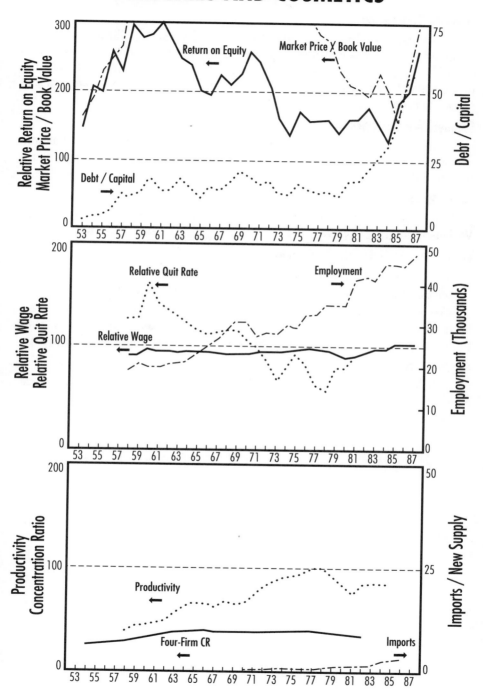

Industry Description

The industry includes Colgate, Procter and Gamble, Clorox, and some smaller firms. The four largest firms control 60 percent of the industry, the eight largest control 73 percent. Employment in this small industry amounts to only about 27,000 nonsupervisory workers. This is a subindustry of the marketing conglomerates.

Competitive Classification

The industry is clearly long–term monopolistic in the sense that it has had the market power to hold profit margins substantially and persistently above the all–industry average.

Labor Market

Unionization in the industry is apparently substantial, but irregular. Various unions are involved.

Who Pays the Union Wage Premium?

Wages apparently have not been taken fully out of competition.

Labor costs are small in relation to sales and to pretax profits.

In view of these facts, we conclude that the union wage premium *could* have been absorbed through lower profits, but also the industry probably has had the market power to shift the wage premium on to the public in higher prices.

Productivity

Productivity rose substantially until about 1973, but has slowed down since. No explanation is available.

SOAP AND DETERGENTS

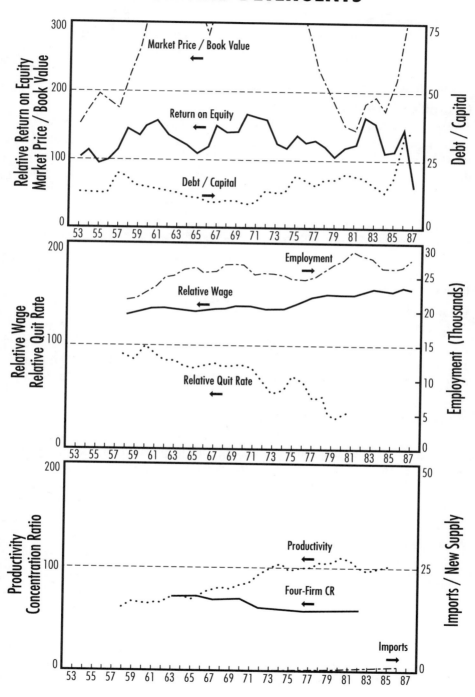

Industry Description

Included in the industry are the three major networks, some smaller networks, individual stations, and cable. Unfortunately, the corporate data are limited to the two publicly held networks and a few smaller firms. Most independents are not included in the data.

Competitive Classification

The above–average profitability of this industry is indicated by the corporate data shown on the chart. The profit margin figures are dominated by CBS and ABC. But the profitability of the industry is repeatedly demonstrated by the high prices that have been paid for individual stations and groups of stations.

But even in this industry competition is rapidly building. Several new networks are expanding and seriously challenging the big three. Many new independent stations are appearing as ultra–high–frequency channels become available. Cable, VCRs, and educational TV are vying for viewer attention and advertising dollars. It may well be that the peak of monopolistic power has been seen.

Labor Market

Unionization in the networks is substantial. Unions include the National Association of Broadcast Employees and Technicians, the American Federation of TV and Radio Artists, and the Electrical Workers, among many others. In individual stations unionization is spotty. The union wage premium is apparently substantial.

Who Pays the Union Wage Premium?

A world of additional information is needed to judge what part of the union wage premium has been absorbed through lower profits and what part has been passed through to the consumer in higher prices.

But in any event, as in the case of other monopolistic industries, if the union wage premium has been paid out of profits, it has still left a handsome residue of reported profits.

Productivity

No productivity data are available.

RADIO AND TV BROADCASTING

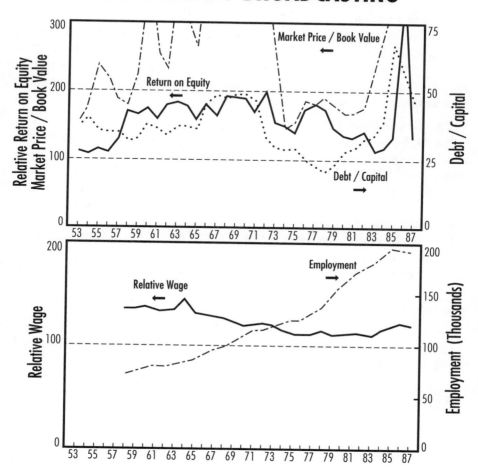

Industry Description

There are thousands of advertising agencies in the country. The four largest have about 10 percent of the industry, and the twenty largest about 30 percent. Obviously, the industry is highly fragmented. But the concentration ratio for those firms large enough to handle national accounts is much greater. Most of the large firms are now international in scope.

Competitive Classification

This industry has reported profit margins persistently and substantially above the all–industry average. Therefore, it must be classified as long–term monopolistic. Profit margins are computed as return on *book value*. Book value for these firms includes large amounts of goodwill created in acquisition programs. If profit margins were computed as return on tangible book value, they would be much higher.

It is not clear why competition has failed to push profit margins down. It probably eventually will do so. But in the meantime, selection of agencies seems to be based on perceived professional abilities rather than on the size of the fee, which does not appear to regularly enter into the competition.

Labor Market

The industry is minimally unionized. The work force appears to include a large number of creative and technical types. No evidence is available as to who pays the union wage premium.

ADVERTISING AGENCIES

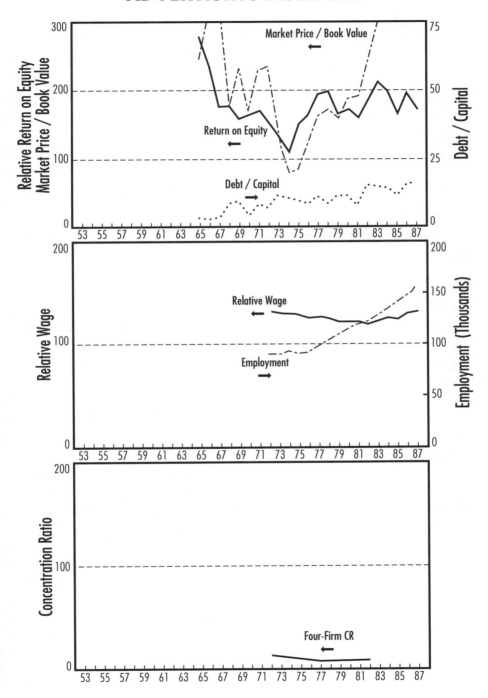

Industry Description

The industry includes the well–known computer firms plus a number of smaller firms making specialized computing equipment. The four largest firms have 43 percent of the industry. The twenty largest have 71 percent of the industry. (The classification of computer equipment is very broad, including equipment beyond the narrow perception most people have of the computer industry.)

Competitive Classification

This dominant–firm industry has clearly recorded profit margins persistently and substantially above the all–industry average, and, therefore, must be counted as long–term monopolistic. The industry without IBM would be classed as long–term competitive with average profit margins. IBM's return on equity has persistently been way above the all–industry average. We would hazard a guess that the increased competition hitting IBM from all sides will take a toll on those profit margins and that in the years to come, the industry's profit margins will be much nearer the all–industry average than in the past.

Labor Market

The industry is only minimally unionized. As would be expected, the union wage premium appears to be small.

Who Pays the Union Wage Premium?

Wages have not been taken out of competition. Labor costs are small in relation to both sales and pretax profits. Therefore, the union wage premium could have been absorbed in lower profits or passed on to the consumer in higher prices.

Productivity

A remarkable growth in productivity has been evidenced in this industry, probably due to the opportunity for so many technological changes. Technological competition is the primary form of competition. Could it be possible that the acceleration of productivity in recent years has been due to the greater competition in the industry?

COMPUTER EQUIPMENT

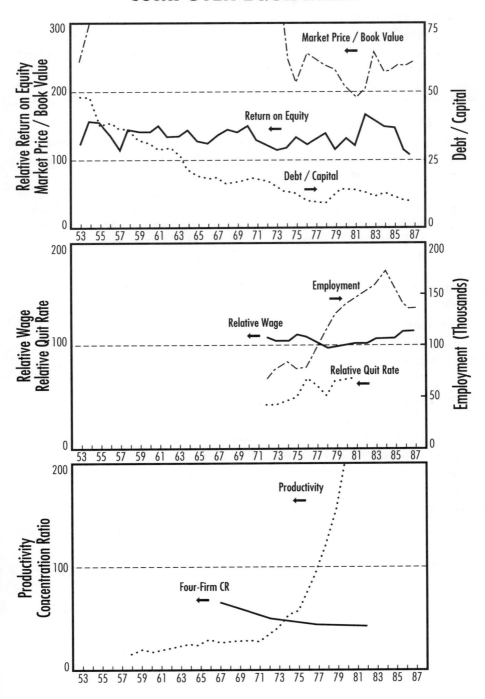

Industry Description

This rapidly growing industry is dominated by the well–known firms such as Merck and Squibb. But there are many smaller firms in the industry. Both ethical and proprietary drugs are included. Although the industry is best known by a few large firms, the eight largest firms have only 47 percent of the industry, and the twenty largest 72 percent.

Competitive Classification

Because of its continuing high relative profit margins over three decades, this industry has been classified as long–term monopolistic. But it shows many characteristics of increasing competition.

Imports in total are rising slightly. In some niche areas they are becoming important. Several new firms have been organized to exploit the new leading area of drug research, biotechnology. There has been a sharp expansion of firms producing and selling generic drugs that have come off patent, a development made possible by changed government regulations. Whether high profit margins can be maintained depends in large part on whether enough new blockbuster drugs can be developed to offset the declining margins in those that are coming off patent.

Labor Market

The industry is only moderately unionized, by several unions including the Oil, Chemical and Atomic Workers and the International Chemical Workers, among others.

Who Pays the Union Wage Premium?

Wages have not been taken out of competition.

Labor costs are small in relation to both pretax corporate profits and to technical and supervisory salaries.

Under these circumstances, union wage premiums *could* have been absorbed through lower profits or shifted on to the consumer.

Productivity

As would be expected in a high–tech industry, productivity has grown substantially.

242

DRUGS

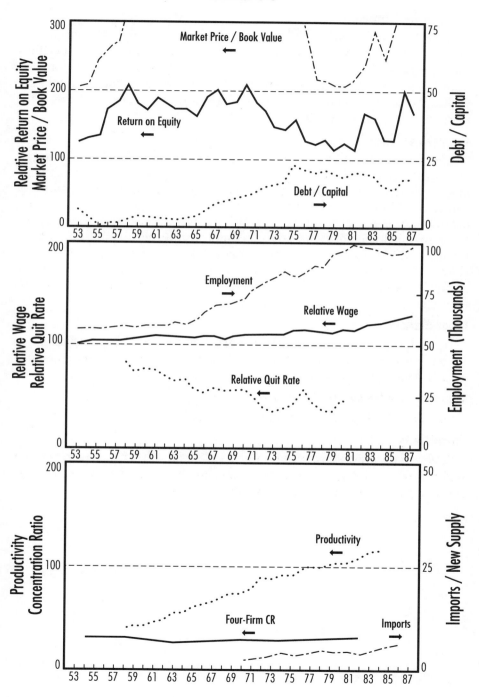

Industry Description

Since the mid–1950s, the drugstore industry has gone from largely independent stores to largely chain stores. The corporate chart is not fully representative of the industry since it includes only a dozen largely publicly owned and generally prosperous chains. The consolidation movement still has a considerable way to go. The industry is still fragmented. Over a third of the stores are still independents.

Competitive Classification

Since the chains covered by our corporate data have reported profit margins persistently and substantially above the all–industry average, we must place *this sector* of the drugstore industry in the long–term monopolistic category. But it is not likely to stay there. Competition from grocery and discount stores, increased payments by sophisticated third–party payers, and head–to–head competition as the chains continue to invade each other's territory will increase competition to the point where profit margins will be close to the all–industry average as for grocery and general merchandise stores. (All data shown on the charts other than the corporate data cover the entire industry, not just the large chains.)

Labor Market

The industry is only moderately unionized by several unions including the United Food and Commercial Workers. As far as can be estimated, the union wage premium is smaller than for grocery stores.

Who Pays the Union Wage Premium?

Insufficient information is available to hazard a judgment.

Productivity

Productivity grew substantially until 1973. Since then it has grown but slightly. No information is available to pinpoint the cause for the earlier rise, but it may have been due to the consolidation movement.

DRUGSTORES (CHAINS ONLY)

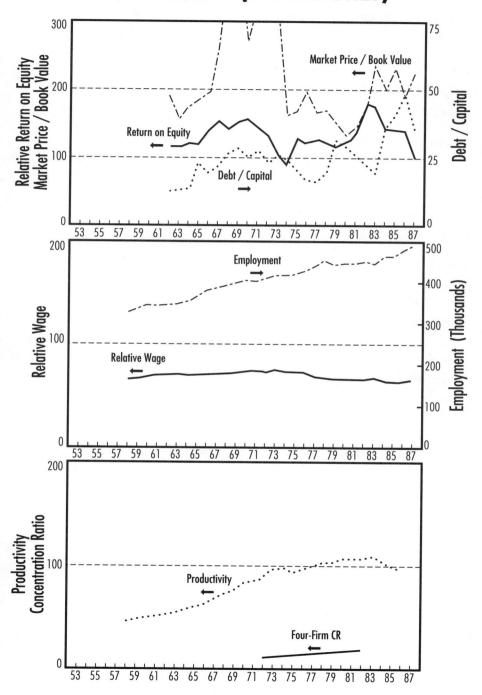

EATING PLACES (CHAINS ONLY) LONG–TERM MONOPOLISTIC

Industry Description

This very large industry employs about 5 percent of the workers in the United States, and employment is growing rapidly. Of course, it is highly fragmented, with the fifty largest firms having only 20 percent of the industry.

Competitive Classification

Corporate data shown on the chart represent only about twenty of the larger chains for which information is available. These publicly held chains account for only 10 to 15 percent of business done in the industry.

This sector has reported above–average profit margins and hence must be counted as long–term monopolistic. It is a subsector of the eating place industry, mostly involving fast–food outlets.

With the considerable buildup of new outlets, the inexorable pressure of competition will likely drive profit margins down to the all–industry average. Indeed, more complete data might show such competition already in place.

Labor Markets

The industry is very lightly unionized, mostly in the larger cities. But the union wage premium does appear to be fairly high.

Who Pays the Union Wage Premium?

Information is not available to allow a judgment as to who pays the union wage premium.

Productivity

The chart shows that productivity is not growing. However, literature describing the industry indicates substantial improvement in productivity at the large fast–food chains.

EATING PLACES (CHAINS ONLY)

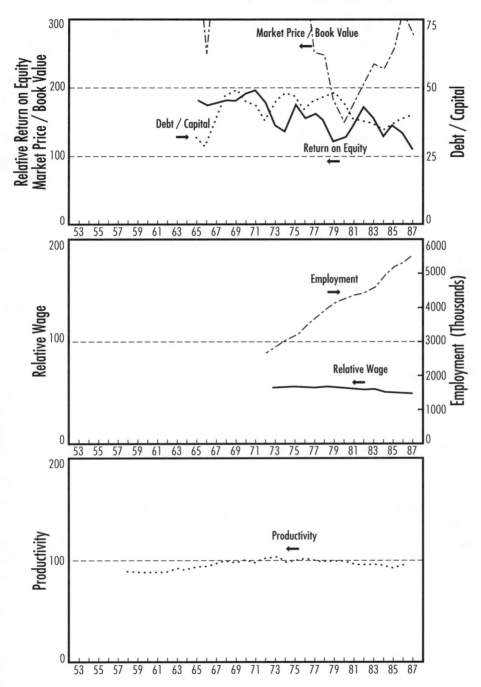

Industry Description

This rapidly growing industry consists of very many large and small firms dealing in a tremendous variety of financial and commodity instruments. The volume of business is now in the tens of billions of dollars a day.

It is a highly cyclical industry.

The corporate chart shows data for only publicly traded firms. These firms are not fully representative of the industry, especially in the early years.

Competitive Classification

Because of the short period for which even limited data are available and because of the erratic nature of the relative profit margins, this industry has been difficult to classify. Since relative profit margins have averaged 40 to 50 percent above the all–industry average for the period studied, we have classified the industry as monopolistic.

However, the industry is becoming increasingly competitive, and in the years to come profit margins will likely approach the all–industry average, for the following reasons:

- Much of the recent prosperity has been due to the enormous growth of the industry, partly due to the introduction of wildly popular new products such as stock options and financial futures, and partly due to the growing popularity of short–term trading as opposed to long–term investing. Such phenomenal growth is not likely to continue for many years.

- Markets are becoming international, thereby increasing competition.

- Many participants are present in nearly every niche of the financial markets. Banks and discount brokers have entered the business with commissions far below those of the full–service brokers.

- Huge amounts of new investment capital are flowing into the industry in response to the high profit margins.

Labor Market

Unionization in the industry is trivial, below 3 percent. The industry is very labor–intensive, but much of it is in technical and supervisory employment.

No labor market or productivity data are available.

SECURITY AND COMMODITY BROKERS

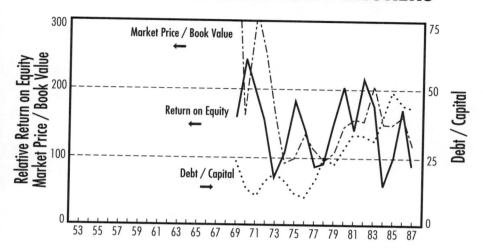

APPENDIX B

SURVEY OF RELATED LITERATURE

Most of the appendix B analyses were prepared by Garry K. Ottosen, Senior Research Analyst. The remainder were written by Peter A. Lawson, also Senior Research Analyst.

THE ANTITRUST DEBATE

In recent years, antitrust law has come under attack from both the left and the right. Antitrust has been attacked before, but this attack is unprecedented in terms of its success. The attackers have succeeded in staffing the two federal agencies in charge of antitrust enforcement largely with economists and lawyers opposed to the previously accepted structure-conduct-performance paradigm of antitrust law. In addition, many judges at the federal level have abandoned traditional antitrust enforcement in favor of a "new learning," and much of the law and a significant part of the economics profession now seriously question the usefulness of antitrust litigation. Here we shall briefly review the mainstream view of antitrust law which held from 1950 to 1980, the attack from the left, which has unwittingly played into the hands of those on the right, and the attack from the right, which is often called the Chicago school or revisionist view.

The Mainstream View

The mainstream view of antitrust law has been described in several papers (see, for example, Harris and Sullivan 1986; Pautler 1983). The mainstream view has at its core the so-called structure-conduct-performance paradigm. This paradigm holds that higher levels of concentration result in higher prices and profits, higher costs, reduced innovation, and reduced mobility. In other words, monopolistic or tight oligopolistic market structure results inevitably in conduct that hurts the public by bringing about higher prices and transferring wealth from consumers to monopolists. In recent years, some mainstreamers have argued that the major problem comes not from concentration but rather from the market power of the largest firms within concentrated markets.

The U.S. Supreme Court adopted the mainstream view in its prima facie rule of Philadelphia Bank (1963). The Philadelphia Bank rule states that a merger is unlawful if it increases concentration "significantly" and results in an "undue" market share, unless proponents can convincingly establish through specific evidence that it will not injure competition. The Philadelphia Bank rule allowed room to learn. How narrowly should a market be defined? What is an "undue share," a "significant" increase in concentration? Since the rule was a prima facie proposition, it left open the possibility of incorporating other structural evidence such as entry barriers. In other words, concentration data are the beginning, not necessarily the end, of structural analysis under Philadelphia. (See Harris and Sullivan 1986.)

Mainstreamers see a too-stringent antitrust law as being less risky than a too-lax antitrust law. Too-stringent enforcement might carry the social cost of reduced efficiency, but that cost is timebound. In other words, the market can eventually correct this type of error. On the other hand, too-lax enforcement results in social costs (monopoly induced inefficiencies, higher prices, and so on) that may never be corrected by the market.

Mainstreamers value well-functioning markets for their efficiencies, their distributional properties, and because they tend to result in a wide dispersion of economic power. Mainstreamers fear excess power, and they recognize that markets do fail. Therefore, they see a need for a strong antitrust policy to protect competition and to correct market failures.

Attack from the Left

Antitrust laws have been attacked from the left by two well-known economists: John Kenneth Galbraith and Lester Thurow. We shall review their attacks separately.

In his book *The New Industrial State*, Galbraith (1978) presents his view that antitrust laws are an anachronism. He argues that the antitrust laws were placed on the statute books to preserve the power of the market against those who would subordinate it to the purpose of monopoly. But, he argues, today the mature corporations through their oligopolistic market structures have taken control of the market "to serve not the goal of monopoly but the goals of planning." He argues that controlled prices are necessary for this planning. In Galbraith's mind the market is a mere illusion; the reality is industrial planning. He therefore sees the antitrust laws as anachronistic, seeking to preserve not the market but rather the illusion of the market. Galbraith sees no need for antitrust laws and would like all such statutes removed because they give legitimacy to a charade and help conceal the reality of industrial planning.

Lester Thurow's attack on antitrust law (see Mueller 1983) seems to be somewhat more schizophrenic than Galbraith's. Thurow's arguments are schizophrenic because instead of attacking antitrust entirely from the left as Galbraith does, he attacks it from the left but uses arguments one would expect from the right.

Thurow first argues that if antitrust laws have had any effect at all, it has been to hinder U.S. competitors in the international market. These U.S. firms must live by a code that their foreign competitors can ignore. Second, he belittles the idea of effective monopoly power on the basis that the general rise in income that the U.S. has experienced tends to greatly increase the relevant market in which firms compete. In other words, such goods as a Rolls Royce, a summer home, and a swimming pool are all in the same market. This expansion of the relevant market tends to limit the power of any one firm in any one market. Third, Thurow suggests that people should simply be smarter than to buy overpriced products, and the government has no business stopping people from making "silly decisions." Thurow also defends price premiums on the grounds that consumers are better off because their "psychic utility" has somehow been enhanced by the amount of the premium. Fourth, Thurow argues that even if a particular industry, such as breakfast cereals, is monopolized, our modern economy provides plenty of substitutes such as bacon and eggs. Finally, Thurow argues that conglomerate enterprises so enhance competition as to make the antitrust laws unnecessary. This is so because, according to Thurow, conglomerates are ever ready to enter any industry that earns high profits. In other words, Thurow argues that effective entry barriers do not exist in today's conglomerate-dominated economy.

For all these reasons Thurow sees no need for antitrust laws and argues that they should be dumped.

The arguments from the left by Galbraith and Thurow have been more or less a sideshow to the debate between the mainstream view and the Chicago school. The appeal of their message has apparently been limited.

Attack from the Right: The Chicago School

The debate between the mainstream view and the Chicago school has been developing at least since the mid-1960s. The debate leapt to the forefront of antitrust theory in 1974 with Columbia Law School's Conference on Industrial Concentration and the publication of its conference volume, *Industrial Concentration: The New Learning*. (See Baker and Blumenthal 1986.)

The Chicago school has as its major principles the following:

(1) The exclusive goal of the antitrust laws should be economic efficiency. Economic efficiency consists of two relevant parts: allocative efficiency and productive efficiency. All business conduct should be evaluated in terms of its contribution to efficiency as predicted by the neoclassical model of the firm, which assumes profit maximization. Since the model also assumes that rational decision makers are always motivated by a quest for greater efficiency, all disputes concerning the intent and consequences of particular practices should be resolved in favor of the business executives making them.

(2) Most markets are competitive, even if they contain a relatively small number of sellers. Industry concentration may not matter at all. Large firms are probably large because they are efficient. In addition, product differentiation tends to undermine competition far less than many economists believe.

(3) Monopoly, when it exists, tends to be self-correcting; that is, the monopolist's higher profits generally attract new entry into the market.

(4) Entry into many markets is relatively easy and many markets are contestable. As a general rule, investment will flow into any market where the rate of return is high. The one exception is in the case of government- created barriers to entry.

(5) Economies of scale are far more pervasive than economists once thought. Therefore, many industries operate most economically at fairly high levels of concentration.

(6) Technological change in many industries is quite rapid. A monopoly in a rapidly changing industry is little cause for antitrust concern because the monopoly will disappear before enforcement action could be effective.

(7) More and more industries function in international markets today. If a domestic cartel attempts to utilize market power and raise prices, a quick foreign response is often forthcoming.

(8) If the government tries to intervene in the market system, it will likely cause more problems than it solves.

(See Hovenkamp 1985; Mueller 1986; and Sims and Lande 1986.)

Based on these principles, the Chicagoists see a very limited role for antitrust laws. Some Chicagoists would use such laws to challenge blatant cartels, especially where the erosion of the cartel is hindered through government policies. And some would probably challenge single-firm monopolies, at least where natural market erosion is encumbered. Other Chicagoists would not even go this far.

Judge Frank H. Easterbrook's (1986) paper described the Chicago approach as a "profoundly skeptical program–skeptical of simple models, skeptical of simple analysis, skeptical of the ability of courts to make things better even with the best data" (p. 1701). Easterbrook points out that this skepticism is why Chicagoists favor little more than prosecuting "plain vanilla cartels" and monopolies.

Empirical Work

At the core of the debate between the mainstream view and the Chicago school has been the empirical work on both sides. An exhaustive survey of this work is beyond our scope here. What follows is a very brief sketch of the direction the empirical work has taken.

Joe Bain began the empirical inquiry with his study of concentration, entry barriers, and profits. He found a significant relationship between high concentration, high entry barriers, and high profit levels. Since then, the empiri-

255

cal work has been both vast and varied. (For reviews of the literature see Pautler 1983; Mueller 1986; and Harris and Sullivan 1986.) In the 1950s and 1960s most research followed Bain's lead and appeared to confirm the existence of a positive relationship between concentration and profits. Beginning in the 1970s, however, a reinterpretation of the concentration/profitability literature has been gaining adherents. Many of the findings of previous studies have been cast into doubt, and some new studies have found no relationship between market structure and profitability. But at the same time other relatively new studies have appeared that seem to reaffirm the structure-profitability relationship.

Members of the Chicago school have cited studies showing no relationship between structure and profits as support for their position. And they have argued that even if a positive relationship is found, their position is not challenged because increased efficiency can explain the increased profitability just as well as, if not better than, increased market power.

At present the empirical literature on structure and profits does not seem to overwhelmingly support either side of the debate; although some reviewers give an edge to the mainstreamers. The literature on market structure and profits is not the only available or relevant literature, however.

Other relevant literature includes several papers showing that concentration has a positive impact on *price*. These papers include studies of financial markets, the airline industry and the food industry. (See Kahn 1987 and Mueller 1986 for citations.) All of these studies showing a positive concentration-price relationship add weight to the mainstreamist side of the empirical debate.

Another relevant set of literature that adds weight to the mainstreamers view is the literature on market structure and X-inefficiency. Leibenstein (1979) has argued that market power can lead to X-inefficiency, where X-inefficiency is simply defined as excessive costs. Several papers have found that concentrated market structures lead to excessive labor costs. Other authors have argued that market power leads to inefficient work rules, inefficient purchasing practices, and/or excessive staffing. Harris and Sullivan (1986) have hypothesized that "if there is a Picasso in the CEO's conference room; if the firm has a well-financed corporate responsibility program; if the firm makes generous contributions to charity; if it buys significant amounts of time on public television; and/or if it engages in extensive image advertising, the firm has market power" (p. 922). The point Harris and Sullivan and other authors make is that firms with market power can enjoy the quiet life and may not worry unduly about minimizing costs. The implication is that concentration-profit studies cannot accurately measure the effect of market structure on performance because profitability is only one aspect of performance.

In sum, the empirical literature seems to favor the mainstream view of market structure and performance and therefore the mainstream view of antitrust enforcement.

In spite of this, the Chicago school still holds sway in the present-day world of antitrust law, so much so that many mainstreamers such as Willard F. Mueller and William G. Shepherd are quite worried about the future of capitalism. William Shepherd (1986) has stated that if the enemies of antitrust succeed in removing the foundations of antitrust law, as they are now succeeding, "there will be great economic mischief for many decades to come and, worse, the integrity of capitalism itself will be in danger" (p. 27).

References: The Antitrust Debate

Baker, Donald I., and Blumenthal, William. "Ideological Cycles and Unstable Antitrust Rules." *Antitrust Bulletin* 31 (Summer 1986), pp. 323-339.

Easterbrook, Frank H. "Workable Antitrust Policy." *Michigan Law Review* 84 (August 1986), pp. 1696-1713.

Galbraith, John Kenneth. *The New Industrial State*. Boston: Houghton Mifflin, 1978.

Harris, Robert G., and Sullivan, Lawrence A. "Horizontal Merger Policy: Promoting Competition and American Competitiveness." *Antitrust Bulletin* 31 (Winter 1986), pp. 871-933.

Hovenkamp, Herbert. "Antitrust Policy After Chicago." *Michigan Law Review* 84 (November 1985), pp. 213-84.

Kahn, Alfred E. "Deregulatory Schizophrenia." *California Law Review* 75 (1987), pp. 1059-68.

Leibenstein, H. "X-Efficiency: From Concept to Theory." *Challenge* (September-October 1979), pp. 13-22.

Mueller, Willard F. "The Anti-antitrust Movement and the Case of Lester Thurow." *Antitrust Law & Economics Review* 13, no. 3 (1983), pp. 59-91.

_____. "A New Attack on Antitrust: The Chicago Case." *Antitrust Law & Economics Review* 18, no. 1 (1986), pp. 29-66.

Pautler, Paul A. "A Review of the Economic Basis for Broad-based Horizontal-merger Policy." *Antitrust Bulletin* 28 (Fall 1983), pp. 571-651.

Shepherd, William G. "The Twilight of Antitrust." *Antitrust Law & Economics Review* 18, no. 1 (1986), pp. 21-27.

Sims, Joe, and Lande, Robert H. "The End of Antitrust-or a New Beginning." *Antitrust Bulletin* 31 (Summer 1986), pp. 301-22.

COMPETITION AND PRODUCTIVITY

In the past, most of the literature on productivity has ignored the effects of competition among firms on productivity growth. This is so mainly because of the neoclassical roots of productivity research. In recent years, however, a few economists have suggested that the neoclassical framework cannot fully explain the forces influencing productivity advance. Among those few economists, Burton H. Klein in particular has suggested that competition among firms is a major factor influencing the rate of productivity advance.

The neoclassical model of productivity growth has as its wellhead the work of Robert Solow. In a 1957 empirical article, Solow showed how to attribute output growth to the growth of inputs and technological advance. Solow's model assumes firms to be the key productive actors that transform inputs into outputs according to a production function. The production function defines the maximum output achievable with any given quantity of inputs and is determined by technological knowledge. Technological knowledge is assumed to be public. Firms are assumed to be profit maximizers, and markets are usually assumed to be perfectly competitive. The model attributes output growth to increases in inputs as firms move along their production function and to technology advances that shift the production function. Proportional output growth due to input growth along the production function equals the sum of share-weighted proportional input growths. The residual is defined by Solow to be a measure of technological advance. (See Nelson 1981 for a review.)

This neoclassical growth model, also known as the growth accounting model, has been used by many authors to try to identify the sources of productivity growth. As in Solow's model of economic growth, authors have attributed productivity growth to the share-weighted proportional growth of inputs and a residual. Significant efforts have been made to identify changes in the inputs. Thus, the labor input has been disaggregated according to education, sex, and age. And the capital input has been disaggregated into machinery and structures, and its vintage has been considered. These efforts have largely been aimed at reducing the size of the residual. Identification of the various "leftover" factors that affect the residual has also been the subject of much research. Reviews of this literature can be found in Denison (1979) and Kendrick and Grossman (1980).

As pointed out, the neoclassical or growth accounting model simply assumes that perfectly competitive conditions exist. Most authors appear to accept this assumption with little critical analysis and without mention of the importance of this assumption. Therefore, competition is usually not mentioned as having a major influence on productivity. For instance, Edward Denison, one of the foremost authorities on the growth accounting model of productivity, noted in

1979 that competitive pressure may have influenced the residual in his model by affecting the quality of management. But in 1984 he rejected this possibility and made no other mention of competition.

One of the few growth-accounting economists to recognize the importance of the assumption of competitive markets is John W. Kendrick. Kendrick (1977) argues that the major factor influencing productivity growth is investment spending, which affects the development of the inputs. He defines investment spending broadly to include outlays for tangible goods or capital formation and for intangible goods such as education. He specifically recognizes that within his framework competition performs the critical function of ensuring the efficient allocation of resources. In 1984 Kendrick again points out the important effect competition has on productivity growth. He argues that "throughout most of American history, main reliance for increasing productivity has been placed on the workings of competitive markets" (p. 387). He uses this point to argue that the United States should continue to rely on competitive markets and should avoid attempts to stimulate productivity via national productivity or industrial policies.

Richard Nelson (1981) suggests that evidence exists of unrest in the economics profession over the inability of the neoclassical model to adequately explain productivity growth. This unrest is at least partly the result of the model's inability to adequately explain the slowdown in productivity that occurred after 1967 and especially after 1973. He reviews several areas of research in which economists have deviated significantly from the tenets of the neoclassical theory. One of these areas is evolutionary modeling of economic growth. Evolutionary modeling differs significantly from neoclassical modeling in its dynamic (as opposed to static) analysis.

Neoclassical models of productivity growth assume that firms are profit maximizers and that the industry and economy as a whole are in equilibrium. The equilibrium concept, as it is usually employed, depicts a static economic system. This presumption makes the analysis of such phenomena as diffusion, competition, and other dynamic processes extremely difficult. To overcome this problem some economists have looked to the dynamic analysis biology provides in its evolutionary theory and have attempted to apply a similar analysis to economic systems. Nelson notes that evolutionary modeling is primitive when compared to neoclassical modeling and involves more complexity than economists are used to dealing with. But productivity growth is a complex, dynamic process that can best be explained using dynamic models.

Burton H. Klein (1977, 1984, 1988) has provided an evolutionary description and model of productivity growth with competition at its core. His 1988 paper, which foreshadows a soon-to-be-published book, is the focus of the following paragraphs.

Klein (1988) argues that the driving force in economics is the competitive games firms play: economic and technological progress is most rapid when those games are positive-sum games. Positive-sum games are characterized by a high degree of opportunistic risk taking. Opportunistic risk taking, when it is successful and results in innovations, puts pressure on other firms to take risks and to be dynamically flexible. Dynamic flexibility is defined as the ability to make speedy adaptations in the face of new circumstances. Dynamic flexibility, according to Klein, is the key to the innovation and productivity growth process. And dynamic flexibility is the result of competitive pressures. In fact, Klein states that, "it is the quest to remain competitive that is the fundamental reason why productivity gains come about" (p. 4). In essence, Klein's argument is that competitive pressure leads firms to pursue dynamically flexible strategies which are characterized by a high degree of opportunistic risk taking. The result is a positive-sum game.

To support this hypothesis, Klein first analyzes the internal workings of several highly productive firms. He finds that these firms place a great deal of emphasis on dynamic flexibility, and competition is the primary motivating factor.

As further support of his hypothesis of productivity growth, Klein examines productivity growth of all manufacturing industries in the United States as it relates to the degree of competition. He hypothesizes that "in the era before the U.S. economy was challenged by foreign competition, firms in many uncompetitive industries, including automobiles, tended to become overly specialized and routinized–and, as such, became highly adapted to a very slowly changing environment. Hence, a lack of dynamic flexibility prevented both the realization of larger productivity gains and better results in international competition" (p. 24). To test this hypothesis, Klein formulates a model that has three principal assumptions. First, the differences in the propensity to engage in risk (PERK) are smaller within industries than between industries. This implies that competition between firms in an industry forces firms to undertake the same average level of risk. Second, a high degree of risk taking in developing new products goes hand in hand with splendid productivity performance. And the primary condition necessary for a high degree of risk taking is the new entry of firms into an industry, either in the form of new establishments or in the form of foreign competition. Third, when the value of PERK is fairly high and luck and necessity go hand in hand, productivity gains at the level of both the firm and the industry come about in the form of highly irregular cycles having no relation to the business cycle.

To test this model, Klein argues that the value of PERK can be inferred from the relative price performance of an industry. The basis of this argument is that firms typically compete by lowering the prices of their less-expensive products and improving the quality of their more-expensive products. However, even in the latter case, such competition occurs within tight price constraints. Thus, by looking at relative price restraint, which implies the level of PERK, Klein argues that predictions can be made about the relative rates of productivity advance. Klein divides all 387 four-digit manufacturing industries into four groups, based on their price performance during the 1960s and again during the 1970s. The A group is comprised of industries that, during either or both periods, raised their prices one standard deviation or more less than the average, which means that there was a marked decline in their relative prices. The D group is comprised of industries which, during either or both periods, raised their prices one standard deviation or more above the average. The B and C groups were obtained by splitting the middle of the distribution.

Of the total 387 industries, 145 exhibited roughly the same degree of price restraint during the 1970s as during the 1960s (that is the A's remained A's, the B's remained B's, and so on). Of this group, Klein found that those industries with the highest inferred values of PERK (that is, those exhibiting the most price restraint) had the highest rate of productivity advance. About one-third of the industries (136 out of 387) exhibited more price restraint in the 1970s than in the 1960s. And about one-fourth of the industries (106 out of 387) exhibited less price restraint in the 1970s than in the 1960s. Klein found that those moving up in terms of relative price restraint had a far greater average rate of productivity advance than did those moving down in relative price restraint.

Klein also found that the primary factor leading firms to restrain prices was import competition. Industries exhibiting strong price restraint tendencies were primarily those facing stiff import competition. Industries exhibiting weak price restraint tendencies were primarily those that for one reason or another were shielded from import competition. In addition, Klein found that those industries with high PERK were involved in positive-sum games in terms of output.

Klein's model of productivity growth is undoubtedly less elegant than many of those following the neoclassical theory. His measure of competitive pressure or PERK is indirect, and his theory is somewhat conjectural. Yet in at least one important respect Klein's model is superior to neoclassical models. Klein's model recognizes that productivity growth is a dynamic process. In the end, a model should be judged not on its elegance but on its relationship to the real world.

References: Competition and Productivity

Denison, Edward F. *Accounting for Slower Economic Growth*. Washington, D.C.: Brookings Institution, 1979.

____. "Accounting for Slower Economic Growth: An Update." in John W. Kendrick (ed.), *International Comparisons of Productivity and Causes of the Slowdown*. Cambridge, MA: Ballinger, Publishing Co., 1984.

Kendrick, John W. *Understanding Productivity: An Introduction to the Dynamics of Productivity Change*. Baltimore: Johns Hopkins University Press, 1977.

____. "U.S. Economic Policy and Productivity Growth." *Cato Journal* 4 (Fall 1984), pp. 387-400.

Kendrick, John W., and Grossman, E. *Productivity in the United States: Trends and Cycles*. Baltimore: Johns Hopkins University Press, 1980.

Klein, Burton H. *Dynamic Economics*. Cambridge, MA: Harvard University Press, 1977.

____. *Prices, Wages, and Business Cycles: A Dynamic Theory*. New York: Pergamon Press, 1984.

____. "Making Luck and Necessity Go Hand in Hand." Mimeo from author, 1988.

Nelson, Richard R. "Research on Productivity Growth and Productivity Differences: Dead Ends and New Departures." *Journal of Economic Literature* 19 (September 1981), pp. 1029-64.

Solow, Robert M. "Technical Change and the Aggregate Production Function." *Review of Economics and Statistics* 39 (August 1957), pp. 214-31.

COMPETITION FOR FOREIGN INVESTMENT
AMONG DEVELOPING COUNTRIES

The role foreign investment plays in less-developed countries is an oft-debated subject in the literature. Foreign investment has been both castigated for promoting exploitation and dependency and praised for promoting development and growth. Policies to either limit foreign investment or encourage it have been pursued by various nations, depending on their viewpoint. Recently, however, a growing number of developing countries seem to have shucked their fears of being exploited and are beginning to compete with each other to attract foreign investment. In the following paragraphs we review evidence in the literature and from economic reports prepared by U.S. embassies to support this observation.

The Literature

In a 1981 address before the Economic Policy Council of the United Nations, Robert D. Hormats, Assistant Secretary for Economic and Business Affairs, stated that "increasingly many countries are turning to investment incentives to attract foreign investment in specific industries." He noted that this trend was likely to continue throughout the 1980s and that the 1980s were likely to be a time of intense competition for foreign investment, especially among developing countries. Hormats stated that a major reason for this increase in competition for foreign investments was the slowing in investment flows and the relative capital scarcity of the 1980s.

Harvey D. Shapiro (1983) has documented the trend that Secretary Hormats alluded to. Shapiro notes that a shift to foreign investment among developing countries is picking up momentum. He believes this trend to be the result of efforts by developing countries to deal with the "twin LDC demons—overindebtedness and underdevelopment" (p. 209). Shapiro also notes many examples of countries pursuing policies aimed at attracting foreign investments. Among these countries are Sudan, Tanzania, Jamaica, India, Egypt, Indonesia, the Philippines, Turkey, Brazil, Algeria, Mexico and China. He concludes that "it's clear that an increasingly integrated global economic system is emerging—one that is largely a market system, not a system run by a dictatorship of the proletariat or a former army colonel" (p. 212). And those nations opting to participate in this global system must open up their domestic economies to investment from abroad.

Jurgen Kuhn (1984), of the West German Federal Ministry of Economics, has also noted that an opening toward the outside economic world is occurring among developing nations, and that many such nations are moving to attract foreign investment. He argues that the example of several countries that have pursued open policies toward foreign investment is beginning to convince even those skeptics who, for ideological reasons, previously tended to view foreign capital simply as a source of exploitation and a restriction imposed upon national sovereignty. Kuhn believes that the international debt crisis has accelerated this change of attitude.

In 1985 the United Nations Centre on Transnational Corporations published its third survey of Transnational Corporations in World Development. As part of this survey, trends in the policies of developing nations toward foreign investment were analyzed. The Centre's survey places developing nations into one of three groups depending on their foreign investment policies. The first group consists of developing nations that have traditionally maintained liberal policies toward foreign investment, but have been unable to attract significant investments because of the small size of their markets or their limited natural resources. The Centre's study found that most of these countries have been intensifying their efforts to promote new foreign investment flows. A second group consists of developing countries that established control-oriented regulatory mechanisms in the early 1970s. These countries typically have lucrative domestic markets, natural resources, or other significant inducements to foreign investors. And these countries have attracted the bulk of the foreign investment in the past. The Centre's study indicates that this group of countries has recently shown a considerable liberalization of policies toward foreign investment. The third group of countries in the study includes nations that originally excluded or severely restricted foreign investments. Included in this group are several socialist countries. The Centre's survey indicates that many of these countries are now moving to reverse their previously restrictive policies.

The Centre's study notes that several factors account for these policy changes. Many developing countries have recently experienced severe balance-of-payments difficulties, sluggish economic growth, and other economic problems. The establishment of an attractive climate to encourage the inflow of foreign capital and the promotion of export-oriented or import-substituting investments has been seen as a way to help solve these problems. In addition, over the past years, many countries have gained experience and expertise in dealing with foreign investment and in the process have gained confidence in their ability to use such investment to develop their countries without being exploited.

A study not unlike the Centre's is that of Katherin Marton (1986, December 1986). Marton looked not at developing nations' policies toward foreign investment but at their policies toward foreign technology. She found that a few nations, during the 1970s, adopted policies to explicitly regulate foreign technology. But in the 1980s most of these countries pursued policies of increasing relaxation and liberalization in terms of their regulatory content. Her study, like other studies, indicates that developing countries are increas–

ingly concerned with improving their business environments in order to attract foreign investment.

Stephen E. Guisinger and Associates (1985) conducted a study for the World Bank of competition for foreign investment among developing countries. Their objective was to assess the intensity of competition and determine the effectiveness of incentives and performance requirements in altering the investment and operational decisions of foreign investors. The study was conducted by a team that gathered information on foreign investment decisions of companies from interviews with corporate executives and government officials. Four industries were intensively analyzed: automobiles, computers, food products, and petrochemicals. In all, more than thirty companies were interviewed, from which more than seventy investment decisions spread over twenty host countries were selected for study.

Results of the study indicate that "the intensity of competition among countries for foreign investment was an important determinant of policy choices." In fact, "it was hard to explain a country's foreign investment strategy without taking into account the type of competitors it faced and the strategies that competitor countries deployed" (p. 10).

In summary of the literature, studies reviewed here indicate that competition for foreign investment is an important element of developing countries' present-day environment. The studies also indicate that the 1980s have witnessed and are continuing to witness a trend toward increasing competition among developing nations for foreign investment as more and more countries step up their efforts to attract foreign capital. Causes of this increasingly competitive environment include the stagnation, overindebtedness, and consequent increased need for capital of many developing nations; the example of several very successful countries that have used foreign investment to their advantage; and the reduction in the concern of developing countries' governments over being exploited that has come about as they have gained experience in dealing with transnational corporations.

Embassy Economic Reports

To gain further insight into LDC competition for foreign investment, we looked at economic reports prepared by U.S. embassies around the world and published in 1985 (U.S. Department of Commerce 1985). Approximately every two years, United States embassies throughout the world prepare reviews of investment climates in their respective host countries. These reviews include information on the laws and policies pertaining to foreign investment; the condition and quality of host country infrastructure; the state of the host country's economy; and host country policies in the areas of taxation, nationalization, foreign exchange, investment incentives, and performance requirements. The conclusion we reached from an analysis of these reports is that most developing countries are indeed improving their business environments in an effort to attract more foreign investment.

To ascertain whether a particular country is or is not improving its investment climate we carefully studied the embassy's review of the country and made two observations. First, we observed the country's current investment climate and assigned each country a rank from 1 to 6 depending on how liberal or restrictive the country's current investment climate is. If a particular country has very few restrictions on foreign investment including the type of ownership arrangements allowed, industries that can be entered by foreigners, geographic locations that can be utilized, and so on, and the country has very few performance requirements such as local content laws, then the country is assigned the "liberal" current investment climate classification and given the rank of 1. At the other extreme, if a country severely restricts foreign investment and has many performance requirements, then it is assigned the "restrictive" current investment climate classification and given the rank of 6. Recognizing that the liberal or restrictive nature of a country's policies is a matter of degree, we assigned the countries to one of six separate "current investment climate" classifications (1 to 6) roughly corresponding to liberal (1), fairly liberal (2), moderately liberal (3), moderately restrictive (4), fairly restrictive (5), and restrictive (6).

Second, we observed recent or anticipated *changes* in a country's foreign investment policies, and assigned each country a classification ranging from "improving" to "regressing" depending on the nature of the changes. The specific classifications are "improving," "no change," and "regressing." The "improving" classification indicates that a country has made or is making changes in policies or laws the intent of which is to attract more foreign investment. The "no change" classification indicates that a country has not and is not making changes in policies or laws concerning foreign investment. The "regressing" category indicates that a country is moving to further restrict foreign investment.

Table B.1 shows the 111 developing countries involved in this analysis, as well as their current investment climate rank and their "improving," "no change," or "regressing" classification. The countries are also placed in one of the following four categories depending on their per capita income: low-income countries, lower-middle-income countries, upper-middle-income countries, and high-income oil exporters.

266

TABLE B.1 INVESTMENT CLIMATE IN FOREIGN COUNTRIES

Country	Current Investment Climate	Recent Policy Changes
Low-Income Countries		
Bangladesh	5	improving
Benin	2	improving
Burkina Faso	4	no change
Burma	6	no change
Burundi	4	no change
Central Afr. Rep.	2	improving
Chad	3	no change
China	5	improving
Equatorial Guinea	4	no change
Ethiopia	6	improving
Ghana	4	improving
Guinea	3	improving
Haiti	3	improving
India	5	improving
Kenya	4	improving
Laos	6	regressing
Madagascar	5	improving
Malawi	2	improving
Mali	5	improving
Mozambique	3	improving
Nepal	5	no change
Pakistan	4	improving
Niger	2	improving
Rwanda	3	regressing
Senegal	3	no change
Somalia	4	improving
Sri Lanka	5	improving
Sudan	5	no change
Tanzania	5	no change
Togo	2	improving
Uganda	3	improving
Zaire	3	improving
Zambia	5	no change

Lower-Middle-Income Countries

Belize	3	improving
Bolivia	4	no change
Botswana	2	improving
Cameroon	2	improving
Cape Verde	5	no change
Chile	2	improving
Colombia	5	improving
Congo	3	improving
Costa Rica	4	improving
Dominica	2	improving
Dominican Republic	4	improving
Ecuador	3	improving
Egypt	5	improving
El Salvador	3	improving
Grenada	4	improving
Guatemala	2	no change
Guinea-Bissau	5	improving
Guyana	5	improving
Honduras	3	improving
Indonesia	5	improving
Ivory Coast	2	improving
Jamaica	3	improving
Jordan	4	improving
Lesotho	2	no change
Liberia	3	improving
Mauritania	3	improving
Mauritius	3	improving
Morocco	3	improving
Nicaragua	5	regressing
Nigeria	5	no change
Papua New Guinea	3	no change
Paraguay	5	improving
Peru	3	no change
Philippines	4	no change
Seychelles	4	regressing
St. Kitts-Nevis	2	improving
St. Lucia	2	improving
St. Vincent	2	no change
Swaziland	1	improving
Syria	6	no change
Thailand	4	improving
Tunisia	3	improving

Turkey	2	improving
Yemen Arab Rep.	3	improving
Zimbabwe	4	no change

Upper-Middle-Income Countries

Algeria	6	no change
Argentina	3	improving
Bahamas	3	improving
Brazil	3	no change
Djibouti	1	improving
Fiji	3	improving
Gabon	3	improving
Greece	5	improving
Hong Kong	1	no change
Hungary	6	improving
Iraq	6	no change
Israel	2	improving
Malaysia	4	no change
Malta	4	improving
Mexico	5	improving
Netherlands Ant.	2	improving
Oman	4	no change
Panama	2	improving
Portugal	3	improving
Rumania	6	improving
Singapore	2	improving
South Africa	1	no change
South Korea	3	improving
Surinam	5	regressing
Taiwan	3	improving
Trinidad & Tobago	4	no change
Uruguay	4	no change
Venezuela	5	improving
Yugoslavia	6	improving

High-Income Oil Exporters

Kuwait	4	no change
Qatar	6	no change
Saudi Arabia	4	regressing
United Arab Emir.	4	no change

Table B.2 summarizes the information contained in table B.1

TABLE B.2   SUMMARY STATISTICS

Current Investment Climate	Improving	No Change	Regressing
Low-Income Countries			
1 (liberal)	0	0	0
2 (fairly liberal)	5	0	0
3 (moderately liberal)	5	2	1
4 (moderately restrictive)	4	3	0
5 (fairly restrictive)	6	4	0
6 (restrictive)	1	1	1
Total	21	10	2
Lower-Middle-Income Countries			
1 (liberal)	1	0	0
2 (fairly liberal)	8	3	0
3 (moderately liberal)	12	2	0
4 (moderately restrictive)	5	3	1
5 (fairly restrictive)	6	2	1
6 (restrictive)	0	1	0
Total	32	11	2
Upper-Middle-Income Countries			
1 (liberal)	1	2	0
2 (fairly liberal)	4	0	0
3 (moderately liberal)	7	1	0
4 (moderately restrictive)	1	4	0
5 (fairly restrictive)	3	0	1
6 (restrictive)	3	2	0
Total	19	9	1
High-Income Oil Exporters			
1 (liberal)	0	0	0
2 (fairly liberal)	0	0	0
3 (moderately liberal)	0	0	0
4 (moderately restrictive)	0	2	1
5 (fairly restrictive)	0	0	0
6 (restrictive)	0	1	0
Total	0	3	1

All Countries

1 (liberal)	2	2	0
2 (fairly liberal)	17	3	0
3 (moderately liberal)	24	5	1
4 (moderately restrictive) 10	12	2	
5 (fairly restrictive)	15	6	2
6 (restrictive)	4	5	1
Total	**72**	**33**	**6**

Table B.2 indicates that a large majority of all developing countries we studied are striving to improve their investment climates to attract more foreign investment. In fact, 65 percent of all countries fall in the "improving" category while only 30 percent fall in the "no change" category and 5 percent fall in the "regressing category." These results generally hold for developing countries in the low-income to upper-middle-income groups. Only in the high-income oil-exporters group do we find a majority of countries not opening up their economies to foreign investment. High-income oil-exporting countries are the exception because with their abundance of wealth they have less need to attract additional foreign investment in order to either alleviate debt problems or promote development.

Table B.2 also shows that most countries are moving to improve their investment climates no matter whether such climates are currently liberal or restrictive.

The results of this review of the embassies' reports must be qualified by recognizing the subjective nature of both the original source of information and the analysis presented here. The original source of information is subjective because U.S. embassy personnel in compiling their reports must interpret and summarize a myriad of policies and laws in the host country. Our analysis of the embassy information is subjective because without actually interviewing officials from each individual country it is difficult to know how flexible the policies and laws governing foreign investment are in practice.

Even with this qualification, the results presented here are strong enough to leave little doubt that a majority of all developing countries are moving to attract more foreign investment. This is consistent with the literature reviewed earlier.

References: Competition for Foreign Investment among Developing Countries

Guisinger, Stephen E., and Associates. *Investment Incentives and Performance Requirements: Patterns of International Trade, Production, and Investment.* New York: Praeger, 1985.

Hormats, Robert D. "New Challenges in International Investment." *Current Policy No. 316*, Washington, DC: U.S. Department of State, September 18, 1981.

Kuhn, Jurgen. "Developing Countries Rethink Their Approach to Foreign Investment." *Intereconomics* (November/December 1984), pp. 280-84.

Marton, Katherin. *Multinationals, Technology, and Industrialization.* Lexington MA: D.C. Heath and Co., 1986.

___. "Technology Transfer to Developing Countries via Multinationals." *World Economy* 9 (December 1986), pp. 409-26.

Shapiro, Harvey D. "LDC's: Courting the Private Investor." *Institutional Investor* 17 (November 1983), pp. 209-12.

United Nations Centre on Transnational Corporations. *Transnational Corporations in World Development: Third Survey.* London: Graham & Trotman Limited, 1985.

U.S. Department of Commerce, International Trade Administration. *Investment Climate in Foreign Countries* I-IV (August 1985).

HOW DO UNIONS AFFECT CORPORATE PROFITS?

Recent studies attempting to empirically demonstrate a relationship between unionization and profits confront problems common to most labor studies, including the determination and measurement of the dependent (profit) variable and accurate model specification. The model specification problem relates to the endogenous/exogenous nature of the union variable. Regardless of these problems, all current studies using single-stage models (that is, assuming exogenously determined unionism) find that unions reduce profits, notwithstanding the profit measure used. The finding that unions lower profits implies that profit studies that do not explicitly allow for union effects may underestimate the actual profits of firms with market power.

Another issue commonly addressed in these studies is monopoly rent and its distribution. This issue generally is considered in its relation to the union wage effect. The inquiry is directed at determining if the union wage effect comes from monopoly rents or is in fact paid for from some other source, either by consumers through higher prices, or, interestingly, through unions capturing Ricardian rents, which accrue to long-term capital. Union effects paid for from monopoly profits infer a benign effect, while other sources imply resource misallocation (Hirsch and Addison 1986).

Aside from the similar finding that unions lower profits, few other areas of general agreement can be found in the literature. Two studies address the issue of whether unionization should be treated as endogenous as opposed to exogenous. Both find that treating unionization as endogenous significantly affects the results of their studies, albeit in opposing directions. One study by Caves, Porter, Spence, and Scott (1980), using Canadian data, found that the union variable loses its significance in a simultaneous estimation. The other study by Voos and Mishel (January 1986) found that making unionization endogenous actually increases its significance. Voos and Mishel looked at a number of specifications, and although results differed slightly, all supported the general conclusion that unions have a negative effect on profits. These conflicting results may be due to different data sets (Canadian vs. U.S.), or they may be due to different model specifications. Whatever the cause, based on these two studies, no conclusion can be made regarding the effect of such treatment.

Results vary somewhat in assessing unions' impact on profits in various market structures (concentrated vs competitive). Clark (1982), using data for product-line businesses rather than industries, found that unions have a significant impact on the profits of firms with product market shares of less than 10 percent (theoretically competitive firms) but have little effect on profits of firms with market share greater than 35 percent (theoretically noncompetitive firms). Clark attributed this to noncompetitive firms' greater ability to pass price increases on to consumers without having their profit margins affected. Clark's study has been criticized for covering only the largest corporations in the United States and thus being unrepresentative of the U.S. economy. Conversely, studies by Freeman and Medoff (1984), Karier (1985, 1988), and Voos and Mishel (August 1986) found opposing results.

Freeman and Medoff looked at three different data bases, regressing the price-cost margin and the return on capital on unionization and various other independent variables for each data set. Their data sets were 139 manufacturing industries (1958-76), 168 Internal Revenue Service major industries (1965-76), and state-by-industry data for 400 observations in 1972 and 360 observations in 1977. Freeman and Medoff found that unionism significantly lowers profitability in concentrated firms but does not affect the profitability of competitive firms. Karier (1985) used price-cost margins calculated from data in the 1972 Census of Manufactures. His analysis supports the view that unionization interacts with concentration to affect the profits of concentrated and moderately concentrated industries but does not affect the profits of competitive industries. In 1988 Karier published a follow-up study that used basically the same data but incorporated controls for import levels. He again found evidence that unions reduce profits more in concentrated industries than in competitive industries. Voos and Mishel (August 1986) in an analysis of the supermarket industry found that while unions reduce profit margins in all unionized supermarkets, they reduce profits more in concentrated markets than in competitive markets. They found that unions reduce profits in concentrated markets by 65.8 percent but in competitive markets by only 13.2 percent.

These studies suggest that noncompetitive market structures augment labor unions' ability to redistribute rents from capital owners to laborers.

Several studies have addressed the issue of how much unions actually capture of the monopoly rents in the U.S. economy. In the first, Michael Salinger (1984) used Tobin's q as a measure of monopoly rent. Tobin's q is the ratio of the market value of a firm to the replacement value of its physical assets. He found that in the U.S. economy, Tobin's q is quite low. This implies that monopoly rents are generally not being earned in the United States or that unions are capturing most of the monopoly rents in the economy. When Salinger made explicit allowance for unionization, he found that unions were capturing most of the economy's monopoly rents. He estimated that in the average firm, unions capture 90-100 percent of the monopoly rents. Tobin's q, however, has been the object of much criticism when it is used as a measure of monopoly rents (see this appendix, "Measures of Monopoly Power"). Therefore, results from studies using Tobin's q to measure monopoly rents should be viewed with caution.

The Karier (1985) study also examined this issue. Karier found that in the concentrated sector, unions capture 68 percent of the monopoly profits on average. For industries with nearly 100 percent unionization, such as transportation equipment and primary metals, he argued that unions capture virtually all of the monopoly profits. In his second study (1988), Karier found somewhat lower estimates. He found that total monopoly profits are divided between imports (14 percent), unions (47 percent), and firms (39 percent). Karier's studies, like most other studies examining monopoly rents, suffer from the problem of accurately measuring monopoly and/or monopoly profits. Karier used concentration as a measure of monopoly and census-based price-cost margins as a measure of monopoly profits. Both have been criticized in the literature (see this appendix, "Measures of Monopoly Power").

Voos and Mishel (January 1986) examined a similar yet different aspect of the union profit effect. They asked how much of the union wage effect could be paid for through union-induced reductions in the profit level. Under their assumption that the union profit effect is constant across all levels of unionization, Voos and Mishel estimated that from 80 percent to 100 percent of the union wage effect could be paid for from union-induced reductions in profits. When they dropped the assumption that the union profit effect is constant across all levels of unionization, these researchers still found that at least 45 percent of the union wage effect could be paid for from the union profit effect. Voos and Mishel, like Karier, used census-based price-cost margins as their measure of profits. Because of the question of whether census-based price-cost margins accurately measure profits, their results must be viewed with caution.

In a theoretical work, Baldwin (1983) speculated that unions could conceivably capture returns to long-term capital. This would happen in a situation where an industry had substantial long-lived capital investment. Baldwin states that once the fixed capital is in place, "it is economically advantageous to keep a facility open as long as revenues are greater than ongoing cost. Knowing this, an adversary such as a labor union may be able to expropriate the surplus that provides the return to capital" (p. 155). The theory also explains that informed investors would then react by lowering investment, thereby producing in a less-than-optimum manner, given no union extraction of capital rents. If this is the case, then unions induce a misallocation of resources.

An additional noteworthy study, by Ruback and Zimmerman (1984), looks at union profit effects via changes in the price of corporate stocks during the period when a union petition and election is being conducted. Ruback and Zimmerman estimate the normal return of a stock from looking at a sixty-month period before the union petition and a sixty-month period after the union election certification. Any movement in the stock away from its normal return during the election period is assumed to be due to union activity. The authors found that union elections significantly reduce the equity of the involved firm. This implies that unions have a negative impact on corporate profits.

This approach has at least two drawbacks that cast doubt on its conclusions. First, this approach assumes that any movement away from the "normal" price during an election period is due to election activity. Perhaps union activity is not the only causal factor. Second, this approach implicitly assumes the validity of the efficient market theory but gives no empirical evidence or overwhelming theoretical basis to support it.

In general, the literature agrees that unions lower the profitability of firms. And a consensus seems to be emerging that unions affect profits more in concentrated industries than in competitive industries. In addition, several studies have examined the issue of how much of the monopoly rents in the economy unions actually capture. These studies seem to indicate that unions capture a considerable portion of the monopoly rents in the economy. Problems with the measurement of monopoly rents preclude hard and fast conclusions and suggest the need for more research on this issue, however.

References: How Do Unions Affect Corporate Profits

Baldwin, Carliss Y. "Productivity and Labor Unions: An Application of the Theory of Self-enforcing Contracts," *Journal of Business* 56 (April 1983), pp. 155-85.

Caves, Richard E.; Porter, Michael E.; Spence, A. Michael; and Scott, John T. *Competition in the Open Economy: A Model Applied to Canada*. Cambridge MA: Harvard University Press, 1980.

Clark, Kim B. "Unionization and Firm Performance: The Impact on Profits, Growth and Productivity. *NBER Working Paper* no. 990, (September 1982).

_____. "Unionization and Firm Performance: The Impact on Profits, Growth, and Productivity." *American Economic Review* 74 (July 1984), pp. 893-919.

Freeman, Richard B. and Medoff, James L. *What Do Unions Do?* New York: Basic Books, 1984.

Hirsch, Barry T., and Addison John T. *The Economic Analysis of Unions: New Approaches and Evidence*. Winchester MA: Allen & Unwin, Winchester, 1986.

Karier, Thomas. "Unions and Monopoly Profits." *Review of Economics and Statistics* 58 (February 1985), pp. 34-42.

___. "New Evidence on the Effect of Unions and Imports on Monopoly Power." *Journal of Post Keynesian Economics* 10 (Spring 1988), pp. 414-27.

Ruback, Richard S., and Zimmerman, Martin B. "Unionization and Profitability: Evidence from the Capital Market." *Journal of Political Economy* 92 (December 1984), pp. 1134-57.

Salinger, Michael A. "Tobin's q, Unionization and the Concentration-Profits Relationship." *Rand Journal of Economics* 15 (Summer 1984), pp. 159-70.

Voos, Paula B. and Mishel, Lawrence R. "The Union Impact on Profits: Evidence from Industry Price-Cost Margin Data." *Journal of Labor Economics* 4 (January 1986), pp. 105-33.

____. "The Union Impact on Profits in the Supermarket Industry." *Review of Economics and Statistics* 68 (August 1986), pp. 513-17.

MARKET STRUCTURE AND INNOVATION

Three views relating market structure to innovative activity can be found in the literature. First, classical economists believe that a perfectly competitive market structure will bring about optimal innovative performance. These economists follow Adam Smith's (1937) tradition in their belief that the "invisible hand" will operate among many atomistic firms to bring forth innovation and progress. Second, economists following Joseph Schumpeter (1947) believe that a monopoly-profit potential must exist in an economy to induce innovative activity among entrepreneurs. These economists believe that a less-than-competitive market structure will bring about optimal innovative performance whereas a perfectly competitive one will not. Finally, those following John Kenneth Galbraith (1956) agree with Schumpeter in his rejection of perfectly competitive market structure but for different reasons. Galbraith and his followers argue that only large firms with vast resources have the wherewithal to undertake the large R & D projects necessary to produce new innovations in today's economy. Firm size, not monopoly power, is the key variable in the Galbraithian argument.

Empirical literature on this subject has not provided overwhelming support for any of the three views. Nonetheless, the literature seems to indicate that a market structure somewhere between atomistic competition and pure monopoly is optimal in terms of innovative performance.

The relationship between market structure and innovative activity has been empirically examined in several ways. Researchers have tested for relationships between (1) firm size and innovative input, (2) firm size and innovative output, (3) concentration and innovative input, (4) concentration and innovative output, and (5) other aspects of market structure and innovative activity. Studies examining firm size are considered tests of the Galbraith hypothesis. Firm size is used in these studies to measure the effect of "bigness" on innovation. Studies examining concentration are considered tests of the Schumpeter hypothesis. Concentration ratios are used as proxy variables for market power, and therefore these studies test the relationship between market power and innovation.

Firm Size and Innovative Input

Studies relating firm size to innovative input typically use one of several different variables to measure the level of innovative input. R & D spending and employment of R & D personnel are the two most widely used variables to measure innovative input. These studies test the hypothesis that large firms devote a greater proportion of their activity to R & D than do smaller firms.

Horowitz (1962) used research expenditures per sales dollar to measure the level of innovative input, and value added to measure firm size. He found a weak positive correlation between innovative input and firm size. Hamberg (1966), using data on 340 of Fortune's 500 largest firms in 1960, also found only a weak positive correlation between firm size (total employment) and innovative input (ratio of R & D employment to total employment).

Scherer (1965) found that the relationship between R & D employment and firm size tended to be quadratic, with R & D employment increasing faster than firm size among smaller firms but more slowly among larger firms. Loeb and Lin (1977), using data on six major pharmaceutical manufacturers, also found a quadratic relationship between firm size and innovative input. Grabowski (1968) found a similar relationship in his analysis of the drug industry, but he found a steadily increasing relationship in the chemical industry. Results from Shrieves' (1978) study on 411 firms support this view. These results imply that innovative input as a percentage of each sales dollar increases with firm size up to a point but declines thereafter.

Comanor (1967), using log-linear regressions, estimated that the elasticity of research employment with respect to firm size (total employment) was never significantly greater than unity and was significantly less than 1 in seven of twenty-one industries. Comanor's results cast doubt on a more-than-proportional positive relationship between firm size and innovative input. Results from Mueller (1967) support those of Comanor. He found a negative relationship between research intensity and firm size. Using data for ten chemical firms, nine petroleum firms, eight drug firms, seven steel firms, and four glass firms, Mansfield (1968) found that except for chemicals the largest firms in these industries spent no more on R & D than did the somewhat smaller firms. Kelly (1970) found no relationship between R & D employment and either the log of total assets or weighted market share. Rosenberg (1976), from a sample of 100 of the Fortune 500 firms found that the percentage of R & D employees declined with firm size. Link (1978) found that beyond some modest level, size in utilities is not especially conducive to R & D.

In a review of the literature, Kamien and Schwartz (1982) concluded that "with the possible exception of the chemical industry, there is little support for the hypothesis that the intensity of innovative effort increases more than proportionately with firm size" (p. 81). In addition, our review indicates that evidence exists of a quadratic relationship between firm size and innovative input. Innovative input seems to increase with firm size up to a point, but not beyond.

Firm Size and Innovative Output

Innovative output, like innovative input, is difficult to measure. Studies have typically used the actual number of new inventions and/or the number of patents as measures of innovative output.

Jewkes, Sawers, and Stillerman (1969) compiled case histories of sixty-one important twentieth-century inventions. They found that less than a third of them originated in industrial research labs. Over half of these inventions came from independent researchers or academia. Hamberg (1963) investigated twenty-seven major inventions of the 1946-55 period. Only seven were originally conceived in large industrial labs, while twelve could be traced to independent inventors. Mueller (1962) examined twenty-five important innovations that du Pont pioneered during the 1920-50 period. He found that only ten came from du Pont's laboratories. The others came from other firms or independents. Mansfield (1968) examined the major innovations during the 1919-38 period and the 1936-50 period in the coal industry, the petroleum industry, and the steel industry. He found that the largest four firms in the coal and petroleum industries were responsible for a larger share of their respective industry's innovations than of its productive capacity. The largest four steel producers, on the other hand, were responsible for fewer. Pavitt, Robson, and Townsend (1987) conducted a survey of over 4000 significant innovations in Great Britain during the 1945-83 period. They found that firms with fewer than 1000 employees commercialized a much larger share than is indicated by their share of R & D expenditures.

Scherer (1965) used the number of patents issued in 1959 as a proxy for average inventive output four years earlier. He found that the smaller firms were responsible for a higher relative share of inventive activity than sales. As in his analysis of firm size and innovative input, Scherer again found a quadratic relationship between firm size and innovative activity. In 1984 Scherer reexamined the issue of firm size and innovative output using both patent data and data on the number of inventions. He found that innovative output increases with firm sales but at a less than proportional rate. Scherer (1984) also reported on a study done by Gelman Research Associates. This study looked at 500 technological innovations first introduced between 1953 and 1973. The study found that small firms contribute more to the generation of important technological innovations than do large firms.

The literature on firm size and innovative output does not provide conclusive evidence supporting the Galbraith hypothesis. After an examination of the qualitative and quantitative evidence, Scherer (1970) concludes that there is a kind of threshold effect. "A little bigness . . . is good for invention and innovation. But beyond the threshold further bigness adds little or nothing, and it carries the danger of diminishing the effectiveness of inventive and innovative performance" (p. 361).

Concentration and Innovative Input

Several studies have analyzed the relationship between concentration and innovative input. Horowitz (1962) found the four-firm concentration ratio to be positively but weakly associated with research expenditures per industry sales dollar but negatively correlated with the percentage of industry research labs in the largest 20 percent of the firms. Hamberg (1966) found a weak positive correlation between company-financed R & D per sales dollar and industrial concentration. Brozen (1965) found a similar positive correlation.

As pointed out by Scherer (1970), these early studies did not adjust for differences in technological opportunity across industries. Scherer (1967) did make such an adjustment and concluded that the hypothesis of a positive association between concentration and the intensity of research effort was generally supported. He further found that the proportion of technological employment reached a maximum at a four-firm concentration ratio of 50 to 55 percent. He also tested the hypothesis that increases in concentration are conducive to increases in technical vigor only in relatively atomistic industries, becoming unimportant once a certain threshold is crossed. He found the threshold level to be approximately a four-firm concentration level of 10 to 14 percent. Kelly's (1970) work supports that of Scherer in that he found a maximum research intensity at a 50 to 60 percent four-firm concentration level. Comanor (1967), like Scherer, made adjustments for technological opportunity. He found a significantly positive association between R & D intensity and concentration in cases where prospects for product differentiation are relatively weak. Globerman (1973) looked at the effect of concentration and technological opportunity on research effort in Canadian manufacturing. He found that for industries with greater technological opportunity research intensity varied inversely with concentration. For industries with lesser technological opportunity no significant relationship was present. Scherer (1984) reexamined the relationship between concentration and employment of technical engineers and scientists. His results indicate that, even after adjusting for technological opportunity, a modest positive correlation between technical employment and concentration exists.

Concentration and Innovative Output

Studies testing for a relationship between concentration and innovative output have sometimes used productivity as a proxy of innovative output. For example, Stigler (1956) compared the rate of technical progress (measured by the decline in unit labor requirements over the 1899 to 1937 period) in fourteen industries of high concentration with seven industries in which concentration was declining and eight in which it was low. His results suggest that competition of new rivals (that is falling concentration) is a significant spur for rapid technical advance. Allen (1969) updated Stigler's study. Using nineteen industries over the 1939-64 period, he found no significant differences in productivity growth rates by industry concentration class. Phillips (1955-56) found that for the 1899 to 1939, period industries with high concentration or large factories showed greater technical progress than other industries. Weiss

281

(1963) found no significant relationship between concentration and productivity change. Bock and Farkas (1969), on the other hand, did find a positive association between productivity and concentration for 1963. Greer and Rhoades (1976) found seller concentration to have a positive and significant impact on labor productivity growth. Scherer (1984), using data for eighty-one SIC three-digit industries, found concentration to be positively and significantly related to productivity when R & D numbers were not included; concentration lost its significance when R & D numbers were included, however.

The divergent results found in these studies make it problematic to come to a conclusion concerning the relationship between concentration and productivity.

Other studies not using productivity to examine the relationship between concentration and innovative output include Scherer (1965), Williamson (1965) and more recently Acs and Audretsch (1988). Scherer (1965) tested the hypothesis that technological output tends to increase with concentration. Using patents as his measure of technological output, he found no support for a positive relationship between technological output and concentration. Williamson (1965) analyzed the influence concentration has on the relative innovational performance of the largest four firms in an industry. He found that highly concentrated industries actually perform worse than less concentrated industries. For a concentration ratio above 30 to 50 percent, the largest firms appear to supply less than their proportionate share of innovations. Results by Acs and Audretsch (1988) support those of Williamson. Acs and Audretsch used a data base of 8,074 innovations introduced in the United States in 1982 to test for a relationship between concentration and innovation (among other variables). They found that concentration exerted a negative influence on innovation, implying that highly concentrated industries perform worse than more competitively organized industries in terms of innovative activity. These three studies definitely do not support the Schumpeter notion that innovative activity increases with concentration.

Other Elements of Market Structure and Innovative Activity

Comanor (1967) argued that a principal goal of research activity is the creation of entry barriers through product differentiation; therefore, research outlays tend to be high when entry barriers are high. His results indicate, however, that both high entry barriers and low entry barriers have no impact on the number of research personnel employed. Moderate entry barriers, on the other hand, appear to have a positive and significant impact on the number of research personnel employed, after other factors are taken into account. Rosenberg (1976) also examined entry barriers in relation to innovative activity. He found that entry barriers, as measured by capital requirements, necessary advertising levels, and economies of scale, tended to have a positive effect on R & D intensity. More research is needed to clarify the relationship between entry barriers and innovation.

Grabowski and Baxter (1973) examined another aspect of market structure: rivalry. They tested the hypothesis that firm R & D expenditures respond positively to a rival's R & D outlays. They found evidence that firms do respond to each other's inventive activity. They also examined the hypothesis that rivalry in R & D is stronger the more oligopolistic the industry. They found that concentration appears to produce a conformity in R & D expenditure among firms. In other words, the more oligopolistic an industry is the more likely it is that firms will match each other's R & D expenditures.

Summary

Studies on the relationship between market structure and innovative activity do not lend unwavering support to the classical hypothesis that a perfectly competitive structure induces optimal innovative activity, the Schumpeter hypothesis that monopoly power is an integral part of an optimally functioning innovative environment, or the Galbraith hypothesis that large firm size must be present in order for innovation to occur. Rather, the evidence seems to suggest that a healthy innovative environment consists of a mixture of large and small firms. As Scherer (1970, p. 361) pointed out, the most favorable industrial environment in terms of innovative performance probably includes a preponderance of medium-sized companies, pressed on one side by many small technology-oriented enterprises and on the other by a few large corporations with the capacity to undertake large projects.

References: Market Structure and Innovation

Acs, Zoltan J., and Audretsch, David B. "Innovation in Large and Small Firms: An Empirical Analysis." *American Economic Review* 78 (September 1988), pp. 678-90.

Allen, B. T."Concentration and Economic Progress: Note." *American Economic Review* 59 (September 1969), pp. 600-604.

Bock, B., and Farkas, J. *Concentration and Productivity: Some Preliminary Problems and Findings*, The Conference Board Studies in Business Economics No.103. New York: National Industrial Conference Board, 1969.

Brozen, Y. "R & D Differences among Industries." in Richard A. Tybout (ed.), *Economics of Research and Development.* Columbus: Ohio State University Press, 1965.

Comanor, W. S. "Market Structure, Product Differentiation, and Industrial Research." *Quarterly Journal of Economics* 81 (November 1967), pp. 639-57.

Galbraith, J. K. *American Capitalism*, Rev. Ed. Boston: Houghton Mifflin, 1956.

Globerman, S. "Market Structure and R & D in Canadian Manufacturing Industries." *Quarterly Review of Economics and Business* 13 (Summer 1973), pp. 59-67.

Grabowski, H. G. "The Determinants of Industrial Research and Development: A Study of the Chemical, Drug, and Petroleum Industries." *Journal of Political Economy* 76 (March-April 1968), pp. 292-306.

Grabowski, H. G., and Baxter, N. D. "Rivalry in Industrial Research and Development." *Journal of Industrial Economics* 21 (July 1973), pp. 209-35.

Greer, D.F., and Rhoades, Stephen A. "Concentration and Productivity Changes in the Long and Short Run." *Southern Economic Journal* 43 (October 1976), pp. 1031-44.

Hamberg, D. "Invention in the Industrial Research Laboratory." *Journal of Political Economy* 71 (April 1963), pp. 95-115.

___. *R & D; Essays on the Economics of Research and Development*. New York: Random House, 1966.

Horowitz, I. "Firm Size and Research Activity." *Southern Economic Journal* 28 (January 1962), pp. 298-301.

Jewkes, J.; Sawers, D.; and Stillerman, R. *The Sources of Invention*, 2nd Ed. New York: Norton, 1969.

Kamien, M. I., and Schwartz, N. L. *Market Structure and Innovation*. Cambridge: Cambridge University Press, 1982.

Kelly, T. M. *The Influences of Firm Size and Market Structure on the Research Efforts of Large Multiple-product Firms*. Ph.D. dissertation, Oklahoma State University, 1970.

Link, A. N. "Rates of Induced Technology from Investment in Research and Development." *Southern Economic Journal* 45 (October 1978), pp. 370-79.

Loeb, P. D., and Lin, V. "Research & Development in the Pharmaceutical Industry–A Specification Error Approach." *Journal of Industrial Economics* 26 (September 1977), pp. 45-51.

Mansfield, E. *Industrial Research and Technological Innovation–An Econometric Analysis*, New York: Norton, for the Cowles Foundation for Research in Economics at Yale University, 1968.

Mueller, D. C. "The Firm's Decision Process: An Econometric Investigation." *Quarterly Journal of Economics* 81 (February 1967), pp. 58-87.

Mueller, W. F. "The Origins of the Basic Inventions Underlying du Pont's Major Product and Process Innovations, 1920-1950," in Nelson, R. R. (ed.),

The Rate and Direction of Inventive Activity: Economic and Social Factors. Princeton NJ: Princeton University Press, 1962.

Pavitt, K.; Robson, M.; and Townsend, J. "The Size Distribution of Innovating Firms in the UK: 1945-1983." *Journal of Industrial Economics* 35 (March 1987), pp. 297-316.

Phillips, A. "Concentration, Scale and Technological Change in Selected Manufacturing Industries 1899-1939." *Journal of Industrial Economics* 4 (1955-56), pp. 179-93.

Rosenberg, J. B. "Research and Market Share: A Reappraisal of the Schumpeter Hypothesis." *Journal of Industrial Economics* 25 (December 1976), pp. 101-12.

Scherer, F. M. "Firm Size, Market Structure, Opportunity, and the Output of Patented Inventions." *American Economic Review* 55 (December 1965), pp. 1097-1125.

_____. "Market Structure and the Employment of Scientists and Engineers." *American Economic Review* 57 (June 1967), pp. 524-31.

_____. *Industrial Market Structure and Economic Performance.* Chicago: Rand McNally, 1970.

_____. *Innovation and Growth: Schumpeterian Perspectives.* Cambridge, MA: MIT Press, 1984.

Schumpeter, Joseph A. *Capitalism, Socialism, and Democracy,* 2nd Ed. New York: Harper & Brothers Publishers, New York, 1947.

Shrieves, R. "Market Structure and Innovation: A New Perspective." *Industrial Organization Review* 4 (1978), pp. 26-33.

Smith, A. *The Wealth of Nations.* New York: Modern Library, 1937.

Stigler, G. J. "Industrial Organization and Economic Progress," in White, L. D. (ed.), *The State of the Social Sciences.* Chicago: University of Chicago Press, 1956.

Weiss, L. "Average Concentration Ratios and Industrial Performance." *Journal of Industrial Economics* 11 (July 1963), pp. 237-54.

Williamson, O. E. "Innovation and Market Structure." *Journal of Political Economy* 73 (February 1965), pp. 67-73.

MEASURES OF MONOPOLY POWER

Monopoly power can be defined as the power to control the market rather than be controlled by the market. This definition of monopoly power is both simple and generally accepted. A similarly simple and generally accepted practical *measure* of monopoly power is, however, not available on a cross-sectional basis. Most economists agree with Lerner (1934) that monopoly power, in theory, can be measured by the excess of price over marginal cost. In practice, however, marginal cost is not observable. Furthermore, reliable, comprehensive data on price is difficult, if not impossible, to obtain on a cross-sectional basis. Therefore, economists have turned to second-best measures of monopoly power when doing cross-sectional work. Many have used census data to approximate Lerner's price-cost margin (PCM). Others have chosen to exploit noncensus data bases in attempting to approximate price-cost margins. Some have turned from the use of price-cost margins and have used Tobin's q (market value of a firm divided by its replacement cost) as a measure of monopoly power. For simplicity's sake, many have used easily obtained concentration ratios or accounting profits to approximate the degree of monopoly power in industries. Still others have taken the comprehensive approach and have analyzed monopoly power on the basis of a variety of structural variables (for example, concentration ratios) combined with performance variables (for example, profits). Here we shall very briefly review the primary methods used to measure monopoly power with an emphasis on the debate over accounting profits as a measure of monopoly power.

Measures Based on Lerner's Price-Cost Margin

Lerner (1934) proposed what has become known as the Lerner Index of monopoly power. The Lerner Index is simply the price of a good minus the marginal cost of the good, all divided by the price of the good. The Lerner Index, while useful in helping one understand monopoly power, cannot be observed in practice. As already mentioned, the central problem is that marginal cost cannot be observed. Collins and Preston (1969) popularized a method of measuring monopoly power that is based in theory on the Lerner Index. Collins and Preston argued that the Lerner Index can be approximated by total revenue minus total variable costs, all divided by total revenue. The critical assumption is that variable costs equal or closely approximate marginal costs. Collins and Preston then used census data on value added minus payroll, all divided by the value of shipments, to estimate their variant of the Lerner Index.

Since its introduction, the use of census-based price-cost margins has been widespread. In 1982 Liebowitz noted that in just three popular economic journals, thirty-four articles had been published using census-based price-cost margins. Not all of these papers used the version of the PCM developed by Collins and Preston. Variations have appeared such as the one developed by Feinberg (1980). Feinberg argued that rental costs, advertising expenditures, and the opportunity cost of capital should be deducted along with payroll to get a true measure of monopoly or economic profits.

Liebowitz (1982) criticized the use of census-based price-cost margins as a measure of monopoly power. He used data from the 1963 and 1967 Government Link Projects to construct PCMs that were more closely related to the theoretical standard of the Lerner Index. He then showed that census-based PCMs are not only *not* related to other measures of monopoly power, but are also not related to the theoretical price-cost margin. Liebowitz's work has cast doubt not on the correctness of Lerner's Index but on the correctness of its approximation when based on census data.

Other Price-Cost Margin Estimates

Several other data sources and methodologies have been exploited in an effort to measure Lerner's theoretical price-cost margin. Three such attempts are represented by Nickell and Metcalf (1978), Sumner (1981), and Shapiro (1987).

Nickell and Metcalf used data obtained from price tags observed in super-markets to estimate price-cost margins. They argued that price-cost margins can be estimated by observing the difference between the price of proprietary brand products and similar products marketed under the name of the super-market itself. Looking past a host of theoretical problems with this methodology, the major stumbling block of the Nickell and Metcalf approach is its limited potential for practical application. Only a few industry PCMs can be estimated this way.

Another unique approach to estimating PCMs has been pursued by Sumner (1981). Sumner argues that the price elasticity of demand can be used to estimate the degree to which a firm is not a price taker. Furthermore, estimates of the price elasticity of demand can be obtained for products that carry excise taxes by observing the effect that different excise tax rates (due to differences across states) have on the price of the products. The price-cost margin can then be estimated. Sumner applies this approach to the cigarette industry. The principal drawback of Sumner's methodology, like the Nickell-Metcalf methodology, lies in its limited potential for practical application over a broad spectrum of industries. This point is admitted by Sumner.

Shapiro (1987) also bases his estimate of monopoly power on the theory of PCMs and observations of elasticities. Shapiro points out that in order to accurately measure market power, price-cost margins should take into account differences in elasticity of demand. This Shapiro does by using the ratio of the market elasticity of demand to the elasticity of demand implied by the price over cost markup as a measure of market power. The market elasticity of demand is measured by exploiting the covariance restriction between a productivity shock and the disturbance in the demand equation. The elasticity of demand implied by the price over cost markup is estimated using Hall's (1986) methodology which exploits the cyclicality of productivity. Hall reinterprets the well-known fact that productivity varies procyclically as follows: "As output expands in the trough of a recession, labor increases less than is warranted by a standard production function. Hence, price exceeds marginal cost. Put differently, when output is low, price does not fall enough to allow the sale of goods that can be produced at very low marginal cost" (Shapiro 1987, p. 1). Shapiro accepts Hall's reasoning that this finding is only consistent with a high degree of monopoly power. Therefore the cyclicality of productivity can be exploited to determine whether or not particular industries have monopoly power.

Shapiro's measure of monopoly power is somewhat complicated and seems to be a bit indirect and possibly a little conjectural; but because of the relatively recent nature of Shapiro's work, it has not been critiqued in the literature.

Tobin's q as a Measure of Monopoly Power

Several papers have proposed Tobin's q as a measure of monopoly power and have argued that it is a better measure of monopoly power than many other proposed measures including PCMs. Among these papers are Lindenberg and Ross (1981) and Salinger (1984).

Tobin's q is the ratio of the market value of a firm to its replacement cost. The heart of the argument linking this ratio to monopoly power lies in the definitions of market value and replacement cost. In theory, market value is said to be equal to the capitalized values of rents attributed to invested capital or replacement capital plus firm-specific rents (such as favorable access to raw materials) plus monopoly rents. In theory, replacement cost is said to be equal to rents attributable to invested capital. Thus in theory, if the q ratio is greater than 1, it must be due to either firm-specific rents or to monopoly rents.

Tobin's q can be criticized as a measure of monopoly power on several points. First, the existence of firm-specific rents in the numerator may cause Tobin's q to exceed 1 even though the industry is competitively organized. Lindenberg and Ross admit this problem and point out that Tobin's q can therefore only be used as an upper bound. Second, as pointed out by Gordon (1985) and Shepherd (1986), Tobin's q measures only the extent to which the benefits from perceived monopoly power are expected to flow through to the corporation's investors. Shepherd notes that Tobin's q is at best an indirect and subjective measure of monopoly power, based as it is on speculation about future possibilities. Investors may be mistaken or misled about the potential monopoly power of a firm or may mistakenly bid up the market value of a firm for reasons totally unrelated to monopoly power, especially in today's speculative markets. On the whole, leaving it up to investors to determine whether or not monopoly power exists seems to assign to investors a role that economists themselves find difficult to fulfill. Third, Shepherd (1986) also points out that the measurement of the q ratio is difficult and complicated and introduces many possibilities of error and bias.

Readily Available Measures

Because of their availability, concentration ratios and accounting profit rates have often been used to give a general impression of the level of monopoly power.

(1) Concentration Ratios

Concentration ratios indicate the extent to which a market is dominated by large firms. In theory, the fewer the firms in an industry (that is, the higher the concentration ratio), the easier it is for firms to collude and exercise monopoly power. A worldwide one-firm concentration ratio of 100 percent obviously is a strong indication of market power (because one firm controls the entire market). A domestic four-firm ratio of 100 percent is not an unambiguous indication of monopoly power, however. Even though four firms make up the entire domestic supply, those four firms may either compete vigorously with each other, compete not at all with each other, or anything in between. Concentration ratios give no information about the intensity of competition. Concentration ratios also give no information about the level and intensity of import competition, an increasingly important element.

William Dugger (1985) has also pointed out that concentration ratios miss two important dimensions of economic concentration and power: aggregate concentration in the entire economy and conglomerate concentration. If firms from different backgrounds continue to get into each other's business and the merger wave continues, then aggregate and conglomerate measures of concentration will become increasingly relevant and simple industry-based concentration ratios will become less relevant.

In summary, concentration ratios are useful as clues when analyzing monopoly power but probably cannot be used by themselves to indicate market power.

(2) Profits

Stigler (1963) pointed out that "there is no more important a proposition in economic theory than that, under competition, the rate of return on investment tends toward equality in all industries" (p. 54). This proposition can be referred to as the convergence proposition. All studies that use accounting profits to measure monopoly power either explicitly or implicitly have this proposition as their base.

Bain and Qualls (1987) have provided a more thorough justification for using profits to measure monopoly power. Bain and Qualls point out that economic profits can be defined as

$$R - C - D - iV$$

where R equals revenue, C equals currently incurred costs, D equals the aggregate costs incurred in past years that are allocable to the earning of this year's revenue (for example, depreciation and amortization), V equals the value of owners' investment, and i equals the net interest rate that funds can currently earn in the best available capital markets if invested for time periods comparable to those for which owners' funds in the firm are invested. Thus, economic or excess profits can be defined as revenue minus allocable current costs minus allocable past costs minus the interest cost on owners' investment. Accounting profit differs from economic profit mainly in that the interest cost on owners' investment is not deducted. Accounting profit is thus defined as

$$R - C - D.$$

Bain and Qualls show that accounting rates of return on equity are convertible into economic or excess profit rates on equity by deducting the applicable interest rate:

$$\frac{R - C - D - iV}{V} = \frac{R - C - D}{V} - i$$

The work of Bain and Qualls provides theoretical justification for using accounting profits to measure monopoly power.

The use of accounting profits as a measure of monopoly power has not gone without criticism. The following paragraphs outline the major criticisms.

The first major criticism of using accounting profits to measure monopoly power argues that accounting profits are not equal to economic or excess profits and, because of accounting profits' treatment of investment flows, accounting profits cannot be converted into economic profits. Fisher (1979) argues that economic profits cannot be calculated from accounting profits mainly because the timing of investment and its treatment in accounting statements causes severe divergence between accounting rates of return and economic rates of return. In an oft-cited study, Fisher and McGowan (1983) continue this line of thought. In 1984 Fisher summarized their argument: "The numerator of the accounting rate of return is current profits; those profits are the

290

consequence of investment decisions made in the past. On the other hand, the denominator is total capitalization, but some of the firm's capital will generally have been put in place relatively recently in the expectation of a profit stream much of which is still in the future. While the economic rate of return is the magnitude that properly relates a stream of profits to the investments that produce it, the accounting rate of return does not. By relating current profits to current capitalization, the accounting rate of return fatally scrambles up the timing" (p. 509).

If Fisher and McGowan are correct, then accounting profits provide no information at all about economic profits and thus about monopoly power. Fisher and McGowan's work has been criticized on several points, however. In particular Kay and Mayer (1986) and Kay (1987) have cast doubt on Fisher and McGowan's unequivocal rejection of the use of accounting profits to estimate economic profitability. Kay and Mayer (1986) show that under the condition of replacement cost accounting, accounting profits provide exactly those measures needed in economic analysis. Kay (1987) continues this work, showing that regardless of the accounting conventions employed, over the whole life of the firm, the average accounting rate of profit is equal to the rate of return on the firm's activities as a whole. This implies that accounting profit data taken over a very long period of time can be used to examine economic profitability.

A second criticism of the use of accounting profits to measure monopoly power involves the long-run nature of the convergence proposition. Several papers have pointed out that the theory of all profits converging to equality under competitive conditions applies only in long-run equilibrium. And long-run equilibrium may be impossible to observe due to repeated disturbances. This point has been made by Stigler (1963), Howe (1978), and Devine et al. (1985), among others. One point can be made concerning repeated disturbances. In theory at least, disturbances in the positive direction should be averaged out by disturbances in the negative direction.

Another problem with accounting profits is that observed high accounting profits may be due to high risk and not to monopoly power (see Howe 1978). Bain and Qualls (1987) have pointed out, however, that individual firms within an economy as a whole or within individual industries can for short or long periods earn excess profits properly describable as risk rewards. But not all firms in the economy or in an industry can do this. If every firm in an industry persistently earns excess profits, it is hard to describe these earnings as risk rewards.

Another problem with the use of accounting profits in economic analysis is that unfavorable demand and cost conditions may cause accounting profits to be low even though the firm has monopoly power. This point has been made by Stigler (1963) and Howe (1978). In addition, accounting profits may differ across firms or industries because of accounting treatment of management services and salaries (see Asch 1983; Clarke 1985; Devine et al. 1985). A similar argument is that high profits of monopolistic firms may be either hidden or simply squandered (see Howe 1978 or Asch 1983). Treatment of research and development and advertising expenditures has also frequently been cited as having a distorting influence on accounting profits (see Fisher 1979; Clarkson 1982; Asch 1983; Devine et al. 1985). Another problem frequently cited in the literature has to do with firms that operate in several industries. Few large firms today operate in one single industry. Profits for such firms are extremely difficult, if not impossible, to disaggregate on an industry level. Therefore, monopoly power in an industry may not be observable via the profit level (see Asch 1983; Clarke 1985).

Many of the problems just cited can be minimized by careful selection of data and examination of relatively long time series. In the long term, some of the disturbances and accounting discrepancies should average out. But some of the problems cited, will remain no matter how carefully data is selected and no matter how long the employed time series is.

Combining Structural and Performance Measures

Some authors have recognized the problematic nature of using just one cross-sectional variable to assess the monopoly power of industries. These authors have argued that the best approach to cross-sectional measurement of monopoly power is to look at several variables, including both structural variables, such as concentration and barriers to entry, and performance variables, such as profits and prices. For instance, Preston and King (1979) argue that assessment of monopoly power should include analysis of market structure to determine if a sufficient number of buyers and sellers exists, analysis of profits to determine if excess profits are being earned, and examination of price and price-cost relationships for evidence of monopolistic pricing. Shepherd (1982) also argues that a combination of structural and behavioral variables should be used to analyze monopoly power. He uses observations on market shares, concentration, entry barriers, pricing behavior, profitability, and innovation to assign industries to competitive categories.

Given the inexact nature of the measurement of monopoly power and the continuing debate over proper measures of monopoly power, the safest methodology appears to be to follow the example of Preston and King, and Shepherd, and include a variety of structural and performance variables. Unfortunately, time and data constraints do not always permit such in-depth analysis. Furthermore, some types of analysis require the use of only one variable in assessing market power. In such cases, single variable measures of monopoly power should be recognized as inexact and caution should be used in forming conclusions.

References: Measures of Monopoly Power

Asch, Peter. *Industrial Organization and Antitrust Policy*, rev. ed. New York: John Wiley & Sons, 1983.

Bain, Joe S., and Qualls, David P. *Industrial Organization: A Treatise.* Greenwich, CT: JAI Press, 1987.

Clarke, Roger. *Industrial Economics.* Oxford: Basil Blackwell, 1985.

Clarkson, Kenneth W., and Miller, Roger LeRoy. *Industrial Organization: Theory, Evidence, and Public Policy.* New York: McGraw-Hill, 1982.

Collins, Norman R., and Preston, Lee E. "Price-Cost Margins and Industry Structure." *Review of Economics and Statistics* 51 (August 1969), pp. 271-86.

Devine, P. J.; Lee, N.; Jones, R. M.; and Tyson, W. J. *An Introduction to Industrial Economics*, 4th ed. London: George Allen & Unwin, 1985.

Dugger, William M. "The Shortcomings of Concentration Ratios in the Conglomerate Age: New Sources and Uses of Corporate Power." *Journal of Economic Issues* 19 (June 1985), pp. 343-53.

Feinberg, Robert M. "The Lerner Index, Concentration, and the Measurement of Market Power." *Southern Economic Journal* 46 (April 1980), pp. 1180-86.

Fisher, Franklin M. "Diagnosing Monopoly." *Quarterly Review of Economics and Business* 19 (Summer 1979), pp. 7-33.

____. "The Misuse of Accounting Rates of Return: Reply." *American Economic Review* 74 (June 1984), pp. 509-17.

Fisher, Franklin M., and McGowan, John J. "On the Misuse of Accounting Rates of Return to Infer Monopoly Profits." *American Economic Review* 73 (March 1983), pp. 82-97.

Gordon, Myron J. "The Postwar Growth in Monopoly Power." *Journal of Post Keynesian Economics* 8 (Fall 1985), pp. 3-13.

Howe, W. Stewart. *Industrial Economics: An Applied Approach.* London: MacMillan Press, 1978.

Kay, J. A. "Assessing Market Dominance Using Accounting Rates of Profits." in Hay, Donald, and Vickers, John (eds.), *The Economics of Market Dominance.* Oxford: Basil Blackwell, 1987.

Kay, J. A., and Mayer, C. P. "On the Application of Accounting Rates of Return." *Economic Journal* 96 (March 1986), pp. 199-207.

Lerner, Abba P. "The Concept of Monopoly and the Measurement of Monopoly Power." *Review of Economic Studies* (June 1934), pp. 157-75.

Liebowitz, S. J. "What Do Census Price-Cost Margins Measure?" *Journal of Law and Economics* 25 (October 1982), pp. 231-46.

Lindenberg, Eric B., and Ross Stephen A. "Tobin's q Ratio and Industrial

Organization." *Journal of Business* 54 (January 1981), pp. 1-32.

Nickell, Stephen, and Metcalf, David. "Monopolistic Industries and Monopoly Profits or Are Kellogg's Cornflakes Overpriced." *Economic Journal* 88 (June 1978), pp. 254-68.

Preston, Lee E., and King, Benjamin. "Proving Competition." *Antitrust Bulletin* 24 (Winter 1979), pp. 787-806.

Salinger, Michael A. "Tobin's q, Unionization, and the Concentration-Profits Relationship." *Rand Journal of Economics* 15 (Summer 1984), pp. 159-70.

Shapiro, Matthew D. "Measuring Market Power in U.S. Industry." NBER Working Paper no. 2212. Cambridge: NBER, April 1987.

Shepherd, William G. "Causes of Increased Competition in the U.S. Economy, 1939-1980." *Review of Economics and Statistics* 64 (November 1982), pp. 613-26.

Shepherd, William G."Tobin's q and the Structure – Performance Relationship: Comment." *American Economic Review* 76 (December 1986), pp. 1205-10.

Stigler, G. J. *Capital and Rates of Return in Manufacturing Industries* Princeton, NJ: Princeton University Press, 1963.

Sumner, Daniel A. "Measurement of Monopoly Behavior: An Application to the Cigarette Industry." *Journal of Political Economy* 89 (October 1981), pp. 1010-19.

UNION EFFECTS ON PRODUCTIVITY&
UNION WORK RULE EFFECTS ON EFFICIENCY

Unions and Productivity

In an earlier section of this appendix we reviewed the literature relating competition between firms to productivity. In this section we review the literature on a related concept: the relationship between uncompetitive organization of the labor market (that is unionization) and productivity. Currently, no generally accepted answer concerning the relationship between unionization and productivity exists. Several recent studies cite empirical evidence indicating that unions have a positive effect on productivity. But these new studies have met considerable criticism on a theoretical basis as well as contradictory findings on an empirical basis.

The issue of unions' effect on productivity has received a great deal of attention since 1978, with the introduction of an institutional concept of unions in a pioneering study by Brown and Medoff. This new approach differed from the conventional monopoly model view of unions in substance and result. Contrary to the restrictive (productivity inhibiting) monopoly model, in this new model unions are seen as an institutional force acting as a collective voice of the workers and boosting productivity by reducing labor turnover, enhancing worker morale and cooperation, providing efficient grievance resolution, and pressuring management into stricter efficiency. Supportive empirical evidence has been reported in a group of studies, sometimes referred to as the Harvard studies. The Harvard studies include papers by Frantz (1976); Brown and Medoff (1978); Clark (July 1980, December 1980); Brown, Freeman, and Leonard (reported in Freeman and Medoff 1984); Connerton, Freeman, and Medoff (1983); and Allen (1984). All of these studies are used in Freeman and Medoff's book *What Do Unions Do?* to support the argument of positive union productivity effects. Two additional studies by Allen (Winter 1986) and Mefford (1986) also suggest that unions have a positive impact on productivity.

Brown and Medoff's study was a cross-sectional analysis of twenty SIC two-digit manufacturing industries using 1972 data. After controlling for capital per unit of labor and labor force quality, Brown and Medoff estimated that union establishments are 22 percent more productive than nonunion establishments. Frantz found a similar result of a 15 percent positive union effect in a study of the household furniture industry using 1975-76 data. Brown, Medoff, and Leonard found 10 and 27 percent positive effects using 1972 and 1977 manufacturing data. In two studies of the cement industry, Clark found positive union productivity effects of between 6 and 10 percent. Allen conducted a cross-sectional analysis of the construction industry using 1972 data and found a positive union productivity effect of 17 to 22 percent. These studies are the basis of the Freeman and Medoff assertion that unions have productivity effects of similar magnitude to, and that offset, their relative wage effect.

An additional study cited by Freeman and Medoff (Connerton, Freeman and Medoff 1983) found seemingly contrary evidence. In separate yearly studies of the bituminous coal industry, they found positive union productivity effects in 1965 but negative effects in 1970 and thereafter. Freeman and Medoff conclude that this negative effect can be attributed to poor labor management relations in the later time period. Because of the extenuating circumstances, they believe this result does not reject the positive union productivity effect previously postulated.

The second Allen study in this area (Winter 1986) addressed the union-nonunion productivity issue using a sample of union and nonunion contractors working on privately and publicly owned hospital and nursing home projects. The results of this study were consistent with his earlier findings. Allen again found union productivity to be greater than nonunion productivity. But the empirical results of this study were rather weak as the null hypothesis of no union/nonunion productivity difference could be rejected at only an 87 percent confidence level.

Mefford (1986) examined the effect of unions on productivity in thirty-one plants of a large multinational firm in the years 1975-82. Results of his study indicate that unionization's overall effect on productivity is positive. Unionization appears to increase the capital-labor ratio and improve management performance, but it also raises the absenteeism rate. A net positive effect on productivity remains even when controlling for these effects. Mefford suggests that this effect may be due to an improved labor relations climate or improved labor quality. Mefford's conclusions are specific to this one labor-intensive, consumer goods industry and may not be generalized beyond.

Criticisms of studies finding a positive union productivity effect can be placed in three major categories. One type of criticism directly confronts the logical basis of the argument behind the union voice mechanism. This criticism makes the point that the institutional view of unionism lacks theoretical justification. A second type of criticism faults the model specification. Brown and Medoff recognize that their specification of the model may have problems, but they do not believe that these problems are so restrictive as to preclude the usefulness of the test. A third type of criticism presents contrary findings that cast doubt on the robustness of the positive union effect conclusion.

The positive-union-productivity-effect theory is vague on how unions work within the production process to achieve productivity gains. Lower quit rates and improved handling of grievances are reported to be part of the answer. Hirsch and Addison (1986), however, find little other support for the Freeman-Medoff position and speculate that the observed positive effect may be attributable to a shock response by management to the union situation. This would imply differing production functions between union and nonunion firms. Specifically, the difference would be a larger managerial input for the union firms, with this being a contributing factor in the higher productivity apparently found. But as will be described below, the model does not include different production functions for union and nonunion firms.

Several problems are possible with the specification of the model used in the Harvard studies. First, excepting the Clark (1980) studies, all assume identical production functions between union and nonunion firms. Second, the dependent variable used in several of the aforementioned studies (Brown and Medoff 1978; Brown, Medoff, and Leonard cited in Freeman and Medoff 1984, and Frantz 1976) is derived from value added per worker. The use of value added brings with it the distinct possibility of the model's capturing a union price effect instead of an output (productivity) effect. In addition, the quality of other inputs (specifically managerial) as well as organizational factors is not controlled for in these studies. For a fuller treatment of these arguments, see Addison (1982), Addison and Barnett (1982), Addison (1985), and Hirsch and Addison (1986).

Walter J. Wessels (1985) observes that evidence that unions substantially increase productivity is contradicted by evidence that the effect of unions on employment is small. He argues that if unions increase wages and productivity by roughly the same amount, costs and output should be unaffected but employment should fall by as much as wages (and productivity) have increased. Wessels shows that if the union is constrained by the firm's demand function, then essentially the only way to resolve this contradiction is for unions to raise the productivity of capital (not of labor) under conditions where the substitutability between labor and capital is very limited. But, he points out, estimates of the substitutability parameter are near unity. Therefore, he argues that either unions do not substantially increase productivity or they substantially reduce employment. The latter is unlikely to have gone unobserved, however.

Morgan O. Reynolds (1986) has pointed out an additional problem in the model specification. Reynolds argues that reliance on the explicit production function approach initiated by Brown and Medoff contains a flaw "that renders econometric estimates based on it incapable of resolving the question of what impact unions may have on productivity" (p. 443). He points out that if firms maximize profits and trade unions impose higher than competitive wage rates on unionized firms, then the marginal productivity of unionized labor is necessarily greater than that of nonunion labor. Even if statistical controls for the quality of workers and capital/labor ratios are employed, "the firms burdened by union pricing must have higher marginal labor products because managers employ smaller amounts of labor than the nonunion firms that enjoy lower labor prices" (p. 444). Reynolds points out that using the Harvard model, there is no way to discover the independent impact of unionization on productivity because there is no way to statistically separate observed marginal productivity differentials from union/nonunion price differentials. He concludes that unionization simply diverts employment from high-productivity sectors to low-productivity sectors and the observed union/nonunion productivity differential is simply a distortion in the allocation of scarce labor and capital induced by monopoly prices.

Yet another problem in the model specification has been identified by Lovell, Sickles, and Warren (1988). The authors point out that to derive a linear estimating equation, Brown and Medoff and others transformed an "intrinsically nonlinear" explanatory variable via first-order Taylor-series approximation. The use of this approximation introduces a bias that necessarily results in an overstatement of the absolute value of the true union productivity effect.

In addition to the criticisms of the model specification are several studies that find contrary (or at least nonsupportive) evidence for the positive union effect on productivity. These include Pencavel (1977), Clark (1984), Warren (1985), and Bemmels (1987). Pencavel studied the union effect on the production of the British coal mining industry from 1900 to 1913. He determined that unions reduced coal output by 2.3 to 3.1 percent during this period of time. One of the appealing attributes of this study is that there was no union wage effect and therefore the previously mentioned concern about mistaking the price effect for the output effect is mitigated. Warren, in a time-series study of private domestic business from 1948 to 1973, found a negative effect of unionization on productivity. Clark (1984), in an analysis of product-line businesses of North American manufacturers, found a negative 2 to 3 percent union effect on productivity. Bemmels's analysis of forty six manufacturing plants in 1982 also indicates a negative union impact on productivity. He found evidence that unions reduce the effectiveness of some managerial practices designed to increase productivity, and that a poor labor-management relations climate also reduces productivity.

In addition to articles analyzing the union effect on the level of productivity, several analyze the effect unions have on total factor productivity growth. Some of these studies are Mansfield (1980), Link (1981), Sveikauskas and Sveikauskas (1982), Kendrick (1983), Maki (1983), and Hirsch & Link (1984). All of these studies found that unions have a negative effect on total factor productivity growth. In the case of the Sveikauskas-Sveikauskas study, the effect was statistically insignificant. In the other four studies, the effect was statistically significant. These studies provide a good deal of support for the hypothesis that unions hamper total factor productivity growth. But as pointed out by Maki and Hirsch and Link, this finding may not preclude a positive union effect on the level of productivity. A possible scenario would be a one-time positive union effect followed by slower productivity growth thereafter.

The findings concerning total factor productivity growth as well as the papers criticizing the Harvard studies cast considerable doubt on the robustness and generality of studies finding a positive union productivity effect. Therefore, no definitive statement can be made concerning this issue.

Union Work Rules and Efficiency

In the preceding section we came to the conclusion that the literature has not yet satisfactorily determined what effect unions have on productivity. In this section we review the literature's findings relating one particular aspect of unionization to efficiency. Specifically, what effect do union work rules have on efficiency?

Popular literature often depicts union work rules as being archaic, extremely wasteful, a tremendous drain on resources, and a bane to efficiency. Horror stories abound of corporations forced to pay for redundant labor or unable to modernize because of union work rules. With all of the attention paid to union work rules in the popular press, one would expect that economists would spend a considerable amount of research effort clarifying the issue. But, in fact, very little scholarly research has been done on how union work rules affect efficiency. And the little research that has been done relates only to the construction industry and seems to indicate that, in general, work rules have added very little to total costs.

Four studies analyzing construction industry work rules have been published. Three of these use a survey and/or interview technique of evaluation. These interviews or surveys are of both union leaders and contractors to determine the effect work rules have on efficiency. The fourth study uses cost data to calculate union and nonunion factor demand elasticities, which are then used to determine the magnitude of the union-work-rule effect on efficiency.

The most thorough interview study is by Haber and Levinson (1956). They interviewed 268 representatives of labor, management, and government in sixteen cities to determine, among other things, how receptive labor unions are to new techniques, how widespread union work rules are, and how much work rules affect costs. Their "back-of-the-envelope" calculations indicate that union work rules raise costs by 3 to 8 percent. Three-fourths of their cost estimate is attributed to restrictions on labor (for example, crew size, and job classification); the remainder is attributed to restrictions on techniques.

Mandelstamm (1965) surveyed contractors in two Michigan cities in 1957 to obtain cost and man-hour estimates for a standard small house. One of the cities was heavily unionized while the other was dominated by open-shop contractors. After calculating total labor cost numbers for the union and nonunion cities and interviewing contractors on the practical costs of work rules, Mandelstamm concluded that work-rule effects on efficiency are very small. The wage bills in the two cities were virtually identical, but no quantitative estimate of the union-work-rule efficiency effect could be made. In a more recent study, Bourdon and Levitt (1980) surveyed union and nonunion contractors in eight cities in the year 1976. They found relatively few restrictive work practices in the union sector. The authors concluded, "There is no question that at various times and places, various locals of the building trades unions have resisted technological innovation in tools or materials and have established unduly restrictive work rules or practices. Yet, the results of the survey, as of other field research, do not support the contention that this has been a widespread or consistent policy" (p. 63). Like Haber and Levinson, Bourdon and Levitt found that the major restriction imposed by union work rules was on labor usage. No quantitative estimate of the union-work-rule efficiency effect can be calculated from their study, however.

These three studies seem to indicate that restrictive work rules are neither as widespread nor as expensive as popularly believed. Because of their limited and subjective nature, the results of survey/interview studies are less than conclusive. Empirical results from Allen (April 1986), however, lend support to results of the survey/interview studies.

Allen estimated factor-demand elasticities for union and nonunion contractors to determine if union work rules lead to lower elasticities in the union sector. He looked at two models: one to determine if unions affect the employment of capital and equipment, the other to determine if unions affect the allocation and employment of various types of labor (for example, skilled versus unskilled).

Allen employed two different data sets, one for eighty-three commercial office buildings built in 1974 and the other for sixty-eight elementary and secondary schools built in 1972. Both data sets were gathered by the BLS as part of its Construction Labor and Material Requirements series. He ended up with 823 union and 266 nonunion observations in the office building sample and 806 union and 155 nonunion observations in the school sample. Each contractor reported the amount of the contract, union status, type and cost of each material item, fair rental value or depreciation for each type of equipment, and hours and wages for each occupation employed on-site.

Allen's first model dealing with union effects on capital and equipment shows no support for the hypothesis of lower factor-demand elasticities for union contractors. This is consistent with the results of earlier survey/interview studies, which imply that union work rules do not significantly affect the types of equipment and materials used in construction. As pointed out by Allen, this result is also consistent with data on contract provisions showing limits on prefabrication or on tools and equipment to be relatively rare.

Results from Allen's second model dealing with the allocation and employment of labor provide strong support for the hypothesis that union work rules reduce management's flexibility to assign workers to jobs in the most efficient fashion. He found that removal of union work rules could reduce labor costs by 5 percent and total costs by 2 percent.

Allen offers the following conclusions with regard to his and earlier research. First, union work rules are restricted mainly to the allocation of different types of labor and tend to have little effect on the employment of capital or materials. Second, although the costs of such work rules are not as alarmingly large as journalistic accounts and nonacademic studies suggest, sizable increases in productivity would result from their removal. Third, the forces linking unionism and efficiency are very complex, with tendencies pulling in opposite directions simultaneously. The positive influence of superior training and reduced hiring costs seems to override the effects of work rules and wages.

A major criticism of Allen's paper is that he simply shows lower union demand elasticities and attributes this to union work rules. The lower elasticities may in fact be caused by another omitted variable. This could be a case of guilt by association.

References: Union Effects on Productivity and Union Work Rule Effects on Efficiency

Addison, John T. "Are Unions Good for Productivity?" *Journal of Labor Research* 3 (Spring 1982), pp. 125-38.

___. "What Do Unions Really Do?" *Journal of Labor Research* 4 (Spring 1985), pp. 127-46.

Addison, John T., and Barnett, A. H. "The Impact of Unions on Productivity." *British Journal of Industrial Relations* 20 (July 1982), pp. 145-62.

Allen, Steven G. "Unionized Construction Workers Are More Productive." *Quarterly Journal of Economics* 99, (May 1984), pp. 249-74.

___. "The Effect on Unionism on Productivity in Privately and Publicly Owned Hospitals and Nursing Homes." *Journal of Labor Research* 7 (Winter 1986), pp. 59-68.

___. "Union Work Rules and Efficiency in the Building Trades." *Journal of Labor Economics* 4 (April 1986), pp. 212-242.

Bemmels, Brian. "How Unions Affect Productivity in Manufacturing Plants." *Industrial and Labor Relations Review* 40 (January 1987), pp. 241-53.

Bourdon, Clinton C., and Levitt, Raymond E. *Union and Open-Shop Construction*. Lexington, MA: D.C. Heath, 1980.

Brown, Charles, and Medoff, James. "Trade Unions in the Production Process." *Journal of Political Economy* 86 (June 1978), pp. 355-78.

Clark, Kim B. "The Impact of Unionization on Productivity: A Case Study." *Industrial and Labor Relations Review* 33 (July 1980), pp. 451-69.

___. "Unionization and Productivity: Micro-Econometric Evidence." *Quarterly*

Journal of Economics 95 (December 1980), pp. 613-39.

_____. "Unionization and Firm Performance: The Impact on Profits, Growth, and Productivity." *American Economic Review* 74 (July 1984), pp. 893-919.

Connerton, M.; Freeman, R. B.; and Medoff, J. L. "Productivity and Industrial Relations: The Case of U.S. Bituminous Coal." Mimeograph, Harvard University, 1983.

Frantz, J. R. "The Impact of Trade Unions on Production in The Wooden Household Furniture Industry." Senior honors thesis, Harvard University, March 1976.

Freeman, Richard B., and Medoff, James L. *What Do Unions Do?* New York: Basic Books, 1984.

Haber, William, and Levinson, Harold M. *Labor Relations and Productivity in the Building Trades*. Ann Arbor: University of Michigan Press, 1956.

Hirsch, Barry T., and Addison, John T. *The Economic Analysis of Unions: New Approaches and Evidence*. Winchester, MA: Allen & Unwin, 1986.

Hirsch, Barry T., and Link, Albert N. "Unions, Productivity and Productivity Growth." *Journal of Labor Research* 5 (Winter 1984), pp. 29-37.

Kendrick, John. *Interindustry Differences in Productivity Growth*. Washington, D.C.: American Enterprise Institute, 1983.

Link, Albert N. "Basic Research and Productivity Increase in Manufacturing: Additional Evidence." *American Economic Review* 71, (December 1981), pp. 1111-12.

Mandelstamm, Allan B. "The Effects of Unions on Efficiency in the Residential Construction Industry: A Case Study." *Industrial and Labor Relations Review* 18 (July 1965), pp. 503-21.

Mansfield, Edwin. "Basic Research and Productivity Increase in Manufacturing." *American Economic Review* 70 (December 1980), pp. 863-73.

Mefford, Robert N. "The Effect of Unions on Productivity in a Multinational Manufacturing Firm." *Industrial and Labor Relations Review* 40 (October 1986), pp. 105-14.

Maki, Dennis R. "The Effects of Unions and Strikes on the Rate of Growth of Total Factor Productivity in Canada." *Applied Economics* 15 (1983), pp.29-41.

Pencavel, John J. "The Distributional and Efficiency Effects of Trade Unions in Britain." *British Journal of Industrial Relations* 15 (July 1977), pp. 137-56.

Reynolds, Morgan O. "Trade Unions in the Production Process Reconsidered." *Journal of Political Economy* 94 (April 1986), pp. 443-47.

Warren, Ronald S. Jr. "The Effect of Unionization on Labor Productivity: Some Time-Series Evidence." *Journal of Labor Research* 6 (Spring 1985), pp. 199-208

Wessels, Walter J. "The Effects of Unions on Employment and Productivity: An Unresolved Contradiction." *Journal of Labor Economics* 3 (January 1985), pp. 101-8.

THE UNION WAGE EFFECT

Most recent scholarly work concerned with the union wage effect cites, agrees with, or takes as a point of departure the findings of H. Gregg Lewis (1963). Lewis surveyed previous literature, as well as reported finding a 10 to 15 percent wage gap between union and nonunion workers for the years 1957-58. He updated his work in a 1986 book finding a mean wage gap of 15 percent for the years 1967-79. Most of the work in this field provides support for this finding. Most recent studies use a cross-sectional or longitudinal method of regression analysis. Differences from, or perhaps enhancements to, Lewis's work, appear in studies that analyze the union wage effect in relation to specific industry, market, occupational, demographic, or regional settings as well as across the business cycle.

The topic of the union wage effect has generated many articles and books. Overviews of many of the issues discussed here may be found in Reder (1965), Johnson (1975), Parsley (1980), Mitchell (1980), Pencavel and Hartsog (1984), as well as in Lewis (1963, 1986). Earlier studies tend to use some type of mean wage differential between union and nonunion workers to arrive at a union wage effect (Parsley). Later studies incorporating regression techniques regress the log of wages against independent variables measuring industry and personal characteristics as well as a union (or collective bargaining) dummy variable (Johnson). The union wage effect can be derived from the coefficient of the union variable.

In spite of the strong agreement of a number of economists concerning a positive union wage effect, points of contention do exist within the field. One of these is the nature of unionism as it relates to the model generally used in these studies. This argument questions the otherwise accepted exogenous nature of the union variable and postulates that it may in fact be endogenously determined. Results of these types of studies vary and are discussed later.

Aside from the theoretical question about the endogenous/exogenous nature of unionism, is the problem of adequately controlling for individual worker quality within cross-sectional models. These models typically employ average wage data rather than actual union and nonunion wage data, which makes controlling for individual worker quality extremely difficult and can result in significant bias in the wage gap estimates. (See Kumar and Stengos 1985 for a discussion of this problem.) Longitudinal studies attempt to compensate for this lack of control on individual worker quality by examining the changes in wage levels of individual workers either entering or leaving the union sector. By examining changes in the union status of individual workers, longitudinal studies dispense with the requirement of employing elaborate controls for worker quality. (See, for example, Mellow 1981.)

Following Lewis's 1963 work, several studies, notably by Weiss (1966), Throop (1968), and Johnson (1975), found larger estimates of the union wage differential than Lewis. A sample of studies that have approached the question of the union premium on demographic and geographic breakdowns follows. These studies employ variations of the cross-sectional model developed by Lewis and others.

Cross-sectional Analyses

An example of a study of the union wage effect by demographic breakdown is the study by Johnson and Youmans (1971). Their results indicate that "unions benefit less educated workers more that more educated workers and tend to provide much higher wage effects for very young and very old workers" (p. 171). Union effects for blacks, however, appear to be greatest in the middle years of employment. Overall they found a 34 percent union wage effect.

Boskin (1972), in a study with similar demographic breakdowns, also included limited occupational breakdowns. In general he found positive effects that varied over occupations as well as sex, age, and race. He found the greatest union effect for craftsmen, operatives, and laborers.

Paul M. Ryscavage (1974), using May 1973 CPS data, found similar although generally larger union effects over occupational groups than Boskin. This is not surprising given the differing data and model specifications. In another study, Block and Kuskin (1978), also using 1973 CPS data, found that nonunion-sector wages are "more responsive to individual workers' levels of education and experience. Despite the greatest labor market rewards to these characteristics in the nonunion sector, union-nonunion wage differentials are positive for most occupations especially . . . in those that are more highly unionized and less skilled" (p. 191).

In a study focusing upon "the variation in union/nonunion wage differentials across workers classified according to occupational/regional attachment," Oaxaca (1975) found the largest differentials "in the South, in certain unskilled occupations, and among black males and white females" (p. 535). He also noted that his study was narrow in scope in the sense that he attempted to estimate the impacts of union membership rather that unionism per se. This qualification applies to all studies of his type and implies that such studies can only show the difference in the wage rate of union and nonunion members, but cannot account for the union threat effect on wages in general.

Unions tend to be associated with product market concentration. Several studies have looked at the combined effect of unions and concentration on wages. Often these studies examine the possibility of monopoly profits in industries. Generally, concentrated industries tend to pay higher wages; however, the significance of the concentration effect on wages drops when individual characteristics of workers are included in the model. This implies that although concentrated industries pay more, they tend to hire better-qualified (more highly educated and more experienced) workers. (See, for example, Weiss 1966.)

Freeman and Medoff (1984) point out that the union wage effect rose substantially in the 1970s to about 20 to 30 percent. They also show that the union wage effect varies greatly among workers depending on their demographic characteristics and the occupation and industry in which they are employed. In general, Freeman and Medoff found larger union/nonunion differentials for relatively lower-paid demographic groups. They also found that by occupation, unions win much larger gains for blue-collar than for white-collar workers. Unions have larger effects in the relatively unorganized South and West than in the Northeast and Central regions. Finally, they found a great deal of variation in the union wage effect by industry, ranging from a low of near zero to a high of over 35 percent.

Using pooled cross-sectional data from 1967-77, Moore and Raisian (1980) raised the issue of union vs. nonunion wage rate changes over time. Their analysis indicates that "real wages have grown faster in the union sector than the nonunion sector between 1967 and 1977" (p. 65). This they felt was caused by shifts in economic factors affecting the union and nonunion sectors and was not necessarily caused by a shift in union power. When they included a market-force trend variable in their model (unemployment within individual industries), the wage-change difference was not significant between the two groups.

Union Wage Differentials over the Business Cycle

In very broad terms, Lewis addressed the issue of union/nonunion wage differences over the business cycle in his 1963 and 1986 publications. He generally found the union wage premium to be countercyclical. This result was corroborated by Pencavel and Hartsog (1984), who had similar findings in a re-estimation of Lewis's (1963) work. Very generally, the union wage gap was high in the thirties, fell to near zero in the forties, was somewhere between 10 percent to 15 percent in the fifties, was estimated at 11 percent in 1967, rose to 18 percent in 1976, and fell somewhat in 1977 and 1978.

Moore and Raisian (1980), using aggregate data from 1967-74, could not find a significant countercyclical effect in the manufacturing union sector. They did find wage rigidity in the manufacturing union sector. This may in part be due to increased COLA clauses in contracts, as well as the number of micro variables they were able to incorporate in their model. They also found evidence, in the nonmanufacturing union sector, of countercyclical wage patterns. Their study reveals a mixed picture of the union sector, depending on the industry analyzed. Of note is their observation that their study did confirm that "the union wage relationship changes significantly over the business cycle making cross-sectional studies sensitive to the year used for analysis" (p. 115). Their results indicate that much of this change over the business cycle is caused by the greater sensitivity of the nonunion sector to economic forces than the union sector. Haworth and Reuther (1978), using interyear comparisons of peak and trough years of the business cycle, found significant union effects in trough but not in peak years. The results of these studies might help explain the varying estimates of the single-equation regression models or the sensitivity to data changes in the simultaneous-model approach. One article that attempted to measure the union wage effect over the business cycle found results opposite to those already mentioned. Pierson (1968) measured the cyclical responsiveness of the union and nonunion sectors separately. Pierson found the union sector to be more responsive to cyclical variables than the nonunion sector. These results stand in contrast to results of most other articles on this subject.

Intrafirm Analysis

To date most union-wage-effect studies have employed an interfirm or interindustry analysis of the union-nonunion wage gap. One study employing an intrafirm analysis instead is that of Verma (1987). Verma argues that an intrafirm analysis provides unique opportunities to incorporate an historical overview of the organizational context of unionization, which is not feasible at other levels of analysis. Verma's methodology facilitates better understanding of not only the magnitude of wage differences but also of how the differences may be interpreted in the context of industrial relations. Verma measures the union-nonunion wage gap within one large manufacturing firm. The firm has over eighty union and nonunion plants in ten different 2-digit SIC industries that are located in all parts of the country. Verma's analysis shows that unions improved the "low" wage rates within this firm by 27.8 percent over the nonunion wage, but the union effect on the "high" wage rate was insignificant.

Longitudinal Analyses

To corroborate cross-sectional findings and better control for individual quality characteristics, several studies analyze the union wage effect using a longitudinal analysis. This approach notes the change in wages over time as they relate to a worker either gaining or losing union status, controlling for some personal, demographic, industry and occupational variables. Four studies using this method–Duncan and Stafford (1980), Mellow (1981), Freeman (1984), and Cunningham and Donovan (1986)–found evidence that supports the cross-sectional findings of a positive union effect, although the estimated effects are significantly lower (generally between 3 and 8 percent). With regard to the longitudinal estimates, Freeman explains that "measurement error biases [the] estimated effects of union downward by substantial amounts" (p. 1). At the same time he notes that the cross-sectional approach might upwardly bias the union effect. Thus he continues, "the likely upward bias of the cross-section estimates of the effect of union and likely downward bias of longitudinal estimates suggest that, under reasonable conditions, the two sets of estimates bound the 'true' union impact posited in standard models of what unions do" (pp. 1-2).

The Exogenous vs. Endogenous Nature of Unionization

A critical assumption in many union-wage-effect studies is that unionization is an exogenous variable. This implies that unionization affects earnings, but earnings do not affect the degree of unionization. If the degree of unionization is actually affected by the level of earnings, then results of studies not specifically allowing for this will obtain inaccurate estimates of the union wage effect. Instead of unionization bringing higher wages, these studies may actually observe higher wages bringing about unionization (Mitchell 1980, p. 105).

One of the first studies to employ the assumption that unionization is an endogenous rather than exogenous variable was by Ashenfelter and Johnson (1972). They found that the union wage effect in manufacturing declines and becomes insignificant when the union variable is endogenously specified. Their results are supported by Schmidt and Strauss (1976). Kahn (1979), however, obtained results exactly opposite to those of Ashenfelter and Johnson. Hirsch (1982) also found results that contradict those of Ashenfelter and Johnson and Schmidt and Strauss. He found that the union wage effect in manufacturing actually increases when endogenously specified. He obtained opposite results for nonmanufacturing. In a more recent study, Duncan and Leigh (1985) showed that the estimated union wage effect increases under the assumption of endogenously determined unionization.

As pointed out by Hirsch and Addison (1986), the estimates of the union wage effect under the assumption of endogenously determined union status are highly erratic and very sensitive to specification of the wage and union equations. In one of the most comprehensive works on this subject, Lewis (1986) reviewed twenty eight studies that employed the assumption of endogenously determined union status. He showed that simultaneous-equation estimates of the union wage effect, under the assumption of endogenous unionization, were not consistently larger or smaller than single-equation estimates. He also showed that a substantial proportion of the estimates were "preposterously large or outlandishly negative" (1986, p. 47). He argued that results from studies employing the assumption of endogenous union status are sensitive to the specification and data sets used. In other words, simultaneous equations do not produce robust results.

Use of an endogenous union variable in wage models does receive some support in the literature. However, such models do not produce consistent results. To date, the literature has not successfully dealt with the simultaneous determination of unionization and wages.

The Union Fringe-Benefit Effect

A number of articles have examined the effect of unionization on fringe benefits. These articles support an even larger positive union effect on fringe benefits, which implies that the union effect on total compensation is larger than the union wage effect alone. (Freeman 1981 is one of the better articles on this subject. A review of these articles will not be included here.)

Summary

From the evidence it seems safe to say that unions do raise the wages of their members. The problem of accurately determining the relative union wage amount is complicated by the complex relationship between all factors involved and the difficulty in measuring them using current data sources. It is apparent that this relative amount is dependent on age, job classification, regional, and other factors. Along these lines, an interesting point made by Duncan and Stafford (1980) is that unions may be predisposed to certain work places with faster work paces, more automation, and a more interdependent and homogeneous work force. The worker trades the higher wages for less-desirable work conditions, which attract union representation. This mutual dependence of wages and unions appears to be a major difficulty in modeling wage determination because of the current condition of available data. Even so, most models generally point to what seems rather obvious, that unions derive a wage premium for their members.

References: The Union Wage Effect

Ashenfelter, Orley, and Johnson, George E. "Unionism, Relative Wages, and Labor Quality in U.S. Manufacturing Industries." *International Economic Review* 13 (October 1972), pp. 488-508.

Block, Farrell E., and Kuskin, Mark S. "Wage Determination in the Union and Nonunion Sectors." *Industrial and Labor Relations Review* 31 (January 1978), pp. 183-92.

Boskin, Michael J. "Unions and Relative Real Wages." *American Economic Review* 62 (June 1972), pp. 466-72.

Cunningham, James S., and Donovan, Elaine "Patterns of Union Membership and Relative Wages." *Journal of Labor Research* 7 (Spring 1986), pp. 125-144.

Duncan, Gregory M., and Leigh, Duane E. "The Endogeneity of Union Status: An Empirical Test." *Journal of Labor Economics* 3 (July 1985), pp. 385-402.

Duncan, Gregory M., and Stafford, Frank P. "Do Union Members Receive Compensating Wage Differentials?" *American Economic Review* 70 (June 1980), pp. 355-71.

Freeman, Richard B. "The Effect of Unionism on Fringe Benefits." *Industrial and Labor Relations Review* 34 (July 1981), pp. 489-509.

____. "Longitudinal Analyses of the Effects of Trade Unions," *Journal of Labor Economics.* 2 (January 1984), pp. 1-26.

Freeman, Richard B., and Medoff, James L. *What Do Unions Do?* New York: Basic Books, 1984.

Haworth, Charles T., and Reuther, Carol Jean. "Industrial Concentration and Interindustry Wage Determination." *Review of Economics and Statistics* 60 (February 1978), pp. 85-95.

Hirsch, Barry T. "The Interindustry Structure of Unionism, Earnings, and Earnings Dispersion." *Industrial and Labor Relations Review* 36 (October 1982), pp. 22-39.

Hirsch, Barry T., and Addison, John T. *The Economic Analysis of Unions: New Approaches and Evidence.* Boston: Allen & Unwin, 1986.

Johnson, George E. "Economic Analysis of Trade Unionism." *American Economic Review* 65 (May 1975), pp. 23-28.

Johnson, George E., and Youmans, Kenwood C. "Union Relative Wage Effects by Age and Education." *Industrial and Labor Relations Review* 24 (January 1971), pp. 171-79.

Kahn, Lawrence M. "Unionism and Relative Wages: Direct and Indirect Effects." *Industrial and Labor Relations Review* 32 (July 1979), pp. 520-32.

Kumar, Pradeep, and Stengos, Thanasis. "Measuring the Union Relative Wage Impact: A Methodological Note." *Canadian Journal of Economics* 18 (February 1985), pp. 182-89.

Lewis, H. Gregg. *Unionism and Relative Wages in the United States.* Chicago: University of Chicago Press, 1963.

____. *Union Relative Wage Effects: A Survey.* Chicago: University of Chicago Press, 1986.

Mellow, Wesley. "Unionism and Wages: A Longitudinal Analysis." *Review of Economics and Statistics* 63 (February 1981), pp. 43-52.

Mitchell, Daniel J. B. *Unions, Wages, and Inflation.* Washington, D.C.: Brookings Institution 1980.

Moore, William J., and Raisian, John "Cyclical Sensitivity of Union/Nonunion Relative Wage Effects." *Journal of Labor Research* 1 (Spring 1980), pp. 115-132.

____. "The Level and Growth of Union/Nonunion Relative Wage Effects, 1967-1977." *Journal of Labor Research* 4 (Winter 1983), pp. 65-79.

Oaxaca, Ronald L. "Estimation of Union/Nonunion Wage Differentials Within Occupational/Regional Subgroups." *Journal of Human Resources* 10 (Fall 1975), pp. 529-37.

Parsley, C. J. "Labor Union Effects on Wage Gains: A Survey of Recent Literature." *Journal of Economic Literature* 18 (March 1980), pp. 1-31.

Pencavel, John, and Hartsog, Catherine E. "A Reconsideration of the Effects of Unionism on Relative Wages and Employment in the United States 1920-1980." *Journal of Labor Economics* 2 (April 1984), pp. 193-232.

Pierson, Gail. "The Effect of Union Strength on the U.S. Phillips Curve." *American Economic Review* 58 (June 1968), pp. 456-67.

Reder, M. W. "Unions and Wages: The Problems of Measurement." *Journal of Political Economy* 73 (April 1965), pp. 188-96.

Ryscavage, Paul M. "Measuring Union-Nonunion Earnings Differences." *Monthly Labor Review* 97 (December 1974), pp. 3-9.

Schmidt, Peter, and Strauss, Robert P. "The Effect of Unions on Earnings and Earnings on Unions: A Mixed Logit Approach." *International Economic Review* 17 (February 1976), pp. 204-212.

Throop, Adrian W. "The Union-Nonunion Wage Differential and Cost Push Inflation." *American Economic Review* 68 (March 1968), pp. 79-99.

Verma, Anil. "Union and Nonunion Wages at the Firm Level: A Combined Institutional and Econometric Analysis." *Journal of Labor Research* 8 (Winter 1987), pp. 67-83.

Weiss, Leonard W. "Concentration and Labor Earnings." *American Economic Review* 56 (March 1966), pp. 96-117.

UNION WAGE SPILLOVER

Most labor economists agree that unions have a positive effect on the compensation level of their members. But how does one union or a group of unions affect compensation levels in other unions or groups of unions, and how do unions affect nonunion compensation levels? This effect, known as union wage spillover, may be either positive or negative. If unions promote pattern bargaining or force nonunion firms in the same industry to raise wages in order to avoid unionization, then the spillover is positive. If, on the other hand, unions restrict employment in the union sector, thus crowding the nonunion sector, the union wage spillover may be negative. A great deal of anecdotal evidence showing positive union wage spillover exists. In spite of this evidence, economic literature has been able to show positive union wage spillover only within narrow classifications and not within the U.S. economy in general.

The professional literature on wage spillover can be divided into four categories, depending on which groups of workers are analyzed: (1) union-to-nonunion spillover within a single industry; (2) spillover within a group of related industries–for example, the wage levels of heavily unionized, durable goods industries may be interrelated; (3) spillover from blue-collar unions to white-collar compensation levels; and (4) economy wide spillover from union-sector wage levels to nonunion-sector wage levels. We shall discuss each of the four categories of wage spillover in turn.

Union-to-Nonunion Spillover Within an Industry

The "threat effect" is a relative rise in the level of nonunion wages as management attempts to forestall unionization. Many economists believe the threat of unionization is greater in highly organized industries. Therefore, they expect that nonunion wages would be relatively higher in highly organized industries than in industries that are not as highly organized. Substantial evidence of this effect exists.

Using industry-aggregated data on fifty-nine manufacturing industries, Rosen (1969) found evidence of a significant positive threat effect. Rosen's results were called into question by a Freeman-Medoff study (1981) which, using a micro data base of blue-collar manufacturing workers, found no evidence of a positive threat effect. Freeman and Medoff found that the percentage organized affects union wage levels but not nonunion wage levels. These results were, in turn, called into question by several later studies. Using micro data from the May 1973 to 1979 Current Population Surveys (CPS), Moore, Newman and Cunningham (1985) found that, inter alia, an increase in the extent of unionism in an industry has substantial positive effects on the wages of nonunion, as well as union, workers. Podgursky (1986) also used a micro data base and found a significant threat effect. His threat effect was significant for medium-sized and large establishments but not for small establishments. Results from Hirsch and Neufeld (1987), like those of Podgursky and Moore, et al, cast further doubt on the results of Freeman and Medoff. They also used CPS data (1973-1981 and 1983) and found that industry union density is positively associated with both union and nonunion wages. A related study by Kahn and Curme (1987) found that nonunion wage dispersion is lower in more highly unionized industries. Finally, Antos (1983) has examined the effect white-collar unions have on white-collar nonunion workers and found a significant positive threat effect. In spite of the Freeman-Medoff paper, the evidence seems to clearly indicate a positive union threat effect within industries.

Spillover within a Group of Related Industries

Literature on wage spillover within a group of industries often refers to such phenomena as pattern bargaining and wage rounds. The literature provides some support for a pattern-bargaining type of spillover but the quality of the data and methodology leaves room for skepticism.

Three studies—by Soffer (1959), Maher (1961), and Rees and Hamilton (1962)—examine the similarity of wage rate movements within sectors of the economy to show pattern bargaining or spillover. However, mere similarity of wage movement or small variation in wage movement is not enough to determine wage spillover. Wage levels may move similarly because of a similarity of market forces. McGuire and Rapping (1966) provide a well-written critique of this method of identifying spillover.

Another method of identifying spillover used by several authors is to include the average wage of a so-called key group of industries as an independent variable in wage regressions. Eckstein and Wilson (1962) were the first to use this technique. They found spillover within a group of highly unionized, durable goods industries and from this group to the rest of the economy. McGuire and Rapping (1967) criticized the Eckstein-Wilson model for being based on only two degrees of freedom, for using improper statistical comparisons, and for yielding ambiguous results that may be consistent with hypotheses other than pattern bargaining such as highly correlated labor-demand changes. In 1968 McGuire and Rapping specified their own variation, with the steel and auto settlements acting essentially as key group. A criticism of this type of spillover model is that inclusion of a broad average as an independent variable will always improve the fit of a wage model but may not identify actual spillover.

Mehra (1976) used a novel technique of measuring spillover. He first took into account the economic factors affecting wage levels and then analyzed the residuals for interrelationships. He found interrelationships within a group of

313

high wage, heavily unionized, noncompetitive manufacturing industries but no spillover beyond that. Mehra's work takes significant steps toward avoiding the mistake of confusing market forces with spillover. Christofides, Swidinsky, and Wilton (1980), using Canadian data, found results roughly similar to Mehra's. They found spillover within broad industry regional subgroups but the relationship weakened as the industry regional subgroups were expanded in scope. This study has the advantage of using a rich Canadian micro data base of union contracts.

The literature appears to have reached some agreement that spillover does exists within narrow groups of industries, such as highly unionized, durable goods industries.

Spillover from Blue-Collar Unions to White-Collar Wages and Fringes

The limited amount of research done on this subject indicates that blue-collar unions tend to increase the level of wages and fringes of white-collar workers, all other things being equal.

Freeman (1981) found blue-collar unionism to be associated with 10 percent higher fringe benefits for white-collar workers in manufacturing and 13 percent higher fringes in all private establishments. Solnick (1985) found that blue-collar unions raise white-collar wages by almost 19 percent and white-collar fringes by 35.4 percent. His results showed a great deal of variation on an SIC two-digit industry basis.

Spillover from Union Contracts, in General, to Nonunion Wage Levels

Several methods have been used to examine the effect union wage levels have on economywide nonunion wage levels. Pierson (1968) examined a group of strong-union manufacturing industries and a group of weak-union manufacturing industries. Pierson found that the weak-union equation had a better fit when the average wage change of the strong-union group was included, and concluded that these results provided evidence of union-to-nonunion spillover. Pierson's conclusion suffers from the problem of including a broad average in the wage equation. This problem in methodology was explained earlier. Ashenfelter, Johnson, and Pencavel (1972) found that wage changes in union manufacturing and nonunion manufacturing were not significantly different over the 1954-68 period. This, they believe, provides evidence of union-to-nonunion spillover. The Ashenfelter, Johnson, and Pencavel conclusion suffers because, as mentioned previously, correlation of wage movement does not demonstrate causation.

Wayne Vroman (1982) used two-digit quarterly data covering the 1958-78 period to estimate the effect union earnings have on *average* hourly earnings. He found that union wages have a significant effect on average hourly earnings, with union scales explaining much more of average wage changes than just their own wage shares. In addition, Vroman found evidence of spillover from union to *nonunion* wages in seven of his nineteen two-digit industries.

Beladi and Brunner (1987) argued that Vroman's findings are incomplete because he tested only for causation running from union wages to average wages, and did not allow for causation to run in the opposite direction at the same time. Using Vroman's data, Beladi and Brunner showed that average hourly earnings have feedback effects on union wages, and vice versa. In other words, average hourly earnings spill over into union wage scales, and union wage scales spill over into average hourly earnings. The authors used Granger causality tests, not simultaneous equations to come up with these results.

Three studies have used a ratio of union to nonunion wage levels as a spillover measure. Using this type of analysis, two separate wage models are estimated, one explaining the union-sector wages and another explaining the nonunion sector wages. The ratio of union to nonunion wages is included as an independent variable in both models. If the union-to-nonunion ratio or relative wage variable is positive in the union equation, then spillover from union to nonunion is indicated. Conversely, a negative sign in the nonunion equation indicates spillover from nonunion to union. Flanagan (1976) and Johnson (1977) both found spillover from nonunion to union but not vice versa. These two papers were criticized and shown to be sensitive to small changes in data and specification by Mitchell (1980) and Susan Vroman (1980). In a later paper, Susan Vroman (1982) used essentially the same methodology to show spillover from union to nonunion. Mitchell (1982) then argued that the relative wage model cannot under most circumstances be used to identify spillover. He showed how the relative wage model can show spillover where none actually exists. For example, using this model, Mitchell found spillover running from apparel manufacturing to finance, a highly implausible finding.

Kahn (1978) analyzed wage levels in a predominantly union city versus wage levels in a predominantly nonunion city to estimate the level and direction of spillover. After controlling for worker characteristics, he found that high union wage levels actually depress nonunion wages by forcing more workers into nonunion jobs. In 1980 he continued his work by looking at spillover within sex-race groups. He found that union spillover raises nonunion white male income but lowers nonunion white female and nonunion nonwhite male income.

Holzer (1982) addressed an issue similar to that of Kahn (1980). Holzer looked at the effect unionization has on wages and employment in the youth labor market. Using data from the 1978 Current Population Survey, he found that "high rates of unionization in SMSAs appear to raise wages for young white and black unionists and also for nonunion whites but the effect of unionization on the wages of nonunion blacks appears to be quite negative" (p. 399).

Holzer's work provides further evidence that union wage spillover does exist in the economy in general, but is positive only for certain groups of the economy.

References: Union Wage Spillover

Antos, Joseph R. "Union Effects on White-Collar Compensation." *Industrial and Labor Relations Review* 36 (April 1983), pp. 461-79.

Ashenfelter, O. C.; Johnson, G. E.; and Pencavel, J. H. "Trade Unions and the Rate of Change of Money Wages in United States Manufacturing Industry." *Review of Economic Studies* 39 (January 1972), pp. 27-54.

Beladi, Hamid, and Brunner, Lawrence. "Trade Unions and Money Wages Changes in U.S. Manufacturing Industries: Further Empirical Evidence." *Quarterly Journal of Business and Economics* 26 (Summer 1987), pp. 79-86.

Christofides, Louis N.; Swidinsky, Robert; and Wilton, David A. "A Microeconomic Analysis of Spillover Within The Canadian Wage Determination Process." *Review of Economics and Statistics* 62 (May 1980), pp. 213-21.

Eckstein, Otto, and Wilson, Thomas A. "The Determination of Money Wages in American Industry." *Quarterly Journal of Economics* 76 (August 1962), pp. 379-414.

Flanagan, Robert J. "Wage Interdependence in Unionized Labor Markets." *Brookings Papers on Economic Activity* (1976) pp. 635-81.

Freeman, Richard B. "The Effect of Unionism on Fringe Benefits." *Industrial and Labor Relations Review* 34 (July 1981), pp. 489-509.

Freeman, Richard B., and Medoff, James L. "The Impact of the Percentage Organized on Union and Nonunion Wages." *Review of Economics and Statistics* 68 (November 1981), pp. 561-72.

Hirsch, Barry T., and Neufeld, John L. "Nominal and Real Union Wage Differentials and the Effects of Industry and SMSA Density: 1973-1983." *Journal of Human Resources* 22 (Winter 1987), pp. 138-48.

Holzer, Harry J. "Unions and the Labor Market Status of White and Minority Youth." *Industrial and Labor Relations Review* 35 (April 1982), pp. 392-405.

Johnson, George E. "The Determination of Wages in the Union and Non-union Sectors." *British Journal of Industrial Relations* 15 (July 1977), pp. 211-25.

Kahn, Lawrence M. "The Effect of Unions on the Earnings of Nonunion Workers." *Industrial and Labor Relationship Review* 31 (January 1978), pp. 205-16.

____. "Union Spillover Effects on Organized Labor Markets." *Journal of Human Resources* 15 (January 1980), pp. 87-98.

Kahn, Lawrence M., and Curme, Michael. "Unions and Nonunion Wage Dispersion." *Review of Economics and Statistics* 69 (November 1987), pp. 600-607.

Maher, John E. "The Wage Pattern in the United States, 1946-1957." *Industrial and Labor Relations Review* 15 (October 1961), pp. 3-20.

McGuire, Timothy W., and Rapping, Leonard A. "Interindustry Wage Change Dispersion and the 'Spillover' Hypothesis." *American Economic Review* 57 (June 1966), pp. 493-501.

____. "The Determination of Money Wages in American Industry: Comment." *Quarterly Journal of Economics* 81 (November 1967), pp. 684-94.

____. "The Role of Market Variables and Key Bargains in the Manufacturing Wage Determination Process." *Journal of Political Economy* 76 (September/October), pp. 1015-36.

Mehra, Y. P. "Spillovers in Wage Determination in U.S. Manufacturing Industries." *Review of Economics and Statistics* 58 (August 1976), pp. 300-12.

Mitchell, Daniel J. B. "Union/Non-union Wage Spillovers: A Note." *British Journal of Industrial Relations* 18 (November 1980), pp. 372-76.

Mitchell, Daniel J. B. "How to Find Wage Spillovers (Where None Exist)." *Industrial Relations* 21 (Fall 1982), pp. 392-97.

Moore, William J.; Newman, Robert J.; and Cunningham, James. "The Effect of the Extent of Unionism on Union and Nonunion Wages." *Journal of Labor Research* 7 (Winter 1985), pp. 21-44.

Pierson, Gail. "The Effect of Union Strength on the Phillips Curve." *American Economic Review* 58 (June 1968), pp. 456-67.

Podgursky, Michael. "Unions, Establishment Size and Intra-Industry Threat Effects." *Industrial and Labor Relations Review* 39 (January 1986), pp. 277-84.

Rees, Albert, and Hamilton, Mary T. "Postwar Movements of Wage Levels and Unit Labor Costs." *Journal of Law and Economics* 5 (October 1962), pp. 41-68.

Rosen, Sherwin. "Trade Union Power, Threat Effects and the Extent of Organization." *Review of Economic Studies* 36 (April 1969), pp. 185-96.

Soffer, Benson. "On Union Rivalries and the Minimum Differentiation of Wage Patterns." *Review of Economics and Statistics* 41 (February 1959), pp. 53-60.

Solnick, Loren M. "The Effect of Blue-Collar Unions on White-Collar Wages and Fringe Benefits." *Industrial and Labor Relations Review* 38 (January 1985), pp. 236-43.

Vroman, Susan. "Research Note: Union/Nonunion Spillovers." *British Journal of Industrial Relations* 18 (November 1980), pp. 369-71.

Vroman, Susan. "The Direction of Wage Spillovers in Manufacturing." *Industrial and Labor Relations Review* 36 (October 1982), pp. 102-12.

Vroman, Wayne. "Union Contracts and Money Wages Changes in U.S. Manufacturing Industries." *Quarterly Journal of Economics* 97 (November 1982), pp. 571-94.

WAGE NORMS

The term *wage norm* was first introduced in inflation literature in the early 1980s by Arthur M. Okun and George L. Perry. Okun and Perry argued that an important part of the inflation process is the inertia of wage increases. The general concept of wage inertia, although not formally referred to as a wage norm before Okun and Perry, was recognized and analyzed by many earlier authors. In fact, Keynes introduced the concept of sticky wages which implies wage inertia. The concept of wage inertia introduced by Perry and Okun differed from earlier work by specifically describing the stickiness of wages as being the result of habitual wage increases or wage norms. The formal introduction of wage norms also significantly changed the way inflation models are specified by those authors accepting the wage norm concept. Whereas inertia in wage inflation models had previously been captured mainly by including lagged values of wage increases, Perry's and Okun's work suggested that introduction of a specific wage norm variable would significantly improve empirical results.

Okun's Work

Arthur M. Okun is credited by Perry with the introduction of the term *wage norm*. In Okun's (1981) book *Prices and Quantities: A Macroeconomic Analysis*, which was largely completed before his 1980 death, Okun provided a common-sense description of the wage-setting process that employed the concepts of career strategy and implicit contracts. Within these concepts, Okun described various influences on wage setting, including the norm rate of increase. Okun stated that "workers are likely to develop some notion of how fast they expect their wages to rise when they begin employment and when they decide whether or not to go shopping for other jobs. When changes in wages are announced by the employer (or newly negotiated in collective bargaining) they are assessed against the background of these expectations" (p. 93). Furthermore, Okun pointed out that when employers grant wage increases that for any reason do not vary much from year to year, then a norm is formed that takes on inertia.

Perry's Work

George L. Perry (1980) argued that three distinct economic processes potentially act on wages. The first is the response of average real wages to unemployment and changes in demand. Perry argued that, in fact, real wages show no systematic cyclical movement and, therefore, analysis of real wage behavior is unimportant in modeling the economy's cyclical behavior. It is the process by which *nominal* wages are determined that is central to explaining wage inflation, according to Perry. And the process of nominal wage setting has two distinct parts. The first is the response of nominal wages to cyclical movements in the economy. The second is the response of nominal wages to a wage norm for the economy.

Perry is careful to point out that the distinction of the norm from cyclical effects on wages does not imply that the norm is insulated from the effects of demand. He states that "the norm for wage increases is at least partly an adaptive response to past rates of wage increase. Thus a sustained wage inflation will eventually escalate the norm" (p. 216). Other influences on the norm that are recognized by Perry include price changes that are independent of wage changes and direct policies of the government such as wage guide-posts, controls, or standards associated with various tax-based income poli-cies. Perry notes that the norm basically reflects expectations of the rate of wage inflation that are formed largely on the basis of experienced inflation.

Perry tests his model of wage inflation using data covering the 1954-80 period. He argues that two shifts in the wage norm occurred during this period. One was a downward shift after 1961. The other was a substantial upward shift, which occurred after the late 1960s. Perry's model accounts for these shifts with dummy variables. Other variables in the model include the demographically weighted unemployment rate, lagged unemployment, lagged consumer prices, and dummy variables to account for Johnson's guideposts during the 1964-66 period. Nixon's wage and price controls were accounted for by simply excluding the period during which they were in effect. Estimation of the model indicated that the norm shift variables were signifi-cant in explaining the record of wage inflation during the period. In fact, when the traditional measure of inflation inertia–a lagged independent vari-able–was added to the model, it proved to be insignificant. These results pro-vide strong support for the wage-norm model of inflation.

Besides his 1980 work, Perry has produced two other papers dealing directly with the wage-norm concept. In 1983 Perry suggested that the severely restrictive monetary policy begun in 1979 and the subsequent severe recession may have shifted the wage norm down. In 1986 Perry added to his work by confirming that the wage norm had indeed shifted down in the 1980-82 reces-sion. He also reiterated the idea that the wage norm is not affected by the typical business cycle. Only prolonged departures from typical business cycles or other extreme economic developments cause shifts in the norm, according to Perry.

Other Authors

Charles Schultze (1981) employed the wage norm concept to analyze infla-tion over the 1901-80 period. Schultze pointed out that the wage or inflation norm "is a useful way of expressing the proposition that the complex of backward- and forward-looking forces that influenced current wage and price set-ting in most peacetime cycles since 1900 tended to persist with only modest changes across a number of cycles" (p. 528). In other words, the norm concept is a useful tool for analyzing inflation inertia.

Schultze, like Perry, employed a discontinuous norm in his model rather than one that continuously adapts in a smooth manner, as would be the case if lagged inflation were used as a measure of inflation inertia. To express his view of inflation inertia, Schultze kept the inflation norm the same through major subperiods of the prewar and postwar cycles, estimating it by the aver-age of price change over the subperiod.

From his analysis Schultze concluded that inflation norms are fairly stable. And "the learning process by which old norms and rules of thumb are aban-doned for new ones depends on both the magnitude and the duration of the disequilibria that give rise to a deviation of actual inflation from the norm" (p. 565).

In 1986 Schultze continued his work by analyzing U.S. price inflation from 1871 to 1986. Leaving aside the two world wars and the Great Depression, Schultze found only one episode resembling a norm shift in the pre-Depression era despite the many ups and downs of the business cycle. Schultze argues that experience in the prewar era had taught people that one year's rate of inflation had little to do with the next year's. The norm was therefore formu-lated not on a year-to-year basis but over a long period of experience. In the postwar era, Schultze points out, experience showed a change in the nature of the business cycle. Positive swings were likely to be longer and negative swings shorter in the postwar era. Declines in the average price level were also unlikely. Looking specifically at the 1966-86 period, Schultze argues that excessive fiscal expansion and too-accommodative monetary policy coupled with supply shocks from oil and food prices shifted the norm rate of inflation up significantly. He interprets the two recessions of the 1970s as the result of efforts to break this norm. Finally in 1980 and 1981, demand restraint was made ruthless enough to break the high norm rate of inflation. Schultze's work implies that, historically, inflation norms have been fairly stable. But this stability may have weakened somewhat in the postwar era. At least the danger of such a weakening exists.

Daniel Mitchell has employed the concept of wage norms in his work on *union* wages. In a 1985 paper he provides a convincing analysis of a down-ward shift in union wage norms in the first half of the 1980s. In a 1986 article he provides further evidence of a downward shift in union wage norms in the 1980s and argues that the norm concept is more applicable to the union sector than it is to the nonunion sector. In fact, Mitchell suggests that the norm con-cept may not be a useful tool in analyzing nonunion wage changes.

Michael Wachter (1986) also looked at wage norms in the union sector. Wachter found that adjustments in collective bargaining often take place in discrete steps. These adjustments are related to transaction costs and the associated parameters of labor law. Once these transaction costs are over-come, large discrete changes in collective bargaining can occur and changes in union wage norms follow. Thus, Wachter sees shifts in union wage norms as a function of changes in the relative union-management power relationship.

Criticisms

Robert J. Gordon (1980) criticized the wage-norm model of inflation mainly because it rejects the natural rate hypothesis (NRH). The natural rate hypothesis holds that there is no long-run trade-off between inflation and unemployment. In other words, according to the NRH, in the short run policy-makers can trade less inflation for more unemployment and vice versa but in the long-run such a trade-off is not possible. Gordon argues that by replacing the lagged wage-change variable with a norm-shift variable the wage-norm model moves away from the NRH by disavowing any systematic process by which excess demand or supply is converted into a shift in the norm. Gordon implicitly argues that current inflation is continuously adapting to past infla-tion, and he rejects the idea of discrete movements in a norm rate of increase that is part of Perry's model. Using a model that includes lagged wage changes as an explanatory variable, Gordon argues that his empirical results show no need to include the wage-norm concept in inflation analysis.

William Fellner (1980, 1981) criticized the norm concept on the grounds that actual shifts in inflation inertia could be better explained in terms of reactions by economic agents to credible shifts in government policy. In other words, Fellner believes that changes in inflation inertia come about as the result of people's rational, forward-looking expectations of changes in government pol-icy. Past experiences, and thus norms, have little to do with those forward expectations and are thus not very useful concepts.

William Nordhaus commented about Perry's 1980 paper that the norm con-cept may be valid but it is not useful until it is possible to establish how the norm is formed (see Perry 1980, "General Discussion," pp. 258-60). He made similar comments about Schultze's 1981 paper (see Schultze 1981, "General Discussion," pp. 589-92). Several economists, including Alan Blinder, Charles Holt, and William Nordhaus, have criticized the norm-model implication that inflationary expectations move in a steplike manner. They argue that expec-tations ought to change continuously (see comments on Perry 1980 and Schultze 1981).

Summary

Wage or inflation norm is a relatively new concept that began with Okun (1981) and Perry (1980). In empirical work, the norm rate of inflation or wage change has been shown to be relatively stable, requiring fairly large deviations from past experiences to initiate a change. The norm concept appears to be receiving increasing attention but is not without its critics. It has been criticized on the basis of its rejection of a continuously adapting inflation rate and for discounting the role of rational expectations.

References: Wage Norms

Fellner, William. "Inflation in Theory and Practice: Comments." *Brookings Papers on Economic Activity* (1980), pp. 243-48.

____. "Some Macro Foundations for Micro Theory: Comments." *Brookings Papers on Economic Activity* (1981), pp. 577-81.

Gordon, Robert J. "Inflation in Theory and Practice: Comments." *Brookings Papers on Economic Activity* (1981), pp. 249-57.

Mitchell, Daniel J. B. "Shifting Norms in Wage Determination." *Brookings Papers on Economic Activity* (1985), pp. 575-99.

____. "Union vs. Nonunion Wage Norm Shifts." *American Economic Review* 76 (May 1986), pp. 249-52.

Okun, Arthur M. *Prices and Quantities: A Macroeconomic Analysis.* Washington, D.C.: Brookings Institution, 1981.

Perry, George L. "Inflation in Theory and Practice." *Brookings Papers on Economic Activity* (1980), pp. 207-41.

____. "What Have We Learned about Disinflation?" *Brookings Papers on Economic Activity* (1983), pp. 587-602.

____. "Shifting Wage Norms and their Implication." *American Economic Review* 76 (May 1986), pp. 245-48.

Schultze, Charles L. "Some Macro Foundations for Micro Theory." *Brookings Papers on Economic Activity* (1981) pp. 519-76.

____. *Other Times, Other Places: Macroeconomic Lessons from U.S. and European History.* Washington, D.C.: Brookings Institution, 1986.

Wachter, Michael L. "Union Wage Rigidity: The Default Settings of Labor Law." *American Economic Review* 76 (May 1986), pp. 240-44.

NOTES

CHAPTER 1: Basic Considerations in the Management of Competition

1. The source of data for this chart is the U.S. Department of Commerce, Bureau of Economic Analysis, Business Conditions Digest, various issues.

CHAPTER 2: Managing Competition in Corporate Markets

1. William Greider, *Secrets of the Temple: How the Federal Reserve Runs the Country* (New York: Simon and Schuster, 1987).

2. William G. Shepherd, "Causes of Increased Competition in the U.S. Economy, 1939-1980," *Review of Economics and Statistics 64* (November 1982), pp. 613-26.

3. George J. Stigler, *Capital and Rates of Return in Manufacturing Industries* (Princeton: Princeton University Press, 1963).

4. For a different view see David M. Blank, "Television Advertising: The Great Discount Illusion, or Tonypandy Revisited," *Journal of Business,* January 1968, pp. 10-36.

5. *Wall Street Journal,* February 13, 1986, p. 14.

6. The source of data for this chart is the U.S. Department of Commerce, Bureau of Economic Analysis, *Survey of Current Business,* various issues containing the National Income and Product Accounts Tables.

7. Data on the Standard & Poor's 400 return on equity are from the Standard & Poor's Corporation. Data on bond yields are from the U.S. Department of Commerce, Bureau of Economic Analysis, *Business Conditions Digest*, various issues.

8. The data on manufacturing return on equity are from the U.S. Department of Commerce, Bureau of the Census, *Quarterly Financial Report for Manufacturing, Mining, and Trade Corporations*, various issues. The data on capacity utilization are from the Board of Governors of the Federal Reserve System, Division of Research and

Statistics, Industrial Output Section, *Capacity Utilization: Manufacturing, Mining, and Utilities and Industrial Materials.*

9. Frank H. Easterbrook, "Workable Antitrust Policy," *Michigan Law Review* 84 (August 1986), pp. 1696-1713.

CHAPTER 3: Managing Competition in Labor Markets

1. H. Gregg Lewis, *Union Relative Wage Effects: A Survey,* (Chicago: University of Chicago Press, 1986).

2. Richard B. Freeman, and James L. Medoff, *What Do Unions Do?* (New York: Basic Books, 1984).

3. Freeman and Medoff, *What Do Unions Do?* Chapter 3.

4. Gary A. Shilling, "Cartel and Strong Unions Up and Down Together," A. Gary Shilling & Company, Inc., May 19, 1986.

5. Peter Linneman and Michael L. Wachter, "Rising Union Premiums and the Declining Boundaries among Noncompeting Groups," *American Economic Review,* 76 (May 1986), pp. 103-108.

6. See, for example, Freeman and Medoff, *What Do Unions Do?* ch 12.

7. Robert F. Lanzillotti, "Pricing Objectives in Large Companies," *American Economic Review* (December 1958), pp. 921-40.

8. Linneman and Wachter, " Rising Union Premiums," p. 105.

9. Richard Edwards, and Paul Swaim, "Union Nonunion Earnings Differentials and the Decline of Private Sector Unionism," *American Economic Review* 76 (May 1986), pp. 97-102.

10. Charles Brown, and James Medoff, "Trade Unions in the Production Process," *Journal of Political Economy* 86 (June 1978), pp. 355-78.

11. See George Perry, "Inflation in Theory and Practice," *Brookings Papers on Economic Activity* (1980), pp. 207-41; George Perry, "Shifting Wage Norms and their Implications," *American Economic Review* 76 (May 1986), pp. 245-48; Arthur M. Okun, *Prices and Quantities: A Macroeconomic Analysis,* (Washington, D.C.: Brookings Institution,

1981); Daniel J. B. Mitchell, "Shifting Norms in Wage Determination," *Brookings Papers on Economic Activity*, (1985) pp. 575-99; Daniel J. B. Mitchell, "Union vs Nonunion Wage Norm Shifts," *American Economic Review* 76 (May 1986), pp. 249-52; Charles L. Schultze, "Cross-Country and Cross-Temporal Differences in Inflation Responsiveness," *American Economic Review* 74 (May 1984), pp. 160-65; and Michael Wachter, "Union Wage Rigidity: The Default Settings of Labor Law," *American Economic Review* 76 (May 1986), pp. 240-44.

12. The data on average hourly compensation are from the U.S. Department of Labor, Bureau of Labor Statistics.

13. See Jerry E. Pohlman, *Economics of Wage and Price Controls,* (Columbus, OH: Grid Inc., 1972).

14. Mitchell, Daniel J. B. (1980), *Unions, Wages, and Inflation,* Brookings Institution, Washington, D. C.

15. Arnold Ordman, "Fifty Years of the NLRA: An Overview," *West Virginia Law Review* 88 (Fall 1985), pp. 15-24.

16. Irving H. Siegel and Edgar Weinberg, *Labor-Management Cooperation: The American Experience*, (Kalamazoo MI: W. E. Upjohn Institute for Employment Research, 1982); Michael H. Schuster, *Union-Management Cooperation: Structure, Process, Impact*, (Kalamazoo MI: W. E. Upjohn Institute for Employment Research, 1984); Charlotte Gold, *Labor-Management Committees: Confrontation, Cooptation, or Cooperation?* (Ithaca NY: ILR Press, New York State School of Industrial and Labor Relations, Cornell University, 1986); and Edward Cohen-Rosenthal, and Cynthia E. Burton, *Mutual Gains: A Guide to Union-Management Cooperation*, (New York: Praeger, 1987).

17. John Hoerr, "A New Friend for Quality of Work Life," *Business Week,* September 27, 1982, p. 26.

18. William Serrin, "Giving Workers a Voice of Their Own," *New York Times Magazine,* December 2, 1984, pp. 126-32, 136-37.

19. Cohen-Rosenthal and Burton, *Mutual Gains.*

20. Shaun G. Clarke, "Rethinking the Adversarial Model in Labor Relations: An Argument for Repeal of Section 8(a)(2)," *Yale Law Journal* 96 (July 1987), pp. 2021-50.

21. Martin L. Weitzman, *The Share Economy: Conquering Stagflation*, (Cambridge MA: Harvard University Press, 1984); and Daniel J. B. Mitchell, "Gain-Sharing: An Anti-inflation Reform," *Challenge*, (July-August, 1982), pp. 34-40.

CHAPTER 4: Managing Below-Capacity Competition

1. The data contained in this chart are from the National Bureau of Economic Research.

2. Jeffrey A. Frankel, "International Capital Flows and Domestic Economic Policies," in Feldstein, Martin (ed.), *The United States in the World Economy* (Chicago: University of Chicago Press, 1988), pp. 559-627.

CHAPTER 5: Managing Competition to Reduce Poverty

1. Data are from the U.S. Department of Labor, Bureau of Labor Statistics.

2. Wage data are from the U.S. Department of Labor, Bureau of Labor Statistics, *Supplement to Employment and Earnings,* various issues. Fringe benefit data were computed from data in the National Income and Product Accounts.

3. Property income data are from the U.S. Department of Commerce, Bureau of the Census, Current Population Reports, Consumer Income, *Money Income of Households, Families, and Persons in the United States: 1983,* Series P-60, no. 146, April 1985. Mortgage and consumer debt data are from the "Survey of Consumer Finances, 1983: A Second Report," *Federal Reserve Bulletin*, December 1984, pp. 857-68.

CHAPTER 6: Managing Competition to Improve Productivity

1. J. R. Hicks, "Annual Survey of Economic Theory: The Theory of Monopoly," *Econometrica* (1935), p. 8.

2. Capacity utilization numbers are from the Board of Governors of the Federal Reserve System, Division of Research and Statistics, Industrial Output Section, *Capacity Utilization: Manufacturing, Mining, and Utilities and Industrial Materials.* Productivity numbers are from the

U.S. Department of Labor, Bureau of Labor Statistics, *Industry Analytical Ratios for Manufacturing, All Persons.*

3. See Wesely Mitchell, *Business Cycles* (Los Angeles: University of California Press, 1913).

4. Burton H. Klein,, *Dynamic Economics* (Cambridge, MA: Harvard University Press, 1977); Burton H. Klein, *Prices, Wages and Business Cycles: A Dynamic Theory* (New York: Pergamon Press, 1984); and Burton H. Klein, "Making Luck and Necessity Go Hand in Hand," mimeograph, 1988.

5. The data in this chart are from two U.S. Department of Labor, Bureau of Labor Statistics publications: *Industry Analytical Ratios for Manufacturing, All Persons and Industry Analytical Ratios for Nonfarm Business Less Manufacturing, All Persons.*

6. F. M. Scherer, *Industrial Market Structure and Economic Performance* (Chicago: Rand McNally, 1970), p. 361.

7. Ibid.

8. Freeman and Medoff, *What Do Unions Do?*

9. Peter K. Clark, "Investment in the 1970s: Theory, Performance, and Prediction," *Brookings Papers on Economic Activity* 1 (1979), pp. 73-124 and Ben S. Bernanke, "The Determinants of Investment: Another Look," *American Economic Review* 73 (May 1983), pp. 71-75.

10. Joseph A. Schumpeter, *Capitalism, Socialism, and Democracy*, 2nd ed. (New York: Harper & Brothers, 1947).

CHAPTER 7: A Special kind of Competition among Countries

1. Peter L. Berger, *The Capitalist Revolution: Fifty Propositions About Prosperity, Equality, & Liberty* (New York: Basic Books, 1986).

CHAPTER 8: Bringing It all Together

1. The data for this chart are from the *Economic Report of the President.*

2. The data for this chart are from the *Economic Report of the President.*

3. The data for this chart are from the *Economic Report of the President.*

4. Touche Ross, Privatization Council, and International City Management Association, *Privatization in America: An Opinion Survey of City and County Governments on Their Use of Privatization and Their Infrastructure Needs* (New York: Touche Ross & Co., 1987).

Appendix A: Industry Analysis

1. Edward C. Kokkelenberg and Donna R. Sockell, "Union Memberships in the United States," *Industrial and Labor Relations Review* 30 (July 1985), pp. 497-543.

2. Gregg H. Lewis, Unionism and Relative *Wages in the United States* (Chicago: University of Chicago Press, 1963).

INDEX

theory of money supply
growth and, 14
wage-gain norms and, 14

Inflation budget.

See Government, importance of
linking policies to inflation.

Interest rates:
decline in due to three prescribed policies, 4-5
productivity and, 117
reduction in will benefit
marginal workers, 100-101
relationship to the federal
budget deficit, 13
structural competition
and, 1953-1988, 42-43

See also Less-developed countries, responsibility of developed countries toward and
Productivity, managing interest rates to improve.

International City Management
Association and Privatization
Council, 149

Keynes, John Maynard, 90

Klein, Burton H.,107, 111-112,
259-261

Kondratief cycle, 79

Labor Law:
change may be necessary to
reduce union power, 67, 70-
71, 151-152
conflicts over interpretation,
67-68

Less-developed countries:
capitalism and, 123-124
capitalist revolution and, 124-
125
competition for foreign capital
and technology, 123-131

competition for foreign investment, the economic literature, 263-265
competition for foreign investment, embassy economic
reports, 265-272
improvement of economic and
political environment, 124-
125
responsibility of developed
countries toward, 128-129
results of competition
among, 126-128
roadblocks to improvement,
125-126
socialism and, 123-124

Lewis, Gregg, 50

Liberals:
poverty problem and, 104

Linneman, Peter, 51, 55, 116

Long-term competitive
industries:
analysis of seventeen industries, 166-199
description of, 31
list of, 32

Long-term endangered
industries:
analysis of five industries,
214-223
description of, 33-34
list of, 34

Long-term Monopolistic
industries:
analysis of eleven of industries, 228-249
description of, 35-39
list of, 36

Lumber industry:
analysis of, 206-207

336

Shepherd, William G., 25-26

Shilling, A. Gary, 51

Siegel, Irving H., 68

Smith, Adam, 2, 6

Soap and detergent industry:
    analysis of, 234-235

Socialism.

See Less-developed countries and
    socialism, and Management of
    Competition, as an ideology.

Standard of living:
    improved by three prescribed
    policies, 5

Steel industry:
    analysis of, 190-191

Stigler, George J., 27

Structural competition:
    acceleration of inflation
    and, 80
    causes of increase in, 44-45
    definition of, 8-9
    effect on average profit
    margins, 39-40
    effect on productivity, 111
    effects of compared to below-
    capacity competition, 10
    improvement of would benefit
    marginal workers, 101
    interest rates and,
    1953-1988, 42-43
    outlook for,44-47
    policy recommendation, 3
    policy review, 145-154
    tradeoff between below-
    capacity competition and, 7-
    10, 111, 155
    unemployment and, 3-4

Swaim, Paul, 55

Taxes:
    as a percentage of national
    income, 134-135

Tax revolts:
    government spending
    restrained by, 134-135

Telephone communications
    industry:
    analysis of, 198-199

Textile industry:
    analysis of, 33, 222-223

Tire industry:
    analysis of, 192-193

Total competition:
    definition of, 9-10

Touche Ross, 149

Trade deficit:
    effects on attitudes toward
    free trade, 152-153
    fiscal deficit and, 3
    improved by three prescribed
    policies, 5
    protectionism and, 3

Trucking industry:
    analysis of, 212-213

Unemployment:
    caused by weak structural
    competition, 93-95
    competition and, 153-154
    consequence of monopoly,
    93-94
    difference between the rate for
    all workers and black work-
    ers, 94-95
    protectionism and, 153-154
    structural competition
    and, 3-4
    weak structural competition
    and, 10

Okun's work, 319
Perry's work, 319-320
Schultze and others, 320-322
Wages:
  definition of excessive, 50
  gap between high and low-
    wage industries, 96-97

most important factor is wage-
  gain norm, 60
movements in quartiles, 96-97
relationship to changing
  prices, 64-65
See also Marginal workers.
Weinberg, Edgar, 68

Note: The authors cited in appendix B are listed in the reference immediately
following each article of that appendix and are not listed in this index.